Pulse, no. 1 by Jordan E.C. Seyer
Acrylic on paper, six inches by eight inches. 2019.

Moon City Review
2020

Moon City Review is a publication of Moon City Press at Missouri State University and is distributed by the University of Arkansas Press. Exchange subscriptions with literary magazines are encouraged. The editors of *Moon City Review* contract First North American Serial Rights, all rights reverting to the writers upon publication. The views expressed by authors in *Moon City Review* do not necessarily reflect the opinions of its editors, Moon City Press, or Missouri State University.

All other correspondence should be sent to the appropriate editor, using the following information:

Moon City Review
Department of English
Missouri State University
901 South National Avenue
Springfield MO 65897

Submissions are considered at https://mooncitypress.submittable.com/submit. For more information, please consult www.moon-city-press.com.

Cover designed by Charli Barnes,
using *Pulse, no. 1* by Jordan E.C. Seyer.
Text copyedited by Karen Craigo.

moon city press
springfield missouri

Staff

Table of Contents

Fiction

Nonfiction

The Missouri State University Student Literary Competitions

Graphic Narrative

Translation

Contributors' Notes

Regina DiPerna

The Midwestern Book of the Dead

The trees rise as if from a dream, dreary
and spare like my sister and me

walking barefoot down the driveway.
The lilacs grow near the treeline,

a gentle flourish in the face
of a landscape pocked with falling

houses, halves of tractors,
crows ripping soft strands of gut

from roadkill. My brother is smoking
cigarettes in the cornfield. We can't see him

but we know he's there.
Winters later, I drive past the cemetery

on Route 83 and see the gravestones rise
in the snow like a white wave.

They all look the same, even his.
The stereo plays static

like an old clock radio, as if it were
trying to wake someone,

as if we were all late for somewhere
we didn't know we were going.

Angie Macri

In the garden without trees,

two women sit apart, not speaking,
just enough light to see
green and all its shades. One woman

forms her heart from dust and breath
and examines its chambers,
its flow of Latin names, the first

as if you are entering a house,
she was taught, terra-cotta space.
The other thinks about the spot

between her shoulder blades,
muscles between spine
and the bones' edge

where she detached her wings.
It hurts to hold her head up by evening,
but it's the first of spring and suddenly

it seems that night will never come,
light hung after sunset this way,
and even when it does, it might be OK.

In the garden without trees,

There's no sun to cast a shadow
this time of day, no trees as far
as the eye can see. The garden

undulates on its plain, never ending.
It's still too cold for snakes,
the season just beginning.

Dawn Dupler

Opossum

We sleep in separate beds
because we lost the friction

to stay warm. You became the boy prince
who sails to Ibiza by day and returns

before your room changes into a squash
at midnight. I turned into the mother

who pours gasoline over the furniture,
throws a torch then sweeps

the ashes into a bin and grows a new home
with fresh sheets and tuna casserole

before dusk. Whether I use salt or diamonds,
dinner tastes bland, and were I to reach

for your hand I'd find a hook.
When I touch you, you play dead.

Kim Magowan

Women on the Sidelines

Veronica was a competent rather than imaginative cook, and for the last eighteen years had made the same two side salads for barbecues—a cucumber salad with feta, cherry tomatoes, and kalamata olives, and a sesame noodle salad. The third side dish she kept messing with, in an ongoing but unsuccessful attempt to find a good recipe for potato salad that didn't involve mayonnaise. This Fourth of July she felt optimistic about finally getting it right: The Epicurious recipe had involved a number of onions, both purple and green, and a heavy hand with Dijon, capers, and vinegar. But because of the surprising quantity of onions, and thus the chopping of onions, Veronica, usually good at time management, found herself still in blue jeans and a T-shirt that had a long tear of mustard running down her left boob—as if extruding from her nipple—when the doorbell rang and Josh opened it to Nick and Bobbi McPherson.

"So good to see you, Bobbi! It's been way too long," she heard Josh effuse, and she steeled herself. This had not been Veronica's game plan for seeing Bobbi McPherson, formerly Bobbi Talbot, for the first time in three years. She had planned, first of all, on Bobbi being at least an hour late, as she habitually was, rather than the first to arrive. Then Veronica would be surrounded by a phalanx of friends; she'd enlisted Tanya Stapleton to run interference. She would be wearing the red sleeveless dress that was still hanging on the towel hook in the bathroom, where Veronica had suspended it hours ago to steam out the wrinkles, as if the dress were a croupy child.

"You look great, Josh! So fit!" she heard Bobbi chirp: "chirp" was really the only word for that fluty, singsong voice, no more typical of Bobbi McPherson than being early for a barbecue. "Are you doing yoga?"

"Running. Just started again, actually," Josh said. "Nick, we should run together some time. Maybe the ridge trail?"

"Dude, my knees are way too fucked up for that," said Nick. At thirty-nine, Nick McPherson still talked like a Sigma Chi, though only, Veronica had long ago noted, around his former bros. Among others, he sounded perfectly adult.

Josh chuckled—really, with the chuckles and the chirps, Veronica felt like she was in the middle of a pet store, surrounded by budgies. "Bobbi, you look awesome."

At this, Veronica could no longer continue facing forward, one fist on the cutting board; she had to check out Bobbi McPherson for herself, despite her mustard boob. She turned.

Awesome? Well, Bobbi certainly looked distinctive. She was wearing a short silver dress, vaguely armor-like. She looked like a cast member in one of Shakespeare's military plays, or perhaps the Tin Man of Oz. Her face, beaming at Josh, was as pretty as ever. Not visibly older, except for the fine cross-hatching around her blue eyes.

"Hello, Bobbi," Veronica said. She had practiced—literally practiced, in front of the steamy bathroom mirror—intonation: She aimed for civility with just a wisp of chill, undetectable to the men, but audible to Bobbi as a dog whistle to a collie. Instead she sounded croaky, a frog in this pet shop of birds.

Bobbi bent her elegant head, a tilt as opposed to a nod. "Hey," she said succinctly, and Veronica felt a pang. There it was, the tone she had been aiming for: as cool and crisp as a summer salad.

"Babe, don't you need to get ready?" Josh said, and now Veronica was conscious of all three of them staring at her.

"I just need to dress this salad."

"Just add that dressing and toss? I can do that. You get ready," said Bobbi. To someone not listening carefully, like their two husbands, now rummaging in the fridge for beer, Bobbi would have sounded like a friend.

Veronica got dressed as if she were being timed: She yanked the mostly wrinkle-free dress over her head, slid on her heeled sandals, and jammed her favorite dangly earrings, the ones with the smoky stones, through her lobes. Why was she speeding? she asked herself, applying lipstick. It's not like she suspected Bobbi of messing with her salad. Though that was the kind of spiteful, passive-aggressive act of which Bobbi was capable.

Lanie Huckaby: That was the name of that Winona Ryder look-alike all the guys had dated, back in college. Trailing after this name, like streamers, was the thought that produced it: Why are these men so unimaginative?

Back at Stanford, Lanie Huckaby had made the rounds of half that fraternity. Josh had dated her before he and Veronica had started seeing each other, then Malcolm Talbot had, then Nick McPherson. It was the sort of thing that would violate every girl code, but none of the boys had seemed to mind sharing. In fact, Veronica remembered Josh giving Malcolm advice about some present to give Lanie—"Her birthstone is amethyst." She distinctly recalled Josh saying this, because it had struck her as so fucked up. Even today, pushing forty, the men lacked imagination. Josh never wanted to try a restaurant before checking the Yelp reviews. Everything had to be vetted in advance. He avoided the responsibility of having to form his own independent opinion.

Nonetheless: It was one thing to date the ex-girlfriend of your bud. It was another to marry his ex-wife. That was a scenario that Veronica had not seen coming. If she had, she would have avoided the gleeful pyromania, three years ago, of burning all bridges with Bobbi Talbot. Sparks everywhere, the sky blue with smoke.

Though Veronica had been like the Roadrunner getting dressed, condensing her usual routine by half, the barbecue was already underway when she returned downstairs. The Stapletons had come, the Rhinelanders, the Katzes. It was a surreal feeling to walk into her own kitchen and almost collide into Bobbi McPherson, deep in conversation with Tanya Stapleton. The two women looked at her, Tanya sheepishly, Bobbi in an inscrutable way that reminded Veronica of the way she preferred martinis: very cold, the surface almost frosty.

Bobbi said, "I finished your salad. I put it on the table on the deck."

"Thanks," said Veronica, mimicking her tone. So this was the approach: declarative, succinct.

Tanya nodded, taking this in. Over the past week, Veronica had had at least three conversations with Tanya about this very predicament, had said to Tanya at least three times, "Make sure you don't leave me alone with Bobbi McPherson."

"Bobbi McPherson! I'm still getting used to saying that," Tanya had said, and Veronica had replied, "I know! That's why I keep fucking practicing."

Now, Tanya's look at Veronica seemed to transmit both apology—having been caught talking, by all appearances warmly, to the woman Veronica privately referred to as her "mortal enemy"—and confusion, since Bobbi wasn't behaving the way for which they had meticulously prepared. It was like inviting to a dinner party someone who was supposed to be vegan and having them unexpectedly reach for the steak tartare. "Where's the psycho bitch?" Tanya's round eyes inquired.

"Anyone want sangria?" Veronica said, and both women, as well as Kelly Rhinelander and Maribeth Katz, who were standing at the open sliding glass door to better watch their children in the trampoline, said, "Absolutely."

Are all barbecues this gender normative? Veronica wondered. The five men, each with a beer in hand, huddled around Josh's fancy grill, its dials making it look like the dashboard of an aircraft. The seven children were in various postures of gravity defiance, caroming in the trampoline. Veronica and Josh had bought the trampoline when they moved to Menlo Park and suddenly had a yard: It was domed, and the kids bouncing up and down in it increased its resemblance to a giant, transparent Jiffy Pop. The women angled their deck chairs in such a way to view both their popcorning children and their husbands, who were laughing uproariously. Clearly, Veronica reflected, taking a gulp of her sangria, the men were having a better time.

Veronica remembered a class she took in college on gender studies. The professor had told them that the gender symbol for female, that icon that looked like a teaspoon with arms, was a metonym for Aphrodite, the goddess of love and beauty, and represented a hand holding a mirror. Women were the object of their own gazes, the professor explained, anxiously assessing their capacity to attract. Much more typically, women watched men. The professor had the students analyze advertisements in a parenting magazine. The little boys were always doing something: flying about on a tire swing, fishing, swinging a bat. The little girls were literally standing on the sidelines, watching them. Veronica grimaced at how perfectly she and her friends were following their assigned gender role as approving spectators.

"I love this sangria. I've never had white sangria before," said Tanya Stapleton.

"Yeah, I thought it would be more refreshing, in July."

"Absolutely! Tell me what's in it."

"Oh, Sauvignon, and 7 Up, and then I put in a lot of summer fruit, like peaches and raspberries …," Veronica said, but over Tanya's fully attentive face, over Maribeth's "It's so delicious!," she saw Bobbi McPherson smirk. Bobbi never had any patience for what she would call, with acidic contempt, "chatter." Talking to Bobbi was the conversation equivalent of being in those oxygen bars that used to be trendy ten years ago. All content had to be important, meaningful. Tanya was a much easier friend, kind and loyal, always behaving as if everything Veronica said was interesting. But with Bobbi, Veronica actually *was* interesting, because she was forced to be. "Oh, yawn," Bobbi would say, otherwise.

Which is exactly what Veronica hoped Bobbi would say now: "Oh, yawn." These women would find such a comment rude, socially irredeemable; they would not be at all amused. Why wouldn't Bobbi live up to her billing as psycho bitch? Was it just to be obnoxious, to prove Veronica once again wrong?

Veronica sighed, and watched Bobbi's daughter Helen, elbow-hooked with Veronica's daughter Tildy, so the two ten-year-olds resembled joined paper dolls. The two girls hadn't seen each other in three years, yet there was no awkwardness; they were immediately back to normal, literally attached as they bounced in the trampoline. That first year, Tildy would ask from time to time, "When is Helen coming over? When can I have a sleepover with Helen?" Veronica had put her off, and by the time Tildy's birthday rolled around, Tildy had not demanded to put Helen on the Evite.

Not for the first time, Veronica envied children's memory: so sharp in the short term (she could never beat Tildy at one of those matching games, even when she played her hardest), but sketchy in the long term, the memory of a missing best friend smoothed away like a raised bump of frosting on a cake. In contrast, the hole Bobbi had left when she tore out of Veronica's life was the full-body shape that cartoon characters left in walls when they were running away. Fuck her, Veronica thought, and took another gulp of sangria.

"The garden looks beautiful, Veronica," said Tanya. "I love that red camellia."

"It really does look pretty, Ronnie. You have so much space," Bobbi said, and for a stretchy second Veronica and Bobbi looked at each other. Breaking the gaze was like pulling apart a Velcro strap.

"Anyone need a refresher?" Veronica said, holding up her empty sangria glass, and the four women said, "Me," "Me," as if practicing scales.

In her kitchen, Veronica steadied herself, palm flat on the refrigerator door. When Tildy was very little, and having trouble going to sleep, Veronica would sometimes lie in bed with her, and they would intone together the various things in Tildy's room, all keeping her company, standing guard. "Here is the nightlight, here is the Humpty-Dumpty clock": For some reason it had calmed Tildy. Now Veronica found herself seeking the same grounding in material objects. Here was her refrigerator, a compromise, like everything with Josh was a compromise; he'd insisted on an ice dispenser, and she wanted brushed steel. Here was her granite countertop, sand-colored but with little chips of black. She liked that it really looked like stone instead of some synthetic. Here were her yellow ruched curtains with cherries: cheerful, because a kitchen should be cheerful.

When Josh had said, a couple of weeks ago, that they needed to invite Bobbi McPherson to the barbecue, Veronica had said, "Must we?" And Josh had said, "Of course! She's Nick's wife." Josh had seemed genuinely surprised by her question.

It was as if he didn't remember Bobbi ignoring Veronica's text two years ago—"HBD! I miss you! XX." Those two Xs, dangling there, rejected, became increasingly pathetic: markers on a pirate map for an unwanted treasure. "Forget her," Josh had said. As if you could just snap your fingers and forget someone! "She's a bitch." At the time, Veronica had felt comforted by Josh's loyalty, but now she saw she'd misunderstood its source. Bobbi was a bitch for divorcing his buddy, not for blowing off his wife. And now that Bobbi was married to Nick, Josh didn't remember feeling anything other than affection towards her. In the kitchen, he'd seemed genuinely pleased to see her.

Nick McPherson, alone in their set, had always been single. The only one of the wives who had also gone to Stanford, Veronica had known these men since they were all nineteen-year-olds. Back then, Veronica had sometimes thought of herself as Wendy with the Lost Boys, insisting that everyone sit down to dinner and use napkins and the proper utensils. Of them all, Nick had always seemed the most--lost boy: handsome—well, they were all handsome—but in a shaggy way that made you want to scratch his head, as if he were a clumsy, affectionate golden retriever.

Sometimes she and Josh would speculate about the sort of woman who would compel Nick McPherson to finally settle down, and Veronica had always pictured someone a good ten years younger, so having children wouldn't be an issue: Nick always gave everyone's kids piggyback rides. Someone very pretty, with a tinkly sort of laugh, the sound that ice makes shaken in a glass—she could actually hear what Nick's future wife should sound like.

What she had not pictured, of course, and would never have had the imagination to picture, was Nick falling in love with Bobbi Talbot.

Veronica carried out the full glasses of sangria in pairs. It wasn't a surprise particularly, since she had been contemplating the same thread herself, that the women were discussing Nick. Naturally it was Maribeth Katz asking: ferrety Maribeth, who in her way of plucking out information reminded Veronica of one of those fat-bladed oyster shuckers. "So how did you and Nick get together?" That was the cue. Veronica sat back down to with her glass of sangria.

"He called," Bobbi said simply. She stared at the domed trampoline while the four women looked at her, and for a moment Veronica thought Bobbi would leave it at that. "He called and asked how Helen and I were doing. He asked if I needed anything. And of course there were plenty of things I needed, stupid things. All the lights had gone out in our chandelier, and I wasn't tall enough to change them. I thought there was a ladder in the garage but Malcolm had taken it." She made a face. "So Nick came over with a bottle of wine, and he changed all my light bulbs, and he did some other stuff—fixed the fan in the upstairs bathroom—and then we sat in the kitchen drinking wine. He said, 'So really, tell me how you are,' and I just started bawling. I don't think I realized until that moment how fucking lonely I was." She took a sip of her sangria. "He called," she repeated, and looked at Veronica. The briefest of glances, but Veronica felt as if Bobbi had held a lighter to her face and burned her.

"Nick is such a sweetheart," said Kelly Rhinelander. The women watched the kids bounce in the trampoline.

"And how is Malcolm?" Maribeth asked, in her jabbing way.

"Hell if I know," said Bobbi. "He quit rehab. I'm not letting him see Helen until he can stick with the program, and so far it seems like drinking is more important to Malcolm than being a dad. His loss. Nick is wonderful with Helen. Even that very first time he came over, he brought wine and cheese and crackers for us, but for Helen, a bag of toffee-chip cookies that he got at that shop Anthony's in the Mission."

"Oh, I love Anthony's!" said Tanya. Veronica tuned out the discussion of various bakeries. She touched the left side of her face, the side facing Bobbi, as if to protect it.

Three years ago, Bobbi had said to her, "I can't believe you and Josh gave Malcolm booze." As if they had given him a handgun rather than a few beers. "I told you," Bobbi said. "I told you about the time he pissed all over the bathroom because he was too drunk to aim for the toilet. What the fuck is your problem, Ronnie? I told you!"

What Veronica had thought at the moment was—well, so many things. She had known Malcolm Talbot, after all, since he was nineteen, and they all played pool together in Antonio's Nuthouse, the floor of the bar covered in peanut shells. Sure, he drank—all of them drank. But a drinking problem—that was Bobbi's fabrication, Bobbi being crazy and dramatic. Like when Bobbi had told her, right before she and Malcolm had separated, about the time she woke up to find Malcolm on top of her. "He raped me," she had said, and when Veronica had asked, "But how can your husband rape you?" Bobbi's face had turned red. "Veronica, what the fuck, it's not 1850."

What she couldn't say to Bobbi that day was, "Sure, you told me, but you tell me all kinds of crazy shit." She couldn't say, "I don't listen to you, because you exaggerate, and you're completely unreliable." So she had looked Bobbi in the eye—it had taken some courage to do it; Bobbi had been practically shaking with rage—and said, "Look, I've known Malcolm since we were practically kids. He's one of Josh's best friends. I am not going to take sides."

And she could have said more—that Bobbi, who was after all her best friend, should understand exactly why Veronica couldn't take sides. She had told Bobbi all about her parents' insane, messy divorce, both of them catapulting fireballs at each other. Of course Veronica had been the most valuable weapon, her father tricking her into meeting his girlfriend with her scraped-back bun, her mother calling her a traitor, the competing holiday plans that were not about wanting to be with Veronica but rather about forcing her to choose—Bobbi knew all that, knew how it had fucked teenage Veronica up. So where did she get off, scolding Veronica about giving Malcolm a beer, same as she had for the last seventeen years?

Veronica could have said all this, but she never had a chance to, because Bobbi had given her one last molten stare, shaken her head, and then called up the stairs (this is when they were still living in their cramped, cold Victorian in San Francisco), "Come on, Helen, we have to go." And went, leaving behind that full-body cartoon cutout vacancy of herself.

But time appeared to have proven Bobbi right after all. Not nutty and hyperbolic, apparently. Even Josh now pronounced Malcolm Talbot fucked up, said he needed professional help, and refused to meet Malcolm at bars. Nick McPherson had gone so far as to marry Bobbi. It was, perhaps, a bad miscalculation, refusing to take sides.

So she probably owed Bobbi McPherson an apology. It was not the worst thing in the world. She was always telling Tildy, "It's brave to say you're sorry."

Then why did the prospect feel so agonizing?

Gripping her sangria glass, Veronica felt a wash of self-pity. She wished she could be back in that bar with the peanut shells twenty years ago, placing her beer on a felt coaster on the counter and chalking up her cue, wiggling her ass for laughs: the one girl there, while all the lost boys looked on.

A.M. Brant

Before the Iron

"Only help her to know—help make it so there is cause for her to know—that she is more than this dress on the ironing board, helpless before the iron."
—Tillie Olson, "I Stand Here Ironing"

She tells me about the summer they spent in Kansas,
so much dust. How she'd iron everything, even his
underwear. Her hands are crinkled, too, skin like crepes,

papier-mâché peaks. She is in her thin paisley turquoise shirt,
a white Chantilly lace robe, sweatpants, slippers, ironing
a pair of man's pants; they're light brown, soft. They have

cuffs at the bottom. I watch her hands more than I listen
to her direction, pulling the pant leg out straight. Inseams.
Pockets. Sharp. Steam puff. I want to ask about her secrets,

if she regrets having so many children. How do women feel
about their lives when they've lived a life so like their mother
and her mother and her mother and her mother and her mother

and hers back into the beginning of forever. Before ironing,
before Kansas, when we were just coming from dust, when we
were just coming from not remembering never having a world

where the bodies building babies weren't just for bodies that don't.
Coming and coming and girls into mothers into mothers over
and over, or dying. Crisp. Creases. As far back as hot coals used to

smooth clothes of their wrinkles, from bodies moving, sitting, sleeping.
Bodies covered in clothes ironed, soothed, sussed out, with love by
hands of women young to growing old. Show me.

Taylor Fedorchak

Wanting to drive
to Roswell with him

to stay awake on his passenger
side, the entire three hours from our rented
house with the pecan trees in the sandy
back yard. This house, where washing
dishes one night he finally asked me
how many people I had slept with.

Where in our kitchen he backtracked.
Once he told me his number was eight,
but now it's   *I don't really even*
know.   Fractured bits of calla lily
implanted in cabinet handles, our floors.
Permanent souvenirs. His medicine. *Use*

or freeze within one year of test date. Freeze
his gray suit.   My cheap green dress
from Amazon and the petticoat underneath.
His matching tie. Let's freeze anything
that isn't contaminated yet. Ruined
like the groundwater at Holloman Air Force Base

sixty miles from us. He and I should get
away, stay at some alien-themed Airbnb.
Rent lime green sheets and towels I probably

won't want to use. A shower with enough hot chlorinated water for both of us. Where sage dye will bleed from the soap into our skin.

Kimberly Ann Priest

The Scrape

You split sunset with your lean silhouette. I see you
as I need to—godly, in a Carhartt jacket and torn-up jeans,
as you watch the horses stop and break into gallops
and kicks, leaving pockmarks all over the pasture,
the fences holding them in and cutting your body
in three at torso and knees, your elbows curled backward
over the top rung, back straight. And I want to feel
a small pang of pity or sadness to say I am a little
comforted by your pain, a little less angry because
you are hurting, a little understanding because I am hurting
too from the awful scream you tore through me
after dinner in the bedroom, the children's ears barely
out of reach. I want to say it must be heavy to carry
such a secret, to feel your body roving with an unrepentant
shame. To be gay and married to me and able to tell
no one of importance, your family dedicated to
a Christian faith. I watch you through the window
hoping you will not return but stay there with the horses
or run off to be with a man of your choice, not because
I am kind this way or want you happy, but because
you've named me, again, the things you feel are you:
adulterer, liar, insane. You shift your weight
into the fence post, elbow slips. I lift my hand in a motion
to catch it, wincing as you coddle the scrape.

Caitlin Rae Taylor

The Laurel County Clergy Demolition Derby

I spent the night, the one when Anthony finally convinced me to compete in the charity derby, sulking over the humble okra plant. I took pains trying to recreate Anthony's grandmother's recipe for country-fried steak and pan-fried okra. Embosomed in a pink frilled apron, I had already burned one batch. I had the cast-iron skillet too hot, accidentally let the oil smoke before throwing in the lightly dusted, starry vegetables. Their ash like supernova against the dark iron. Anthony, home from work, emerged through the smoke screen, coughed, and brought up the derby for the eighth time that week.

"I ran into Father Killian at the Food Lion," he said, peeling out of his gray windbreaker. North Carolina autumn settled over us from the nearby mountains, cooling the clear mornings and evenings. Anthony tossed his key ring onto the kitchen counter. The jangled bundle of old apartment keys and flimsy plastic discount cards skidded through my pile of flour and cornmeal.

"Ah, Father Killian, the darling of these interfaith charity events," I said, rolling my eyes. Bits of okra flesh, their pearly seeds, stuck to my knuckles as I chopped a new batch.

"Come on, Clara, don't be jealous."

"I am not jealous." I did my best not to make a face as I coated the okra. I nudged Anthony's keys to the side with my knuckle. "Just because he raises more money than any other church combined, what do I have to be jealous of? He probably cheats anyway."

Anthony kicked off his brown loafers and padded over to the kitchen stereo. A coffee-scented breeze wafted off of him. The scent used to comfort me. Now, though, the familiarity of it nauseated me.

He clicked on the radio so the sounds of experimental jazz rankled from the speakers. He hadn't changed the CD, Sun Ra, in four weeks, but still insisted on playing it every night when he got home from work. My home, not his. His home, technically, was that apartment downtown he'd abandoned when his brother, Ned, came back comatose from their last rock-climbing venture. Their parents had chosen to keep Ned on life support, and Anthony had come to me. The two of us had only been together for a few months by then, touches and personal confessions still new and exhilarating. I'd held him while he cried. Kept some complicated truths about Ned from him and made him dinner. A comforting borscht from his childhood. And he had simply never left. The food became my apology. Every chop, baste, buttering. Each edible *I'm sorry* fell like hair from my head into soups, stews, bakes. During every meal, I wondered if he somehow knew. If Ned had risen from his coma and whispered my transgressions in his brother's ear.

Anthony visited Ned every Saturday, though I couldn't bring myself to join. I had never been introduced to Ned as Anthony's girlfriend. As far as Anthony was concerned, I had no idea who Ned really was. I let Anthony believe that hospitals made me squeamish.

In reality, I had known Ned quite well. Could never shake the image of him walking in and out of my office at church. But the idea of visiting him now sent shocks through my body. Paralyzing shocks with the power, it felt, to stop my heart entirely.

Anthony would come home from the hospital on Saturday afternoons, his eyes puffy, their redness diluted from the drive. And he would drag his grief behind him like a broken doll. By the time he'd shaken it off, learned to leave it in another room, in the closet, it would be Saturday again.

When we were just dating, before his brother's coma and before the messiness of his life stuck to me like burrs, he had just been the quiet owner of the coffee shop where I liked to get my espresso every morning.

I didn't break up with him because he needed me. His parents were too emotionally crippled to take care of their healthy son, and my own parents had given up on me as someone to rely on. They did the bare minimum. Called twice a month and boredly asked how the church was. They'd ask if I was calling my sister. I usually wasn't. But Anthony depended on me. He believed, against all proof, that I was a person who could be depended on. I spent my adulthood passively resenting most people for the burdens I collected from them. Their broken marriages and fractured families, their hospital prayers and burials.

"Father Killian said it's a shame we don't have a participant for the charity derby." Outside, the neighbor's dog barked. A front door slammed. A man yelled at his son or wife or potted plant. I dropped a handful of okra into the skillet and let the hiss drown him out. "You've got the skillet too hot again," Anthony said. He strode across the kitchen and turned the stove knob down from eight to six.

"Your mother told me it was eight," I said, which was probably a lie.

"Suit yourself. I can stomach ash as a side dish as long as the steak's cooked OK. Look, I know the job taxes you sometimes, but you still have to be part of the community," Anthony chided. "Even if you think Father Killian's going to win anyway. I don't care what you do, but how's it going to look when you're the only priest in the whole county not participating? What will that say about you?"

"I just don't understand why they had to make it a demolition derby," I said. This was my refrain. I knew it well, had been railing against the event for weeks. Anthony, on the other hand, was thrilled. His people hailed from Indiana. He had grown up on the state-fair, car-crash spectacle. "We can raise money for charity in literally so many other ways, and we choose crashing into each other like morons?"

"Ned would have loved it," Anthony said, his gaze fixed on the green fluorescence of the kitchen clock.

I set the knife down and sighed. Nodded my consent. Ned made every decision in our household.

"Good, because I've already agreed to be the announcer."

When the neglected skillet started to smoke again, it was Anthony who took it off the burner and ran cold water into the mess of charred vegetables. Hot oil sprang from the pan and bit us both on the arm.

"I guess six is still too high," he said. The neighbor man's voice capitulated over the jazz and crackle of ruined sustenance. "Remember that for next time. I'll call in a pizza."

Despite my explicit instructions not to, Anthony arranged for me to meet his buddy Sam after service on Sunday. When he wasn't exterminating roaches, Sam tricked out broken-down vehicles for Laurel County's demolition derby circuit.

Anthony wouldn't be joining us. He rarely came to church. Spent most Sundays in bed, in a black mood that demanded swaddling in blackness. So Sam, easy to spot as the first newcomer to grace St. Paul in almost a year, sat alone in the farthest left pew, twiddling his thumbs in the back.

He had a small distended beer belly, made more prominent by the cranberry polo tucked into his oil-stained jeans. His curly brown hair was combed neatly to one side. I could tell right away he wasn't religious. He kept his eyes downcast during the entire service, like his atheism could be detected. As if it gave off a scent.

The sermon was nothing special on my part. I hadn't prepared well enough and had shirked my memorization routine. I'd spent the evenings that past week watching and re-watching old episodes of *Grey's Anatomy*. Nevertheless, Sam came up afterward in the parish hall to tell me how moving he'd found my words.

"Most preachers are just all fire and brimstone," he told me at the snack table while I attempted to balance a plate of mini donuts and a carafe of coffee. "Your sermon wasn't like that. You talked about history. That was always my favorite school subject."

I didn't enjoy speaking to my congregation about my sermon-writing process. It often involved last-ditch Googling efforts and a lot of time with my old history books from college. But I couldn't tell anyone that I didn't like to be asked questions. I couldn't tell anyone anything real about my life.

I affixed my most convincing priest smile. Soft face. Tilted head. Half-lidded, tender eyes. Like how someone might look if really cared about you. That's how I had to be with everyone. With four hundred and seventeen congregants. Sometimes, I forgot the look of my real face entirely.

Parishioners milled about the bright parish hall, a carpeted room with painted cinderblock walls and tiny, circular tables. They fetched their coffee and cinnamon rolls and ham finger sandwiches. Some could be heard strategically planning their bets on which priest would win the derby, which denomination would nab the gold.

"Well, thank you," I said to Sam over the din. "I'm glad you enjoyed yourself. Where do you usually attend?"

I bit into a powdered donut, careful to hold my breath so a puff of sugar wouldn't descend on the black bosom of my clergy shirt.

"I don't really go anywhere," Sam said. He leaned over behind me to the snack table and procured a bundle of napkins. I set my plate down and used the whole wad to brush the sugar from the corners of my mouth.

"Anthony said he'd introduce us himself, but," Sam continued. "Well, you know how he's been lately."

"Ah, yes," I said, throwing the pile of used napkins behind me onto the table. "It seems I need a car for the charity derby. Can you help me with that?"

"You bet your rear I can, Mother," he said, his blue eyes lighting. "I used to supply about a third of the cars for the county fair every year. I'm happy to donate for a good cause. I live near the track by the fairgrounds, actually, and there's a derby happening Saturday morning."

I raised my eyebrows, slightly intrigued. Who on God's green earth would want to live spitting distance from engine and metal?

"Why don't we meet on Saturday, then?" I suggested. "I can see what I'm getting myself into, and you can show me just how special your cars are."

Sam shook my hand, my knuckles still kissed with powdered sugar. He squeezed tight.

"It's a date," he said, and a peculiar shiver jerked beneath my clerical collar.

"Sam and I have a date," I told Anthony during dinner that evening as he picked at the broiled tilapia I'd cooked. He never had much of an appetite after visiting his brother.

"Hm?" he grunted. Spooned a gooey segment of yellow squash into his mouth. Didn't look away from the old *Tom and Jerry* reruns flashing across the television screen. Cartoons were all he watched on Sundays.

"Sam. He invited me to watch a derby with him next weekend. Point out his cars, show me what they can do. Then I guess we'll work on designs or something." My voice tried for brightness. I wanted to show him my investment. This, too, was an apology.

"Oh. Cool." He fell silent, eyes glazed over as Tom lifted a baseball bat above Jerry's head.

"How was Ned today?" I asked. It wasn't a question I asked often. I usually avoided finding out information about Ned. Most mentions of him spiked my blood pressure. If I pretended I'd had nothing to do with him, maybe that would end up being true.

Frustrated as I could get with Anthony, I always did my best on Sundays. On the rare occasion, if the correct concoction of childhood comfort food and surrogate spousal concern coincided, he could be cajoled into a good session of grief sex. Good grief sex cleansed him sometimes. Sometimes it cleansed me, too. To see him tender again. We had both of us lost so much tenderness.

"Just shut the fuck up Clara, OK?" The timber of his voice was stoic—lifeless. Anthony had only sounded like this once before—the day of the accident. The accident where a highly skilled rock climber with professional equipment somehow slipped, unlatched from that equipment, and fell almost a thousand feet. This was soon after Ned's and my last counseling session. The last time I'd seen Ned's unkempt hair and dirty bomber jacket.

Sometimes I thought about bringing up that Ned and I had been meeting weekly before I'd even met Anthony. Now was one of those times. I thought about how the shock value would bring Anthony immediately to the surface. Like a diver with a depleted oxygen tank. Instead, I opened my mouth and shoveled in the cold rubber of tilapia, its sheen of greasy oil. It coated my tongue like a hospital blanket.

The track by Sam's house, part of the long expanse of the county fairgrounds, roiled with salt-of-the-earthers. Packs of burly men in deer-hunting attire, enthusiastic bleacher women sporting multicolored camo print on their purses and their crop-top sweaters. Late morning saw them with half-empty cans of Coors Light, Michelob Ultra, and Budweiser.

The track itself was a giant circular disk of compacted North Carolina red clay against the backdrop of the foothills. Tire marks crosshatched the track. A rusty chain-link fence secured the perimeter. Bleachers towered on all sides—three different stands of them—and the farthest part of the fence was left open with just enough room for the cars to make their entrances.

I trespassed tentatively, an imposter in my sundress and cardigan. The air was stale and swirling with cigarette smoke. Engines roared from the other side of the track from souped-up clunkers waited in line. Every time a driver revved their engine, murmurs from the crowd stoked into full-blown hollers. Beside me, a couple passed a Black and Mild back and forth between their lips.

Sam startled me as he sidled up and laid a hand on my shoulder.

"Sam. You scared the daylights out of me," I said. Sam smiled wide, his chapped lips showing two rows of perfectly straight teeth—the products of careful dentistry and home whitening remedies. He wore clean, acid-washed jeans and a soft red flannel shirt to ward off the early morning chill. His face was clean shaven. His shoes, though—cheap Walmart affairs that had once been as white as his teeth but were now an orangey mud color. Those shoes, for whatever reason, made me nervous. As if they were some clue to the Sam inside of him. I clasped my hands around the rusted tips of the fence and turned away.

"How do you rest with all this racket going on?" I asked, surveying the cars on the other end of the track.

"It's just on the weekends," he said in his pleasant drawl. "And I'm usually out here in the middle of it all. Gotta see how my cars do."

"And how do your cars usually do?" I wanted to know just how much of a chance I had of getting destroyed. Preachers were competitive animals. St. Paul's had once done a joint fundraiser with St. Mary's Catholic for flooding victims during hurricane season. Father Killian and I had scrambled over one another like baby turtles trying to raise more money than the other. I visualized full-speed vehicular impact.

"Pretty well. I make 'em sturdy. I got a deal with the owner at the scrapyard, and I pay pretty cheap prices for the cars in better condition. He's a little biased, though. My daddy taught his boys how to shoot."

"You hunt?" I asked almost involuntarily. Around Laurel County, everyone hunted. Asking if people hunted was a courtesy.

"Oh, no," Sam said. "I don't hunt. I used to when my dad was alive. But he died when I was in college, so. Haven't hunted since."

"I'm so sorry," I said, another courtesy. It seemed like each day Anthony came home sullen from the hospital, each day he spent in a trance covered up in a dark bedroom, each day some teenager or sick infant landed themselves in the hospital needing last rites, the less I could sympathize with what I had begun to categorize as ordinary grief.

"I'm sure he was a great man," I said.

"He was all right," Sam said. A breeze blew by and caught the ends of my dress. "Did his best. But he didn't believe in God, so. Can't say he's in a better place."

"As long as he was a good man, I'm not sure believing in God is super necessary."

Sam cut his eyes at me in a curious way.

"Mother?"

I laughed, feeling at ease for the first time. Away from parishioners expecting their priest or Anthony expecting his dutiful girlfriend.

"I'm not Mother right now," I said, searching for the root of my comfort with Sam. He harbored a familiarity I couldn't shake. "Just Clara. You have to tell people things when you're of the cloth or whatever. I don't belong to myself when I'm wearing that collar. It's like keeping the peace, I think. I could espouse my own ideologies, but that's not really what I'm there for, is it?"

This kind of compartmentalization kept me sane through the marital problems, the dead family members, the car-crashed sixteen-year-olds. There are things I would never tell my congregation just to appease them. Everybody needed a dash of guilt when it came to religion. But they didn't need to know that I thought all dogs went to heaven or that, sometimes, the people I counseled slipped through my fingers like minnows.

"Don't you think people would be calmer if they thought they didn't have to believe in God to get some peace and quiet when they die?"

"Probably," I said. "But then the church would die, and I'd have to become a plumber or something."

It was a joke, but Sam didn't laugh. I coughed and tried to change the subject.

"Well. Anyway. Which car is yours?"

Sam nodded.

"I usually have a few dogs in the fight, but business has been slow lately." He said. "I've got one today. First one I've worked on in a while. She's back there. Third in line. Teenager. Real talent."

The car in question was a sedan of some sort, but the make and model were unrecognizable. Stripped of all its dealer furnishings, its coat of chromic paint, the car had been transformed, first by the elements, then by Sam's handiwork. It was windowless and the bottom half was painted black, the top half purple. Exorbitantly large tires, the kind found on Hummers and cargo trucks, elevated the car's miniscule frame. Across the body of the car were spray-painted comic book action words in hot pink: *blamow, pow, kerplunk*. The Wonder Woman symbol was emblazoned beneath an odd pipe protruding from the car's hood.

Wonder Woman was up against seven other vehicles, most of them sedans of the same size, spray-painted with their own strange themes and gimmicks. One car was all white and decked in a cape of taffeta. Strings of soup cans trailed from the back with the words JUST DIVORCED in blood red across the side doors. Another car had more common monster-truck stylings with painted-on fangs and reptilian-like foam ridges jutting from the top.

"ARE YOU READY TO RUUUUUMBLE" came the echo from the loudspeaker. Sam joined the chorus of barking fans. From his back pocket, he supplied a pack of red Marlboros and a lighter. Lit one up and returned them without offering one to me.

The announcer, sequestered in a little tin box above one of the bleacher stands, shining against the deep blue, cloudless sky, announced each car individually as they entered the ring.

Wonder Woman entered after a car painted simple silver. When each vehicle was within the fence, a horn blared through a loudspeaker. Car engines revved, and the sound of metal contracting against metal thundered through the arena. I began to sweat even though the weather was still pleasantly cool, no sign of rain, the white-topped mountains in the distance hinting of snow to come when October beseeched November in two more weeks.

JUST DIVORCED circled the ring at breakneck speed before pummeling into a jet-black car marked 007, denting the passenger door inward.

Fresh air gave way to an impenetrable cloud of exhaust, so thick even the cigarette smoke dissipated within it.

Wonder Woman wove in and out of clunkers, whose movements like uncoordinated elephants left them more susceptible to attack. Four cars perished and had to be pushed to the edge of the track by referees before Wonder Woman took any kind of hit. She sped backward in preparation to hurdle into JUST DIVORCED's rear end when Monster Truck took her out from the side. She skidded a bit but regained control before the odd protrusion on her hood spit a tangle of flames into the air.

"Holy shit," I yelled, forgetting myself, grateful that no one could hear me.

In the end, Wonder Woman came in second. As the crowd dispersed and Monster Truck took home the gold, a young Black girl in jet black braids crossed the track and waved to Sam. He waved back, chuckling.

"She's a good kid, Emily. I'm guessing I'll have to be fixing her car up for the next derby."

"Well, your car kept her safe," I admitted. "And second place isn't so bad. Second place in our derby gets about $1,000 for their chosen charity."

"What's your charity?" he asked as we made our way to the side of his house where I'd parked my car.

"I'm actually giving it to the hospital. Laurel Presbyterian. I don't know how much you know about Anthony's brother …."

Sam stopped walking and looked at me.

"I know all about Anthony's brother. Clara, did he not tell you who I am?"

"He just said you were a friend is all."

"Clara …." Sam trailed off. His youthful face drooped, the white skin sallowing before my eyes like a time-lapse of a putrefying mushroom. "Clara, I'm Sam. Ned's fiancé?"

"What?"

"I go to see him every day. I'm there every Saturday when Anthony drops by."

"I … didn't even know Ned was gay."

"Anthony doesn't talk about him much."

"We had just started dating, really, when Ned died," I said, that familiar wave of panic and guilt surfacing, though I tried my hardest to dry it up, convert the rough waves of it into sand inside of me.

Sam rolled his chin forward, sucked in a breath, and spit a glob of saliva onto the compacted clay beside my feet. It landed there with a wet thwack, orange pigment from the clay seeping into its wet, bubbled heart.

"He's not dead," Sam said.

"I know … well, I didn't mean …. Anthony sometimes acts like he is."

"Sometimes I think it'd be easier if he were dead. We wouldn't have to see him. We could … we wouldn't have to see him."

In the trees above us, in the branches that reached across the roof of Sam's house toward one another like lovers, morning birds chirruped.

"Before the accident, he used to tell me how he would kill himself if he ever got up the nerve," Sam said.

My lungs constricted.

"It was usually always pills or a gun to the head. He was seeing someone about it. Every Wednesday he went off to therapy somewhere. I don't know how he paid for it. We didn't have insurance."

A cold slice of paranoia slit me from chest to navel. My lower extremities numbed.

"Goddamn hack is what I say," Sam continued. "I've had a mind for quite a while to track that therapist down. I wonder every night if he told her how he might kill himself if he got brave enough. I wonder if he told her he might just throw himself off a cliff if he got the chance ...."

Anxiety distorted my vision, making it hard to focus on what Sam was saying, but I knew what it boiled down to: Mother Clara Stevens had effectively killed his fiancée.

"Look," he said, endearing his face with a sad smile. "I'm sorry to dump all that on you. I know what you do for Anthony. And usually I'm fine, but ever since Saturday when Anthony's parents told us they want to take him off life support, it's been rough going."

"Paul and Nancy want to take Ned off life support?"

"Well, yeah," Sam said, confusion knitted into his eyebrows. "Didn't Anthony tell you all about it after his last visit? He's been texting me constantly trying to figure out a way to change their minds."

Guiding Ned through counseling had been rough enough, had melted parts of me away with the multitudinous magma of his sorrow. Knowledge of his vegetative state, the product of what I was now sure had been his attempted suicide, was a burden I wasn't equipped to handle.

"I'm sorry," I said, striving to hide the hive of emotions buzzing beneath my denial. "I forgot I've got a meeting with a parishioner in about thirty minutes. I would love it if you could fix me up a car for the race. I trust you."

Before waiting on his response, I swiveled and sped to my car.

"What about a theme?" he called after me.

I pretended not to hear.

I left a note for Anthony to find on the kitchen table the morning of the Laurel County Clergy Demolition Derby. It explained everything.

How Ned had come to me for counseling long before Anthony and I ever started dating. How he'd spoken week after week of the nothingness inside him. How I begged him to find a real therapist. How the Bible, the liturgy, the incense-swinging would never be proper weapons against clinical depression. I wrote about how I'd done my best. And mostly, I wrote about how Ned should be unplugged. It was a note that begged for mercy.

A letter, that was the best way. He would read it, and by the time the race was over that night, we would be able to talk. Unless of course he decided not to come to the race. Unless he decided to pack his things and go. I thought about absence. About how a few days ago I would have celebrated his.

But now as I changed clothes in the church bathroom, I wanted to be forgiven. For him to tell me how right I was, how glad he was that I had been there for Ned, if only for a bit. How it wasn't my fault that he'd fallen to his death. That I had done all I could.

I looked at myself in the mirror under the fluorescent flickering of the white bathroom light. Tried to smooth back my frizzled yellow hair. Makeup applied that morning melted off my face from sweat and the day's many duties. I leaned down and pulled on the ridiculous black jumpsuit I'd purchased for the occasion, sliding my freckled arms into the sleeves. Fastened my clerical collar to the neckline, that familiar choking sensation.

As I drove to the derby track by Sam's house, I decided that it didn't matter if I won or lost; $1,500 to the hospital wasn't going to bring Ned back. Maybe I should have prayed.

You forget to do that, when it's your job. You forget to be sincere. You forget that you must be a cupped hand capable of holding everyone's sorrows. Because when you are holding it all, prayer feels like wading through the feathery fronds of lake weeds, down in the muck with your eyes shut. Waiting to be tangled up.

At the track, I screened the perimeter for Anthony or Sam. The crowd was hushed. There was the mineral smell of the track and the watered-down pig scent of hot dog vendors.

On the far end of the track loitered a group of penitent faces— Laurel County's preachers. Their pastors and priests. They talked in clusters while their cars waited in line behind them. I joined them, waved at Father Killian and Pastor Jeremiah as they chatted by their cars.

I found Sam by a hot dog stand, squirting a line of mustard along the dog's sweaty, pink- and gray-mottled flesh. He turned to me.

"Hey, Sam."

"Hey there, Mother."

"Now, now. You built me a car. I think you can call me Clara."

"I think I'll leave what I call you up to me."

"Well … OK. Anyway. Where's the car?"

Sam bit down on a third of his hot dog and tore it away with a jerk. Pointed to the lineup of cars. The fourth vehicle, a refurbished VW bug, stared back at me with its circuitous headlights. They were painted over like segmented insect eyes. The rest of the car was an unsettling green with slender accents of yellow that carved out mandibles, leaf-like wings lying flat against the rear. Two car antennae had been bent, painted yellow, and affixed above the windshield.

"What is it?" I asked.

"Praying Mantis," Sam said with his mouth full. "Vicious little bug. Made for fighting. Eats its mates."

"Seems a little violent."

Sam shrugged and grunted, shoving the butt of the hot dog in his mouth. He crumpled up the translucent paper holder and tossed it on the ground. Made his way toward my car and gestured for me to follow him as Anthony emerged from behind the closest stand of bleachers with a microphone. I tried to wave him down, but he just jogged to the center of the track without looking my way.

Sam opened the driver's side door, his palm picking up flakes of cheap green spray paint. He dangled a car key in front of my face. I took it from him and sat on the car's worn fabric seating.

"LADIES AND GENTLEMEN," Anthony's voice amplified from the tinny loudspeakers, surprising me with his gusto. I'd had doubts about his ability to emcee on a day when he'd seen Ned. "IF YOU'LL PLEASE FIND YOUR SEATS, WE'VE GOT A DERBY TO GET UNDERWAY."

The crowd cheered, hoisting their signs above their heads. Hand-scrawled poster board with the names of their church or leader in varying stages of legibility. I looked up at Sam, the sight of him cutting deep to that mine of guilt I'd kept sealed off from myself for so long.

"Got any tips so I don't make a fool of myself out there?"

"Advice?" Sam said. "I don't think I owe you any advice, Mother."

"WELCOME ONE AND ALL TO THE FIRST ANNUAL LAUREL COUNTY CLERGY DEMOLITION DERBY." The tail end of Anthony's announcement was eclipsed by the crowd's sudden and violent applause. Little boys and girls sprang from their seats and scrambled down the bleacher aisles to line the track's fence. Men and women shook their poster board in unison.

I turned to Sam, confused by his hostility. He gripped the open door and shook his head slowly from side to side.

"Ned used to talk about your honesty."

"I'm sorry?"

"He never told me who you were, but he went on and on about how you never bullshitted him, about how he could trust anything you said."

"Sam," I said, realizing I had no idea what to say.

"Anthony's parents unplugged Ned today. Just like it was nothing," Sam said, throwing his arms in the air, wild searching eyes roving in his skull. "And don't flatter yourself thinking it had anything to do with that stupid letter of yours. That cruel letter. How could you hold onto him like that … so much closer to him than it turns out I ever was … and let him unravel? Four years of my life I gave to him, keeping him above water. Five weeks with you and he jumps off a fucking cliff."

Here he paused to scoff, raspy and vitriolic.

"Therapy, yeah right," he continued "What exactly did you say to him in that room every week?"

Before I could answer, a horn blew from the track's loudspeakers. All around, clergy members turned the keys of their cars. Sam darted his hand inside the car and turned my key for me. Slammed the door almost before I could retract my arm.

Panic and adrenaline rose deep from the well of me as I pressed my foot to the gas pedal and broke into the arena.

My fellow men and women of the cloth reversed and rammed with the best of derbiers. As I circled the track, trying to keep out of the fray, I watched Father Killian's car veer straight into the side of Reverend Millicent's, crushing metal inward toward her pliant body.

As I dodged the escalating scene, I remembered Ned's and my last counseling session. I drove in circles, hoping to avoid the bloodshed.

Ned, the last time I had seen him, dressed so haphazardly in that dirty jacket, those dim, tattered jeans. His long, curled hair fastened in a loose ponytail at the nape of his neck. His dusky face unshaven.

He had wanted to talk about loved ones, what happened to them when their family members died unexpectedly.

I hadn't combed through my Bible in years, reliant on the church calendar to inform my sermons every Sunday, so I tried to direct all of his queries back on himself. "Well, how might you feel, if you were to lose someone you were close to?"

He'd paused for a moment, letting the silence stagnate.

"Well. Death is peace, right? So, I think maybe I would be happy for them? Because if they felt what I felt, this crushing gutter where I'm sinking and I can't climb out. Where the crest of every hill is lower and lower and it takes fewer and fewer steps to descend back into that place … I would want to take that from them. I would want them to do anything in their power to escape. And I hope that's what they would want for me."

And I hadn't known what to say, aware for the very first time he might mean to kill himself. Like a therapist in a bad movie, I had mumbled something about our time being up. The day had been long and challenging—a hospital visit for a teenager in my parish with cancer. A thirteen-year-old girl who only understood the pattern of her life through God's plan, because that's what her parents had taught her. Because that's what I had taught her. She'd wanted to know how her leukemia fit into all that. How, in God's grand design, her suffering and impending death made the world godlier, more divine, more molded in God's image.

By the time Ned had come to see me, his counseling session, his very person, had become in my mind like a paper to push, a form to sign that I had no energy or desire to read. Because the thought of accessing that ever-shallowing pond of empathy within me presented as a herculean, almost unnecessary task.

I couldn't remember the rest of the session. Just that small exchange.

Beyond the solitude of my praying mantis, the derby escalated, fueled by an unfeeling rage perhaps similar to my own. Fueled by all the losses, all the grief, all the refuse of small human tragedies built up over years of service.

Though I knew he wouldn't have me, I wanted to leave the car and comfort Anthony. To have him fill me up with his fresh anguish. I wanted to hear all his unkind words. I wanted my own well of absence filled.

I parked my car and turned the key. The frame of the car shuddered to sleep. Through the window, I scanned the crowd for Sam or Anthony. Couldn't see them through the mayhem of dust and exhaust.

Which is why I didn't immediately see the rusted fender of Father Killian's car coming toward me. The crumpled metal of his car's hood exposed bits of engine almost coyly, like a new bride on her wedding night.

Right before impact, I saw Father Killian's face, glossed over by the car's shining dashboard. I saw how it had aged since last year's fundraiser. How his skin was now cratered with obsessively picked acne scars. How the grooved lines carved his every feature away, whittling his skin inward to the deep interstellar of his glassy eyes.

And I hoped, just then, that this joining of metal might grant us both some peace.

Justin Carter

Memory in Which We Stare Through the Window All Night

When I think of all the places I'll never
be again, I think of the night
X drank too much & flipped his car
right in front of the house where
the rest of us were still drunk.
We huddled near the window & watched
the police lights turn the night
into a kind of ornament. & I remember
how, right before the cops arrived,
he'd walked back toward us,
his face a cocktail of glass & blood.
I think of Y, another friend,
who had been inside that car until
just moments before it happened,
how he'd asked to be dropped back off
at the party & then watched
as the car lifted off in the distance.
I think of how it could have been
any of us in the passenger seat instead
of none of us. Of how thankful
I am we didn't witness death. We stayed
in that house, behind that window,
until morning. Some of us never left.

We thought if we stayed there forever,
if we never stepped outside & faced
the scarred grass, the field where
we'd find bits of metal for months after,
that we could escape our fear,
could stay drunk & innocent until
the sky returned to darkness,
that maybe then we could have
one more chance to get everything right.

Sam Herschel Wein

I Showed You a Poem About My Car Accident and You Thought It Was About Yourself, Again

I am the car.
I am handgun brakes and steeltoe
inertia, I am not the ice storm.
When I remember it, someone is

always the
ice storm, like the fortune-teller,
spiritual travelers I've said "No
thank you" to, or my dead dog.

I am also the
truck-pickle, pickletruck. Long
and oblong, fuzzy and green in
the roads, a stopping oasis. Who

wants to be the
salt? Iridescent, laneless and alone
in the night? Well none of you get
to be the salt because the salt was

vacant, on a lunch
break, dipping pretzels in gooey

beer cheese. But the ice storm—
so Oscar the Grouch, so Piglet

and nervous and
captivating every space of air,
like white suspended hanging rugs,
the truck-pickle slow and cautious

like a bird new with
flight. So I'm the car, and I'm
impatient. So I'm the car and the
truck and someone is the ice

storm, I say *To*
hell with all this, this fairy world,
wings on the trees. I try to pass
pickle-truck, other me, slower

me, me meets me
next to each other on the road
and me starts to lose it, car me.
Turning me. Turning into

me, me. Lo, truck,
I dreamed of meeting you, my
head leaning to your gruff, bulky
calf, but I had learned

young not to
slide myself into love, so I
watermill-arm swing the wheel
opposite, spinning off the

highway to roses,
highway to iced greens, a salad

turning hurricane, three spins
in and I'm clenched waiting for

the hit, waiting for
the rail for the car, other me's
not the ice storm because that is
not me I *swear* I curse my eyes

watching the
sky as I'm thrown around its nexus
and curve, my shoulder a pinball
going for gold I see white, blink,

I am stopped on
the other side of the highway. A
car heading in my direction.
I steeltoe gas, I handgun steer into

the median. I stop.
I stop. I stop, car me, in the car
me, we all pick our favorite
drops of wet, hoping to finalize

our freedom,
our sight. I breathe the most
important me onto the glass, body
empty. I feel like a fresh snowfall,

completely new,
cold as goat horns, mountains
miniature, so beautiful I wanted
to build them with my hands.

Danielle Kotrla

Dead Dog Corridor

On hot pavement, the bones of coyotes,
strays, melt under Texas sun on their journey
nowhere. Stopped by tire tracks
on dotted white lines, I imagine the howl
of not wanting to die. Not here,
not in the face of so much indifference.

The interstate is no foyer for a funeral home,
but the tune carried by engines almost sounds
like god calling each one of us home
to distant horizons, northbound and bitter.

My morning travels involve avoiding god
and time and Nietzsche—all three turning
on the head of a canine covered in yesterday's
moonlight hunt. The tune, barbaric,
reminiscent of all of the things I have said
under the covers and nowhere else.

When I stop on the side of the road
somewhere between the two borders of Texas
beside the body of a coyote two days dead,
I make no music. I sing no funeral hymns.
The sympathy falls short with the abrupt end
of barbed wire and the morning's traffic.

Dead Dog Corridor

I cannot speak of the dying desires of canines,
but I can put a name to what sits behind the ribs—
like everything else vain-seeking and glorious,
I wish to be seen by so many for so short a time.

Elizabeth Nonemaker

Blue Desert

My mother is a twig in the desert.

The sun is sinking but its rays are still hot. They catch like tinder in the tufts of her hair, forming a halo around her face—so brilliantly white and glowing that I'm expecting at any moment for the whole of her frayed head to spark and to go up in flames.

She sways in the unchecked wind. She clutches my arm, then pushes it away when she finds her footing. At the base of the foothills, the river curls through the land like a snake. It catches the sun and flares red. Behind us, the desert yawns—a hungry thing. It might swallow us up. I see the convergence of sky and earth as a jaw, a white bone churning dust, and the mountains are the teeth of some old desert god.

My mother mutters, "Where *is* this?" Looking to me, her brow wrinkles, as if she can't comprehend my existence here.

She used to know all of my places: the tire swing by the community pool, the cemetery plot on the golf course. If I left the house when she needed me, she'd know where to go. She'd cruise through those humid Virginia suburbs, brights on, keeping her Peggy Lee and Bobby Darin on low. "Oh the shark, babe ...." I imagined that she had every street, back alley, makeshift trail committed to memory.

Now, there is an aimlessness that pools about her like a contagion. In the two days since her arrival in New Mexico, I have often found myself wondering what exactly it is we're supposed to do next, what even brought her out here: Was it me? I know that we've come to this spot to watch the sunset, if only to orient ourselves as to where east and west lay. I know that I'm pleased to see her taking it in. I have wanted to feel her seeing the land, as I did only months ago, as something confounding. How a spacious earth makes the sky seem larger, too. But she is easily pulled into reverie. The wind dissipates, and in the stillness she begins to wander, picking a path through the sagebrush.

I call out. "Where are you going?"

A branch snags at my mother's cashmere cardigan, which she delicately untangles before answering. "I'm looking for a good place to pray."

"Why not here?" She doesn't answer. I resist the urge to follow her.

Other times, when I was a girl, she found me by, as she said, calling to me. I started to get a feeling to walk in a certain direction, and soon enough, there she'd be, parked, drumming her fingers on the steering wheel. I would slide into the passenger seat, she would crank her music, and, shouting over the brass swells, debrief me: It was 3 p.m., and time to say the novena, always more powerful when two or more were gathered in Jesus's name. Or, we needed to repaint the living room, and right now. If it stayed that dark blue, it would always remind her of that horrible fight with my father. She wanted me to look surprised whenever she found me, so that she could tell me I shouldn't be. She insisted we had a special bond—that we were actually the same person, displaced just a little by body, time, circumstance—like how there were three persons in one God.

I keep my eyes on the bright-yellow square of her cardigan. Then there is a thunk, a small "Oh!," and it disappears from sight.

"*Care*ful!" Sighing, I trace her path through the brush. My mother has tripped on a root—a gnarled old thing that pokes through the earth like a finger from the grave. She lies facedown in the dirt, only struggling to raise herself once she hears me arriving. I hook my hands beneath her armpits and hoist her to her feet. "You OK?"

"Now I am." My mother curls an arm around my neck and leans. I stumble, squinting against the sunlight glancing off of her many rings—one, if not two or three, on each finger. "You saved me," she says, teasing. "See how I need you?"

Dusk comes on fast. The air holds neither water nor light. Clear and suddenly brisk, it's a nail inside my throat. With my head bowed, I have a vision that it is actually the root around my neck, pulling me into the earth. I try to turn, to glimpse my mother's expression.

I cannot make it out. The sky darkens. Soon the night is a mask that slips over her face.

This time, it will be different. This time, I won't let her take me back.

As we trudge back to the car, a junky thing I'm borrowing from a friend, I can feel my mother simmering with dislike: for the stones that push through her flats, for the unexpected cold, the dust. I know she doesn't want to be here. She called me every day in the weeks before her arrival, asking me to come home. Cajoling. Threatening. Saying it was where I belonged and where I was needed, that this time it was serious.

But it's always serious. It must have surprised her, the way I skirted her, suggesting a visit to me instead—as if seeing each other were the point. She relented. She can't manage that house all by herself, with all of its purposeless rooms.

In the car, Dolly, my mother—she's never liked me to call her by anything except the pet name she pushes on all other familiar adults—examines her seat belt before allowing it to touch her sweater. She buckles in, and I feel the air grow taut. I brace myself. For the most part she has been apathetic these past two days, but there is a weight between us, and sometimes I catch her looking at me in a way that reminds me of her cat, moments before snapping a bird's neck in its jaw.

She only wants to make an announcement. "I have to go home," she says.

I punch the address of our hotel into the GPS. "Right now?"

"I have to go—I have to go home." Dolly's voice takes on an edge of panic. She curls her hands around the lip of the passenger seat, gripping.

"And do what?"

"I don't know!" she snaps. She drags her nails against the seat's upholstery. "That's the point. I need—I haven't even found an attorney." She pulls herself forward, pushes back. Her nails catch on the scabby part of the fabric where something once spilled and dried there. She pulls them away in disgust. "When we get to the hotel, I'll buy a ticket. How much do you think that will be? I'll fly back tomorrow." She pauses. "You come, too."

I nestle the GPS into its stand on the dash. I put the car in reverse, bracing my right arm against the back of Dolly's seat and twisting to gaze behind us. I might as well close my eyes. It is a moonless night, and the view out the back of the car is opaque. "You want to pay extra just to fly home a few days early?" She says nothing. "You haven't even seen my casita."

My mother rocks forward and backward, clutching her elbows, sucking the air in through her teeth. As we reverse, pebbles clatter against the car's exterior, and she winces at the noise. It must seem a thin barrier between us and the desert, us and everything else that could harm us.

"How far away are we, anyway?" she asks.

"From the hotel? About thirty minutes."

"No," she says. "I mean from *home*."

"Oh." I squint, as if sizing up the distance. "About two thousand miles." When the tires hit a bump and we start to roll smoothly, I know we've reached the road. Before I point the car in the direction of the hotel, I say, "I am home."

Nothing Dolly does has only one reason. Maybe the attorney business really is pressing. But I have a notion that she doesn't want to see my casita on principle, doesn't want to acknowledge that, after years of arrested attempts, I did, after all, manage to leave. We stay up that night at the hotel, arguing. She argues; I placate. We both know she won't change her flight. As the sky grays with morning, she seems to doze, waking to mumble that this is no time for a vacation, and she doesn't expect to enjoy herself. I tell her I know. I don't tell her that I also think that all of this could help her—could show her that it's not so bad to be alone. It's not so bad to start over.

We don't sleep long. Over breakfast, my mother is morose. With one hand she strokes the white fox-fur coat draped over her shoulders—a gift from my father for their twentieth wedding anniversary. The first time she showed it to me, she leaned over, cupping her hand against her mouth, and stage-whispered, "This will make *all* my friends jealous!" I'd been in my room, and there was no one else around.

With her other hand my mother picks at her oatmeal before letting the spoon drop to the table. When I look up, her face is twisted into an expression of almost cartoonish sorrow, the mouth arched perfectly downwards.

"What's wrong with me?" she says.

I arrange the silverware next to my plate. "What do you mean?"

"Why would he leave? What's wrong with me?"

"Nothing's wrong with you." I look off to the side, searching for words. "He just—."

"Do *you* know why he's leaving?"

I hesitate. I say, "Sometimes people need a change. To figure things out." I look at her pointedly. "To be on their own."

Dolly leans forward, unblinking. "Hold my hand," she says.

I pull my left hand from my lap and extend it to her. My mother encloses it in both of her hands, and squeezes. Her rings cut into my skin. She speaks slowly, pressing into the syllables. "Did you put him up to this?"

My blood goes very hot, then cold. "Of course not."

"But you could fix it."

"No." I try to pull my hand away, but Dolly is holding too tightly. "Dad is a grown man," I explain. "He makes his own decisions."

"But he always listens to you. If you come home, you could fix this for me. You could talk him out of it."

"No," I say. "I couldn't." I glance down at our hands, where Dolly's are cinching the soft part just below my knuckles. "Please let go."

I remind myself that this time, it is already different. If you invite someone to come see you, it is not the same as them finding you. It is not the same as them pulling you back.

My mother releases, but she keeps her hands on the table, palms open, as if waiting to receive something. Her need is like a vapor filling the air, forming tendrils, and searching—for me, for someplace to land, like the kudzu back home that eats saplings. She trains her immobile gaze on me until I flag down the server and ask, please, for the check.

The Loretto Chapel is the only part of her trip that my mother seems to enjoy. We visit after breakfast, starting the day as we have the others. Each time we enter, Dolly draws back her shoulders and takes in the sight of the staircase, built without nails and, as believers say, by St. Joseph himself. She recites, "The Lord makes the impossible, possible," and then we take a pew.

Kneeling, my mother mixes the known prayers with her own. "Help me to be as a little child before the Lord," she whispers, not very quietly. "Blind, dumb like an infant in my time of trial, I submit wholly to Your grace." I know enough by now to suspect that the prayer is voiced for my benefit. It is meant to impress me with her helplessness. I sigh. I'm aware of the other visitors in the chapel—tourists, who have come here only for the postcards, and some who are bending their ears toward Dolly's prayer.

It used to work, the helplessness. The need. There's something about heeding it that I miss. As when, only a few months into my first semester at university, Dolly arrived with the announcement that she had been diagnosed with an aggressive cancer. Soon, she would not even be able to feed herself. What was I supposed to do? I remember feeling only a great swell of nobility as I watched, for the last time, the campus recede in the car's side mirror. That Dolly recovered so quickly was a testament to my care, or so I thought at the time. And when, later, she put an end to my craziness with that man, Noah—recalling the name makes me shiver, with both desire and fear—I was so overcome with dawning gratitude that I didn't care what Dolly asked of me; for months afterwards, I doted on her like a servant. She learned to remind me of what could have happened whenever I seemed to tire of her. Noah and I had made it all the way to a motel in Poughkeepsie, with plans to marry the next day, when she found us.

Although, that's what made me wonder. Was my mother more capable than she made herself out to be? Hadn't she supported herself for a few years before marrying? Did she have talents that simply lay dormant—or obscured? How had she tracked us across state lines?

Dolly has started on a rosary. She rocks, rattles the beads. As passion overcomes her, her voice breaks from her whisper, warbling. Two teenaged boys with expensive-looking cameras have taken the pew across the aisle. I can see them nudge each other, glance toward my mother, snicker. I don't want to stay here. I squeeze Dolly's shoulder and whisper, "I'll be outside." As I pass the boys I reach behind and flick one, hard, on the skull.

But as soon as I pass from the chapel I hear Dolly's voice booming from within. "Don't," it intones, "*laugh* at me."

How do you make a person strong?

Outside the chapel, I study a short, twisted tree laden with rosaries that dangle and glimmer like tinsel. Not very long ago, I would have looked upon them for guidance. Now?

I dig through my bag until I find my own rosary, a battered thing I've kept for ten years or more, and drape it over a branch. As I watch it swing in the exposed air, a dull sadness overcomes my body. So many nights lulled to sleep, whispering over the milky beads.

How do you teach someone to let go?

I find myself thinking of the water pump at my casita. The building is very old, built without plumbing, and whenever I want water I have to tramp out to the iron device in the yard, raised upon a mound of dirt like a shrine. The chore annoyed me at first, but gradually I became fascinated by it—how an arm's easy pressure could draw something so pure from the ground, how I could hear the water rushing upwards before it emerged. My fascination for the pump grew until one day, as I watched the water collapse from the spout like an expulsion of words, I felt a barb rise in my throat. I was kneeling. The spaces between things seemed to flatten, and I got a little heady. I felt as if I were praying.

Immediately I pressed my palms against the dirt, startled, and shivering with guilt. What I was doing seemed—I searched for the word—sinful. But when I asked myself why, I couldn't answer it. So I let myself cry a little, and then I pumped the rest of the water and walked back to the casita. The sun sheared off the angular plane of the water as I walked, and I was reminded, too, of the feeling I had when I left my university—but this was vibrant: a new thing.

I startle at the feeling of a hand running through my hair. "Beautiful," my mother murmurs. I didn't notice her emerge from the chapel. She stares into me with that same unblinking gaze from breakfast. Impossibly, she seems shorter than I remember.

"I used to have a mane like this once," she says, taking a bundle of the hair in her hand, seeming to weigh it. "It drove your father wild."

I place a hand on Dolly's shoulder, and realize that she's hunching. "What's wrong with your back?"

Dolly curls her lip. "I'm *old*."

"You're fifty-nine."

My mother's shoulders start to quake. I realize that she's laughing. When she doesn't stop, I feel as if I've missed a cue, and we'll be frozen in this moment until I've told her whatever it is she needs to hear. But I don't know what that is. Finally, she regains her breath. "Hawney," she says, laying on her old Southern accent, "age has a way of catching *up* to you. Where's the car?" She hobbles down the sidewalk, gingerly lifting her feet, hands steadied before her as if she anticipates toppling over at any moment.

We drive north, flanking the river. Slabs of sheer, red rock rise beside us. Sometimes the rock pulls aside like a curtain to reveal the plains speckled with scrub, stretching for miles. I talk about the high country and the river; I name peaks in the distance. I feel that if I can spark her interest just once, a whole ripple of revelations will follow, as they did for me: the world, its beauty, her place in it. Her future. But my mother keeps her head bowed, fingering her rosary.

I find myself fighting the urge to rip the thing from her fingers. The soft clack of the beads, her saliva sticking as she mouths the Hail Marys, are making me sick. I stick my head out the window and gulp dry air.

I am remembering why I left. How every moment in my mother's house felt as if it were clinging to me, both interminable and hopelessly fleeting. How one day, I felt that if I didn't leave soon, I never would.

It was something I'd always dreamed about. Packing a bag, stuffing every last dollar bill in my pockets. Catching a series of buses. Drifting, until I found a place that felt right. I actually shouted "Stop!" to the cargo van driver from Albuquerque when we passed through the town—my town—and nothing since has compared to that first sensation of my worn-out tennis shoes smacking the dust. From there, each day was simply a day: They began and they ended, and one led to another, and a life arose from them all on its own.

Something in the car has changed. I glance over at Dolly. She has put away the rosary. Now she has her flip phone out, and she's plugging numbers in with stiff, deliberate fingers. "Here," she says, and she thrusts the phone against my ear.

I jerk my head away and the car almost veers off the road. "What are you doing?" My hands are shaking.

"Talk to him." My mother is crying now. She extends the phone toward my ear like a priest wielding a crucifix, as the line on the other end bleats again, and again. "It's your father. You talk to him." There's a click, and then a recorded, digital sing-song.

"He didn't pick up."

Dolly snaps the phone shut and her shoulders are shaking again, this time from tears. "Why won't you help me?" she moans.

I handle the car automatically, bewildered. "What would I have even said to him?" My anger surprises me. "'Hey, Dad, I know this impacts your entire life, but don't get a divorce—just my two cents.' Is that what I should say?"

"*His* entire life?" Dolly's voice rises, gaining strength in the way I remember so well. "Here *I* am, approaching my sixties. What, do you expect me to go back to work? Who is supposed to take care of me?" From the corner of my eye, I watch my mother lift her forearms, and feel her glaring. She shakes her arms, jangling her bracelets against each other, as she bellows, "I've *earned* this."

I purse my lips, thinking that since her arrival, my mother has not seemed so vital, so alive as she does now, insisting on her own ineptitude.

We drive in silence, the only sound the shudder of wind coursing in through my window. Then we both speak at once:

"When you were little, I could make you do whatever I wanted," Dolly says.

"You're supposed to take care of yourself, yes," I say.

Again, I feel her eyes, tunneling, sinking into my skin. My mother speaks so softly that at first I wonder if I'm imagining the words. "You," she says, "have grossly misjudged me."

My heart quickens as we approach my town. I've missed it. We start to pass the landmarks: a steep climb up an escarpment, and then, at the peak, a bare, solitary olive tree. At the tree we turn right and nose down the plateau. And there it is: the speckle of structures, ridiculous, nestled between the plateau and the looming mountains.

I draw Dolly's attention to them. "There's a legend about this place. They say there's a spirit living in those mountains. She decides if you can stay, so people either love or hate the town depending on whether or not she accepts you."

Dolly has been slumped against the passenger door. She mumbles into the window glass. "How long does it take her to decide?"

"I don't know," I say. "A few days? So you won't—."

"I'd rather," my mother says, "you be an atheist than a heathen."

We pass ranches, with their wooden arches over the entrances. Then we begin to pass houses, fenced in by crude posts and wire. Some are decorated with the expected things: dried chile ristras, Tibetan prayer flags tattered with age. I slow for a gaggle of dogs with clumped fur and lolling grins. Out of habit, I start to brake for a man sitting on a pack at the side of the road, thumbing for a ride, but my mother reaches across and grabs my forearm. "Don't even think about it," she says. We continue forward, and red grit kicks into the air even though we're driving on pavement.

"Why is everything here …"—she searches for her words—"so degenerate?"

But now I'm suppressing a laugh. We pass through the alfalfa fields that enclose my casita and pull up along the dirt drive, and I can hardly wait. My mother hasn't always been this way. She didn't always live in cavernous houses, didn't always drape herself in jewels. She grew up poor, in Raleigh, in a neighborhood swarming with children; every time she's ever spoken of it, she tears up. It was only when I got older that I started to wonder if she had cast herself as the aloof housewife only because she thought she was supposed to. I don't even mind when she steps out of the car and makes a big pantomime of brushing the dirt off her coat; it strikes me as funny. My mother eyes the little house and says, "Is this where you live?"

It is. The place that I have made for myself, in a desert town thousands of miles from everything I've ever known, and it is mine. I lead her inside, wanting to show her everything. It is small, I admit, but it's all I need. There's the basket for hanging fruit by the stove—something I found and repaired with discarded fence wiring. There's the simple bed by the window, stacked milk crates for bookshelves. Behind the casita, two green plastic chairs—castoffs from the shop where I work—and every morning the magpies gather in the crabapple trees. "They're smart birds," I say. "I'm trying to befriend them." I pause, catching my mother's expression: the lips pressed tightly together, the nose flared. She clutches her fur around her as she rotates, taking it all in. "It's a little dusty," I apologize. "And cold—I'll plug in the heater. And we can make tea. Come on." I grab the pail and lead Dolly outside to the water pump. "When was the last time you saw one of these?" I start to work the handle, waiting for the pressure to build.

My mother stares. "You don't have running water?" Her voice is faint.

"Not in the house, no," I say. "But it's right here." The water bubbles up and splashes into the pail. "See?"

At the sight, my mother bursts into laughter. Harsh, guttural belly laughs that make birds take off from the surrounding trees. I can hear it echoing inside the pail. I focus myself on the task of monitoring the water level. My mother has doubled over now; she is leaning on her knees. "Good Lord," she wheezes. "You left my house for *this?*"

I grind the inside of my cheek between my molars, something I forgot I used to do. My mother recovers, wiping tears from her eyes, but she gives in to the few stray giggles that keep escaping. When have I seen her so happy?

"Come home," she says.

Softly, I answer: "No."

"What is it you want me to say?" My mother's grin is easy and loose; she rocks back on her heels. "Is this why you wanted me to come out here? To beg you to come back? You know I'll always need you." Her jowls droop as she makes a pouting face. "Come home. Please."

I've never really held my own against my mother. Even when I left five months ago it was, as with Noah, in the middle of the night. Otherwise, it would not have been her rage that kept me, but the inevitable collapse, the consolations I would have had to provide afterwards. I didn't even pick up her calls until I had signed the paperwork for my casita. I was so afraid of finding myself at a bus station, filled with remorse and self-loathing.

But this time, I remind myself, it is different. "No," I repeat. "I live here now."

My mother's face is passive at first, and then it begins to contort, as if each muscle below the skin is firing separately from the others. My stomach twists. Dolly takes a step forward, places a hand around her own throat. She gasps against its pressure. Her eyes bulge, and she won't look away. We stand like that for some moments before she explodes from her stillness. Like something else has taken control of her body. She rips the coat from her shoulders and begins beating it against the ground. Between her assaults she spits words. "God," she hisses, "gave me—a husband—and a daughter." Now she's on her knees, trying to claw out the fur. "And I'll be damned"—she takes off a shoe and hammers the heel into the coat—"if you take them—away from me."

Then she crumples. Falls upon the battered coat and sobs as if she is trying to expel her insides. I wait to make sure it is real. Then, cautiously, I approach. Place a hand on her shoulder. Kneel with her, hold her.

☾

The river is the slowest knife. Inexorably it digs, carving away the layers of earth, as if searching for something lost in the hard mud eons ago. Its path runs much deeper here in the high country, a precipice so sudden, that even if you were to walk along the ridge, you would only hear the water in phantom snatches, when the sound, like an old sigh, rides up on the wind.

I have taken my mother here, to the gorge, to watch the sunset again. But we've missed it. Already the night is enclosing the desert in its soft, black mouth, but it's not as if Dolly cares. Limp in the car, she exerts only a loose pressure upon the rosary entwined in her hand. She would not even buckle her seat belt—I had to do it for her. Now, I unclip the buckle and gently ease it back. "Come on," I say. I get out of the car and walk to her door. I open it and guide her to her feet. "Have you ever seen stars like these?"

I shut the door behind her and my mother slumps against it. She has put her coat back on, filthy as it is. Her chin flops to her chest. Next to her, I lean my own back against the car. "I don't want this," I hear her mutter.

I do not know what to say. I fill my lungs with desert air. I don't hear my mother peel away from the car.

When I look down, I notice the rosary first, discarded upon the ground, and then the vacant space where my mother used to be. I pick up the rosary and look around. Nothing—just the dried brush shivering in the breeze. I step back around to the driver's side, turn on the high beams, angle them out over the plateau. I stand inside the opened door, one arm flung over the roof, and scan the landscape for a stab of unordinary movement: a flash of color, the glimmer of rings. At last, I spot a white blur, already far away, and retreating still. Just walking.

Where is she going, and why? The thought of doing nothing makes me ill. I dig the seam of a rosary bead into the tip of my finger and start to jog across the desert. I am surprised at the distance my mother has already covered. I lope awkwardly, jumping over bushes, until the headlights dim behind me, and the stars burst out of the sky and splatter.

Then I slow. The blur seems as far away as it always was. I have the feeling that even if I were to follow it throughout the night, I would never meet it. At times it seems to flicker and then it disappears. Then there are only the striated mountains. The split ache of the canyon, and, cradling me as I cross it, a blue desert, expansive, and holy.

Karaline Stamper

Let's Not Talk About the Feathers

When my mother plucks out all her feathers, I try to glue them back. Saltwater and snot aren't adhesives, at least not for very long. Three days later she slumps out of bed. She asks where her feathers went. Dad tells her she's molting. That her feathers will come back. That the blue pills will help. They keep me from cleaning, she says, and look at this mess. So I gather her feathers into a nest. I ask her if she wants mine, if she can take mine instead. I pluck my own feather and place it behind her ear. Dad fits a pill between her beak and tongue. We are both, in our own ways, willing her to be OK. He asks her to try. I ask her to stay alive.

Autumn McClintock

Houses

Those strange beasts,
how they keep us and kill us, let us rest
a minute, then complain they're full of dust.

When I let one go, it had already become a husk
taken over by those I didn't understand.
Pets dead in the yard. Tree swing swung

from the maple, and into the grand
gathering of pine, under a rock clung
to its pages, a porn mag, eaten through.

No, friend, I won't judge you
for casting them off, even as you love them.
The shed holds each rake and chemical

you'd ever need for digging up, chucking away.
A seed spit from your lips, now chaff left bent awry.

Gary Leising

Something's in the Yard, Moving

When the dog barks and scrabbles at the window,
bowing its panes toward the outside world,
and the night outside is so dark we cannot see
what she hears or smells,
yet we tell her to be quiet, "Enough!
we bark ourselves:

I think of all the times I felt
a blackness thick as blankets stuffed
in the cavity around my lungs and heart,
so much scratchy wool, a feeling I could not name
except that way, and you told me it wasn't
all that bad, get over it,

and the next morning the grass is tamped down,
the yard filled with signs something was there,
its stench left behind, and something like scat
but not, something black, black, so black.

Jennifer A. Howard

Flat Stanley reads Agatha Christie

who was a pharmacy tech, like my sister. AC wrote about ricin as a weapon before *Breaking Ba*d, before television, can I say before men were in charge of stories? In the past, real police officers caught actual suspects because they recognized symptoms from AC's novels. This tell us that cops read books, in the past. Once, AC's boss misfilled a prescription, adding a lethal dose of medicine to the suppositories, ten times what had been ordered by the doctor. Because woman, because whatever, instead of alerting him to the error, AC tripped comically on a pre-placed banana peel and the suppositories spilled to the floor, where she proceeded to fall on them. Flat Stanley is only imagining her slapstick, of course, the bodywork women enact—even Agatha Christie! Even my sister!—when they cannot expect trust. We don't poison each other as much any more, in the U.S. now, is that true? We just shoot them, or let them out of the door where somebody else shoots them. We strangle them, certainly; we beat them with our fists. By "we" I mostly mean our husbands and boyfriends. The world likes to think quiet poisoning is how women get the job done, but we also like knives, and intoxicated victims who have already raped us, and rarely do we poison soon enough—almost never in time. By we this time I mean me, or my sister, and maybe you.

Jennifer A. Howard

Flat Stanley is so often at the post office

where, he learned, watching *Clueless* with his third-grader, that people shoot each other, they go postal. Before people started shooting each other at schools and temples and churches and mosques, people shot each other at factories and banquet halls and grocery stores and Air Force bases. Being a person who works, or studies, or worships, is dangerous. Every time he slides through the sorting machine, he listens to hear how the employees talk to each other. They talk about television, about other people's imaginary love and violence. Either love is easy or love is infuriating; he can't tell. Don't go to work and don't fall in love, Flat Stanley. Probably don't go to school, either, his third-grader warns, or the movies. Let's stay here and I'll show you how to play cards by yourself: red four on black five, aces up top ready for building. Solitaire is also called patience. The foundations, the stock.

Michelle Ross

Fishbowl

I say, "Come give me a hug. I'm cold," but my kid runs from me, her feet sinking into the snow like candles into cake frosting.

It's late in the year for snow. Our daffodils—bulbs my wife, Rhonda, planted a few years before she died—sprung up a few weeks ago, and amongst the snow on the ground and the snowflakes coming down slow as feathers, they look fake, like those plastic, neon plants in my kid's fishbowl.

Those fake plants glow in the dark. I worry about my kid's fish, living in a world like that. The fake plants remind me of images I've seen of Tokyo at night—all those steel buildings lit up with candy-colored lights. How do those fish sleep?

I worry about our old dog, too, how she doesn't do anything anymore but eat and defecate and nap. She used to roll around in the snow. Fish Stick, we'd all called the dog then, because covered in white, she looked like one of the fish sticks Rhonda made from scratch—the way the flour stuck after she coated the cod in egg. Now our dog lies on the porch, shivering. At least she has good reason, I guess—being old and all.

My kid is getting old enough now to notice things about me I wish she didn't see. Like now when I say again, "Get over here and hug your father," she says, "Your breath stinks," and she keeps running around me in circles—too far away to reach, too fast to chase.

Those fish of hers swim in circles, too. They circle round and round those fake, plastic plants that sit there rigid in the middle of the tank, that don't sway the way real plants do, that wouldn't even sway if there were a current in that water. I wonder if her fish pretend they're really going somewhere. Lies like that do more good than harm. Lies probably keep them alive.

When I say, "How about we go pick up a pizza? We can watch a movie. Whatever you want to watch," she calls out, "I'm sick of pizza. I'm sick of watching movies." I bristle at the word "sick." I worry about my kid, most of all.

"Fine," I say, "but we have to eat something, and there's nothing in the house. So let's get in the car and go somewhere."

My kid stops running. She stares at me. Then she says, "We don't have nothing. We have crackers. We have beans. We have cheese. We have cereal. We have spaghetti. We have rice. We have yogurt. We have granola bars. We have frozen berries. We have butter. We have paper towels. We have spoons. We have forks. We have knives. We have tables. We have chairs. We have floors. We have crumbs."

Then my kid's in the back seat of our car. She's buckled in, looking out the window at me. Her breath fogs the glass as she continues to rattle off all that we have. Through the black plastic garbage bag sealing the hole where the passenger window should be, I hear her describe each dish towel folded inside the drawer beside the stove—the white towel printed with brightly colored hummingbirds, the pale-blue towel with the yellow sunflowers. I listen to her list cookie sheets, muffin pans, and the silicon Bundt pan. She will go on like this for hours, maybe until she passes out from exhaustion, if I don't take back my words, admit I'm wrong.

I won't let her go on that long, but for now, I remain where I am. I watch her mouth make shapes on the other side of the glass.

Leigh Camacho Rourks

Eighty-Five Days After
the Second Ship Cast Its Shadow

Henri had seen the girl before. Not like this, he was sure. Not with bare feet digging ruts into the edge of the lapping Gulf. Not with bare scalp. Bare thighs. Bare chest.

The moment of unexpected recognition struck him so hard he stopped and let his own heels sink deep into the cool sand.

He tried to remember, but all that came to him at first was the faint, weathered image of sun on yellow curls, full, blinding light—

> —how quickly he'd come to ache for unfiltered, painful brightness, for the ability to turn upward and see red heat through shut lids.

> THEY were terraforming, for lack of a better word, smogging the sky to a dull and milky memory of what it once was. Shooting blue smoke-trailing *somethings* to the east. Early every morning, more of them.

And then he knew. He knew that many times he'd seen this white girl lit *full up*, back when the sun's cast against concrete was still a yellow sear that haloed and burned. A neon prayer.

The curls were gone. Burned or shaved or maybe even torn from her scalp. He wasn't close enough to see, but there had been enough burned scalps, enough torn scalps, enough horror on his pilgrimage to know what was possible.

He had seen THEY dim the sun, after all.

He'd never known her name. The sort of stranger who was not quite a stranger. Had only seen her in stores or on the street waiting for a bus that might or might not show up. Henri owned a car then, a nice car, four-door, two booster seats in the back, and only did his own shopping occasionally, when he needed something faster than the app on his phone could get it to him.

They shared a general suburb but nothing more. But she was the first person he'd seen in two months who was familiar. And the first in weeks who was alive.

He moved closer, realized she was older than he'd thought. Not that he'd ever thought much about her. A face that smiled and nodded faintly in the cereal aisle.

"You're from Baton Rouge," he said. Felt relief. Her hair had been shaved. Her scalp was not a mass of scars.

Her left arm, though, was wilted. Thin but angry. Limp. Nearly matching his own before strangers had cut it from him like meat and replaced it with a metal and plastic miracle salvaged from the streets.

She did not answer. Did not even take a drag from the cigarillo she was holding, lit, in her bad hand.

They stood there in silence that Henri measured in the shortening, brown cigarillo. But he did not leave. He did not stop looking at her face. He could not.

Finally, as if taking pity, she said, "Yes." Only, "Yes."

And again they stood, until finally she, and then he, sat on the sand. She said, "You shopped at CVS." And then more silence. And then, "Or was it Walgreens? Or was it Walmart? Or was it Target?"

All the choices were exactly the same now. Or maybe always. Didn't matter. It was less than three months since he had parked a car, since he had thought of vitamins or ketchup, since he had seen another human he already knew. "Walgreens, mostly, if I was doing it," he said finally. He had stopped speaking a while ago. His voice, the accent he had tried to lose in his teens, felt wildly unfamiliar.

She put her hand, her good hand, on his foot. Sand caked his black sock and the too-big oxford he'd stolen from another man, a man long dead. A corpse.

"Your kids?" she said.

In the other time, they'd seen each other enough that she knew his girls. "Taken," he said. "First wave." He did not say *aliens*, no one liked to say *aliens*.

Her hand was still, a weight there.

I have stopped looking is the other part he did not say. *If I do not look, it is just easier to believe they are OK,* he did not say. *I do not know—I do not know—I do not know where else to look; I do not even understand how to keep looking. I can't figure out where else to go,* he did not say.

He had said those things to the concrete and the dimming sun and to a dead dog on the street. He had said those things to his hands and to his blistered, bleeding feet. He had said those things too many times already.

He measured their silence in her forgotten cigarillo, the cherry longer than the first and second segments of his pinky. He measured the silence in the way her hand did not leave its strange place on the rise of his foot, measured in how much stranger that gesture was by the second, by the minute, measured by the way the ash on the cigarillo lost its color and became a gray, tottering thing.

"Have you seen one?" she said. And then, "An alien?" Just like that.

He said nothing.

"Smooth," she said. "They are white and glassy," she said.

And he did not want to talk about that.

She finally took a drag from the cigarillo, and it was a saccharine-and-spice smell that came out of her as she exhaled. She offered him a drag, and he, having never smoked, not even in college, not even when his friends teased his straight-laced ways, took it. Inhaled the sweetness.

Coughed.

White and glassy.

Her hand stayed on his foot, and they smoked. Watched the water under the pale, dying sun.

Hannah V Warren

Slipping Between Dimensions & The World Ends

I know what you're thinking, but there is no happy ending. We will not gather as one, our hands over our salivating mouths, our eyes dim as paper. We will not come together arm in arm. We will not photograph ourselves, our hair braided with oil and water, for future evolutionary bipedals to caress. We will claw slick earth. We will bury ourselves like moles and live beneath the ground afraid and alone. We will lose our sight, our trimmed fingernails. We will grow elongated muzzles, furred bellies. Armageddon is already here, living inside the lining of our wombs, the rotten pear skins melting into the soil, the leftovers of a swift's nest. If this ending were a serpent, it would have already swallowed its own tail. It isn't predator or devil or extraterrestrial. I know you feel like you can disappear sometimes, and isn't that enough? Other versions of ourselves propel us as we gorge on the dead, their good deeds syrup on our fingers and lips.

Savannah Bradley

Service of the Light

Once, I opened my mouth to pray
and a horde of mosquitos unfurled
from my mouth.

They festered there, between my teeth,
for all these years I've kept my mouth
shut bowing before the altar—

I've been baptized once before,
a tiny, unassuming thing you'd thought
would keep this sort of promise.

Have I surprised you, Mama, with my ability
to disappoint you? Last Easter vigil, I let my candle
drip its wax down my arm

stared Christ in the face while I burned
not for him, but for you.
I'm sorry, this wasn't meant to be mean.

I wanted to make you proud so I pretended
to pray so hard that I forgot
the world. I thought that the harder

I pressed my palms together the better
God could hear me. But I wasn't even
saying anything,

and Mama, you never did, either.
We are both so good at never speaking,
aren't we?

B.J. Best

from "Ornithoncology"

You think they should be called *seagulls*, not *gulls*. You have said this before.
You are very clear about your preferred nomenclature for birds that circle
stinking mountains of garbage. This world is such a dump. *How can you be
a fuckin' mother and not see your fuckin' kid?* the neighbor said, thinking a
screen door means privacy. She probably wasn't talking about the Virgin
Mary. Jesus was such a bastard. Jesus, does your pet name for me sound so
soft in your mouth.

Maggie Dove

Every Time My Mother Dies

The only time my mother doesn't warn me about her impending death is when she's actually dying.

She had lost her own mother to cancer when she was only nine years old, and nobody had prepared her for it, and she wanted to make sure that her own children always knew that she was going to die someday so that we wouldn't be caught off guard. I was reminded of my mother's imminent death nearly every day, some days more subtly than others, for as far back as I can remember.

"... if I live that long," ended most sentences.

"Women die young in our family."

"Let me tell you again about that time they didn't expect me to make it through the night with pneumonia when I was twenty-two, because it could happen again."

"Parents die, Maggie. You know parents can die, right? I'm just saying that you shouldn't always count on me being alive."

My OCD started when I was six, all of my obsessive counting and touching routines centered on keeping her alive.

It was my twelfth birthday at Bennigan's. If you've never been to a Bennigan's, it was basically TGI Fridays with a slight Irish pub bent. I think their menus were identical except for a turkey sandwich they called "The Turkey O'Toole" that was just a turkey sandwich served on a soft pretzel, and a couple of items with corned beef in them, which meant that it nearly qualified as an "ethnic restaurant" in Boca Raton, Florida.

We lived one town over, in a poor neighborhood in Delray Beach, me and Mom and my two older sisters, but birthday rules dictated that I got to eat wherever I wanted for dinner, within reason. I had decided that this birthday would be *fancy*. I hoped I'd run into a classmate or two who would tell everyone in school that I ate at the kind of establishments that served a $6.50 cheeseburger, hoping they'd forgotten about that time they saw me at the Tuesday Kids Eat Free night at Po' Folks restaurant.

We all got burgers and fries, except for Mom, who ordered the gumbo. Mom was born on the Gulf Coast of Alabama and loved seafood more than just about anything in life. She grew up fishing and trawling, could scale and gut a fish like nobody's business, and often bragged about how she used to go frog-gigging when she was a kid—a perennial tomboy. Crawdads, oysters, shrimp, frog legs—if it came from the water, she was going to eat it. She taught us how to catch bass and would chase us around the kitchen with our catches after she'd sliced the fish bodies open in the kitchen sink, exposing their bloody insides much to our little girl horror.

"Don't you go gettin' attached to those crabs!" she'd say, our kitchen floor skittering with live crabs as she boiled the pot of water on the stove. We sat on the floor playing with them with the tongs she had given us to defend ourselves against their pinches, her warning us that crabs pinched so hard, only a clap of thunder could make them let go.

I loved it when she talked like that, when what was left of her Alabama accent would creep in to warn us about things like crab pinches and thunder, and how mushrooms grew in the yard were where fairies had stepped the night before, and that if we got up out of bed early enough in the morning and spotted a fairy in the yard, it would turn to stone and we could keep it. We knew these stories weren't exactly the truth, in the way that Southern stories often aren't exactly the truth, but we looked out the sliding glass door to see if there were any thunderstorm clouds gathering, just in case, and then fenced with the crabs like little pirates.

"Can't we keep just one as a pet?" I begged, trying to pick up a particularly feisty one with the tongs. "This one likes me!"

Into the pot they all went.

Over the years, Mom noticed that her fingers would start to swell shortly after polishing off a bucket of crabs, and sometimes she would remark that the inside of her ears were itchy after she got done with a lobster po' boy. Nobody thought much of it.

Towards the end of my birthday dinner, her voice started to crack, getting progressively squeakier as she coughed and tried to clear her throat. She coughed and coughed.

I said, "Are you OK, Mom? Can you breathe?"

She nodded her head yes.

We went outside to see if fresh air would help, but the coughing only got worse, until it seemed like she couldn't get a breath at all. The three of us kept asking, "Can you breathe?" and she would nod her head yes.

Finally, my oldest sister said, "We're going to the hospital."

Mom shook her head no, put up both her hands and fought us as we tried to get her into the car. It was like trying to get an unwilling cat into a pet carrier, the fight this woman put up. Luckily the hospital in Boca was just a couple miles away, because she started to black out as we ran inside the emergency room. They took her back behind closed doors and we were told to sit in the waiting room. I watched as they wheeled her through the second set of doors, her body slumped over in the chair.

Then she died.

She died on my twelfth birthday.

For one full minute.

She remembers waking up in the emergency room, her heart pounding and her insides burning from the shots of epinephrine they'd given her to open her airway and bring her back to life. They were just about to cut her trachea open to put a breathing tube in when the shots suddenly kicked in and she opened her eyes and started to breathe on her own.

She heard the nurses talking in the hallway, "Can you believe we almost lost a thirty-seven-year old to a damn shellfish allergy? They had to hit her with so much epinephrine I'm surprised she's not climbing the walls."

Even as a grown tomboy, she was still a Southern woman, so she was irritated that they mentioned her age, and especially irritated when the doctor referred to her as "a middle-aged, obese woman" as he dictated his notes into a tape recorder. She had been clinically dead for a full minute, but this was her main complaint about the incident.

When we finally got to see her, she was hooked up to an oxygen tank, with the little hoses ringed across her face and up around her ears. We walked into the room, our steps delicate with fear, eyes swollen from crying, so thankful she was alive, to find her yelling, "Obese?! I need to lose ten pounds and this guy is calling me obese?!

And middle-aged?! Why didn't he just haul off and call me an old, fat woman?!"

The doctor told her that her shellfish allergy was so severe that she needed to wear a medic-alert bracelet that listed it, but she waved him off with, "I don't wear jewelry," like he was asking her to wear the crown jewels to a monster truck rally.

This was 1988, and allergies were something most people attributed to bees or pollen. We'd never heard of such a thing, being allergic to shellfish. Hell, we didn't even know the term "shellfish." You mean crabs and lobsters? How about oysters? Are conch fritters OK?

Mom took "shellfish allergy" in its most literal sense, and continued to eat all kinds of seafood that couldn't technically be considered "shellfish," the way alcoholics in denial make rules about not drinking brown liquor, or only drinking themselves unconscious every *other* day. She would eat fried catfish, her fingers would swell; her eyes and ears would itch, but it wasn't shellfish, so she declared herself fine.

A couple years later, we were sitting on the couch eating dinner and watching TV, just the two of us, when her voice started to crack again. I looked down at the tuna fish sandwich on her plate.

"Can you breathe?"

She nodded her head yes, coughing.

"Can you really breathe or are you just lying to me?"

She shook her head no, coughing harder.

"So you can breathe then?"

She nodded her head yes, the coughs getting shorter.

"Then tell me with actual words that you can breathe right now."

She shook her head no, rolled her eyes and made a face like I was being ridiculous, the coughing sounding more like muted hiccups; her face turning blue.

"Do you want to go to the hospital?"

She shook her head no, putting her hands up as if to say, "Don't even try it, kid."

"Maybe we should just drive to the hospital since it's not even half a mile away? We can just sit in the parking lot, you know, just in case?"

She grimaced and shook her head no, and got into a fully defensive posture, like she was going to kick my ass Jean Claude Van Damme-style if I tried to get her into the car.

"You know I don't have a license and have no idea how to drive, right? If you start to lose consciousness, I *will* have to call 911, and then all the neighbors will come out and watch you get dragged off on a stretcher. Do you have any idea how much that ambulance is going to cost?"

I think the combination of "What will the neighbors think?" humiliation and poor-person-fear of an ambulance bill must have gotten through to her, because she walked to the front door, picked up the car keys, and drove us up the street to the hospital. She started to black out as she parked the car. I ran to the door for a wheelchair and shouted for help.

After they revived her at the emergency room, they told her that her shellfish allergy, now reclassified as a seafood allergy, had grown so severe that she should not only avoid all seafood, but that she should never eat food that she hadn't personally prepared in her own kitchen. No restaurants, no fast food, no potlucks. Any cross-contamination, no matter how small—even a knife used to cut fish that was then used to cut chicken an hour later—could make her go into anaphylactic shock and die.

So, the next year, she was eating Chinese takeout in her car and bit down on a shrimp that had made its way into the fried rice.

"Can you breathe?"

She nodded her head yes.

A few years after that, Mom was turning blue and coughing from the crab dip that she had mistaken for bleu cheese dressing at a Memorial Day potluck barbecue.

"Can you breathe?"

She nodded her head yes.

I tell you what—if she weren't going to die someday, I would call that woman downright maddening.

J.A. Bernstein

Northern Cowboy

I suppose it's reflective of academia, or at least the contemporary job market, that I, a Jewish vegan and Marxist from Chicago, live in the town of Hattiesburg, Mississippi, population forty-thousand, smack in the heart of the deep South. It's even more foreign for my wife, a Soviet-born Israeli, who also happens to be among the few, if not the only, practicing climate scientists in the state. Last week, a campaigner for Forrest County supervisor knocked on our door. When asked his affiliation, he shrugged. "I don't like either, to be truthful, but my opponent and me iz both Republican." I took his flier and smiled.

Of course, we do have the luxury of being "white" (in my case, male), as well as straight, cis, able-bodied, and fully equipped to conceal our status as academics, or carpetbaggers, as it were. It also isn't lost on us that Jews were rarely seen as "white" in the U.S. prior to the 1920s, and in most parts of the Deep South—outside of a few hubs in Atlanta and New Orleans, where large communities exist—are frequently regarded as foreign, if not Middle Eastern. All that aside, we can pass.

I cite this background to explain how it is that my wife and I came to arrive at a Fourth of July festival in a town called Sumrall, population one thousand, twenty miles west of Hattiesburg, our three sweaty children in tow. Our holiday options were limited, since all the beaches along the coast had been closed for algae blooms. The heat index that morning registered 108 degrees Fahrenheit, which, had this been Duluth, Minnesota, where we'd formerly lived, would have prompted the opening of shelters.

Driving along Highway 42, one leaves behind the used auto lots and the stilted planks of mobile homes for an endless expanse of spruces and loblolly pines—miles thick on both sides. Hattiesburg, like most of the Pine Belt, was largely uncultivated until the twentieth century, when the lumber mills sprang up, and large sections of forestland remain. Towns like Sumrall, and to some extent Hattiesburg, arose to ship wood, and with the industry vanished, the towns have been left to rot. The university where we work, Southern Miss, has helped to replenish the area, as have two hospitals, though both, like most around the country, are struggling with consolidation. Industry has mostly disappeared, minus some plastic and bottle-making plants.

Emerging from the car in blue jeans—this is my attempt to look populist—I immediately regret the decision. To call the town "hot" would be like saying they aren't fond of Obama. A line of police cars is blocking the road, where a parade, it appears, is under way.

My wife runs ahead with our kids, halting on Main Street, where a dozen glinting cars rumble past. BLAKE MATHERNE FOR CORONER, one says. In the front seat of his Buick convertible, Blake (I presume) is decked out in khaki uniform—not unlike Gamal Abdel Nasser, I think—and a baseball cap logoed with guns. Beside him, his wife looks out placidly; she's wearing a camouflage baseball cap emblazoned with the American flag. They pass beside Sumrall Donuts and Breakfast, as indicated by the hand-painted window, beside which a wheelchaired woman gives watch. A few dozen children chase through the street, picking up Jolly Ranchers and Dum-Dums and cherry Laffy Taffy and those New Orleans-style beads that they throw. The sun is unexplainable, like a sheet of fire in the sky, though no one here seems to mind, save for my wife, who takes shelter with our kids behind a Shell gas station sign.

Next in line is some kind of military vehicle, like a mine-clearing truck, something so immense and steaming and loud that my two-year-old son begins to cry, despite his affinity for trucks. Inside in the front seat, a bearded forty-something is wearing a tank top and smokes. A few other classic cars follow him—mostly Corvettes—then finally a half-dozen horses, including a pony, at which my younger daughter gawks. She's probably seen an actual horse two or three times in her life. As a vegan, I don't normally take her to zoos, which means anytime she sees a live animal, she gasps, and will undoubtedly grow up to eat them, probably two at a time.

The lead horse, which I guess is called a colt, though what would I know, has scarlet bands on his ankles—they look like leg warmers—

and an American flag crudely painted on his rump. The heat has smeared the stripes, dying his garlanded tail, and riding atop the worn saddle is a sandy-haired cowboy—replete with blue jeans, I well note—holding a flagpole. Old Glory hangs flaccidly, overwhelmed by the heat, while at its side, a Stetson-wearing boy, who cannot be six, sits erectly on the pony, one hand gripping the pommel, the other clenching a blue popsicle treat. I believe my younger daughter is in love.

Sometime around ten, I discover that my daughters have tattooed their faces with American flags, which were apparently thrown at the parade. Quite a few tears have been shed, with my wife having denied them Goobers, horrifically, their buckets filled to the brim with sweets of every possible brand. Mississippi, of course, boasts the highest obesity rate in the U.S., and while my wife and I love it, we bemoan the lack of fresh produce, not to mention the school-served lunches (sample menu choices: "Oven-Fried Chicken," "Pork Chop Sandwich").

Making our way down to the fairgrounds, we're accosted by tents, nearly all proclaiming local candidates. None show a party affiliation, as I suspect that isn't required. We saddle up next to a lemonade stand, where two kids in MAGA caps dish out a yellowish slime. My wife eyes them warily. As recently as last week, the National Oceanic and Atmospheric Administration, under pressure from the man who would Make American Great Again, began relocating vital data on its servers, crippling her efforts at modeling climate change's effects. At other points, she's been told she can't use the term "climate change" in her government-sponsored research. I hesitate before paying but reconcile myself to the fact that they, too, are wearing blue jeans.

About two-thirds of the attendees are white, the others a mix of Latinx, Asian, and African-American. None of the minorities seem to campaign; most have claimed tables in the park, beneath a stand of willow oaks so towering they provide little shade.

Inside the park shelter, where an auction is about to begin, the fair spokesperson cradles a mic, bowing her head. She gives thanks to the Lord for bringing us together and allowing for the celebration of our great nation. Men doff their Stetsons. Everyone crosses their hearts. This is followed by the Pledge of Allegiance, which my daughter, by

77

virtue of her schooling, faithfully, maddeningly recites. Later, she'll ask me why I didn't cross my heart, to which I have no reply.

My kids scamper off to a playground, which, unlike most in the North, is still made, handsomely, of wood. As usual, smoking parents are gathered nearby, gaping at their phones, while their older children torment mine. At the edge of the playground, two men in gray-and-white-striped uniforms are removing trash from a bin. Their backs say *MDOC*, and my wife quickly moves towards our kids. We begin to settle back, realizing we're far less terrified of the prisoners than the Trump supporters at our sides.

My kids find relief from the heat in a poured cement splash pad, where murky water springs from the jets. My wife does her best not to cringe as an unleashed dog slurps and shakes. We're both aware that flesh-eating bacteria have killed folks in the region, left others maimed. Parents in tank tops and cutoff blue jeans finger their pockets and smoke. We're the only ones using sun lotion, which turns my kids a bright pink. It also isn't lost on us that the fifteen dollars we pay for a bottle of Australian Blue Lizard mineral sunscreen exceeds two hours of minimum wage.

When my wife determines that the heat is unbearable—it isn't eleven—we begin to move to the car, whereupon I take notice of a mechanical bull. It's situated behind the other rides: a bungee-corded trampoline, from which toddlers periodically spring; flying scooters, which vaguely resemble mad gorgons; and some kind of tilt-a-whirl, which looks nauseating to sight; not to mention the stalls with cotton candy and food trucks in which people roast. The bull, as it were, consists of some kind of metal apparatus sheathed in a carpet and bearing two plastic white horns. It's surrounded by a circular, stars-and-stripes-themed inflatable, which emits a faint haze in the sun. My wife looks at me tepidly. This, she knows, is a mistake.

"I'll take it slow," says the operator, pocketing my five-dollar bill. Huddling beneath a tent and a white Lions Club banner, she smirks a bit, gleefully, and dabs her face with her sleeve.

My children gather around the ring, asking for hugs, as if knowing this could be the end. I mount the inflatable, which feels like a moonwalk, except it's four thousand degrees. A handful of passers take note, one pausing to look up from her chicken-on-a-stick. Another nudges her friend.

My only exposure to the sport is the image of John Travolta, buckle and all, riding the device in *Urban Cowboy*. Saddling up, I also recall Borat proclaiming to the rodeo in Texas: "May your George Bush drink the blood of every single man, women, and child of Iraq!" My younger daughter smiles. The spruces quake in the heat.

Flexing my thighs, I inhale the scents of barbecue, the stench of burnt rubber and pumps. The vinyl carpet creaks, and the bull begins jerking, bobbing left and right. "I love you," my wife whispers. Then the plastic horns dip, my whole body contorting as I struggle to grip the rope knob. The operator nods demonically. I'm exercising muscles I didn't know I have, doing my best to stay on, and it will only become apparent to me minutes later—what in fact is ten or twelve seconds, but who's counting—that I'm doing at least three revolutions per second, nearly upside down, fully sideways in fact, and watching the spread of a sun—or what I take to be the sun; it might also be the grin of my wife, or the barrel of a rifle nearby—feeling all the blood in my throat, and the eyes of gaping locals, and the smells of burnt meat on a stick, and, not least of all, the glares of my son, who is watching, confounded now, befuddled, perplexed, amused that I could act like I'm two, which is in fact what such devices are for, if not the American South, though who am I to judge, being a Yankee, and making a fool of myself. Then my cheek hits the mat—what I presume to be the mat—and I come to rest on all fours.

"You were excellent," says my wife, as I turn and limp from the ring.

My children are glowing, melted Goobers in hand, the sun bearing down like a flame.

Sarah Browning

A Beautiful Evening for Baseball in Our Nation's Capital

My friend Pete studies the religious right, goes to conferences,
hangs out at Liberty University. He's just spent his whole day
with lawyers and scholars who were fretting over threats to their
religious freedom. "Like gay people," says Pete. We're meeting

at Nats Park on a sweet September evening. Pete's husband Dan
is in Florida giving a reading and staying with our friends, Gregg
and Rick, who moved to their Florida town, we joke, because it's
even gayer than their gay Chicago neighborhood. Outside the ball-

park, a man with a bullhorn is yelling at the Nats fans. His sign
reads, *The Pope Is the Antichrist. Save Yourself, Sinner.* The Pope
is due to visit DC later this week. Dan and Pete live near
the basilica, had thought to rent their spare rooms. But they realized

they'd have had to make clear: The house is full of gay people and
dogs. This pope is cooler than any past pope but I keep saying
that is setting the bar very low—on the ground, just about.
Pete and I climb to our good seats high above home plate as the

light slips away and the Nats go down two in the first inning to
the Miami Marlins. Maybe it's all those gay people in Florida,
we suggest, putting their powerful juju on the Marlins' starting
lineup. But no—it's a close game, the lead going back and forth

over the course of the beautiful evening, as Pete and I drink beer
and eat greasy ballpark food. The game goes into the tenth until—
glory be—the Nats pull it out with a messy slide into home plate
on a Marlins error and the crowd leaves happy. The Jesus people

have gone home. It's just the press of fans headed down Half
Street to the Metro, men hawking five-dollar caps. In front of us,
two white-haired ladies hold hands in the crush.

Tessa Livingstone

Edinburgh, 1948

A crowd,
crowding around to see,

     in plain brown paper:

the body with soft skin
     and no
     broken bones.

Half a fish   stitched
to a monkey's torso.

A scattering
  of animal hair.

     Scales.

Mouth wide open.

     Teeth bared.

Gawkers,

     in this hour
     of tarot cards,

occult blood,

she is no more a fright
        than   an attraction.

Reach out your hands
and touch her.

      Touch her.

Tessa Livingstone

Traveling Along the Trace

I got lost along the Natchez Trace:/ a trail of pinecones,/ crags,/ leaf litter./ Loose bark./ It's not molting season./ But the snakes are rubbing their arrow heads against rocks,/ and you tell me,/ *There are no snakes here./* And I think, I think, I think—:/ You know, if it weren't for this snow cover,/ the mountain lion,/ lioness,/ whatever,/ would go away./ And when I go away he gives me a present,/ tied special with ribbons./ And it is mine to keep./ And it is mine to be eaten/ without milk/ or sugar./ And it is mine to be pointed at /with a finger/ that almost touches it./ That night I let the horses out/ I felt almost like a devil./ But here is the hunter with the gleaming axe,/ and the full-throated firs itching to meet/ its sharp edge./ If we had a window, you would see them, too./And besides./ Something's hissing.

The Missouri State University Student Literary Competitions

Moon City Review is a journal published by the Department of English at Missouri State University. *MCR* publishes one poem, one fiction work, and one creative nonfiction work annually by its student population, as selected in a competition inititially by our own faculty, and then finally by an outside judge.

For our creative nonfiction contest, Erika T. Wurth—author of *Buckskin Cocaine* (Astrophil Press, 2017), among other books—selected Amelia Fisher's essay, "June 19, 2018." Wurth states of Fisher's essay,

> The slow, lovely, winding descent from a lushly described personal memory to an event that brings us to the bigger, the human, the catastrophic, makes this the kind of essay that will stay long in my mind. I loved reading this piece. I hope to see this author utilize their spectacular talent in the long form soon. Who could ignore the power of lines like this? "Maybe these deaths would matter a little more. Maybe this essay would feel more urgent. There are too many lives lost to unexplainable senselessness for us to dwell on one for much time at all, though. I know this very well."

Other finalists considered in the creative nonfiction category include the following writers: Ryan Davies, Rebecca Harris, Ryan LaBee, Bridgette Noland, Lane Pybas, Tommy Stuart, and Harley Vantuyl.

In fiction, Ron A. Austin—author of *Avery Colt is a Snake. A Thief. A Liar.* (Southeast Missouri State University Press, 2019)—chose Madison Green's story "The Housefly's Head, Thorax, and Abdomen" as the winner. Austin says of Green's story, "'The Housefly's Head, Thorax, and Abdomen' combines Carmen Maria Machado's precision of imagination and genre-bending bravery with Lauren Groff's lyrical prose and careful surrealism to produce a powerful gothic story."

Joining Green as finalists were Victoria Cook, Morgan Dame, Amelia Fisher, Amanda Hadlock, John King, and Harley Vantuyl.

In poetry, guest judge Kathy Goodkin, author of *Crybaby Bridge* (Moon City Press, 2019), chose Amelia Fisher's "Why I Like Bad Boys According to the PCL-5" as the winner. Of Fisher's poem, Goodkin remarks, "I love how this poem uses the framework of a mental health assessment tool to excavate the speaker's interiority. The result is a beautiful example of how a poem can access universal or near-universal emotions using concrete details."

MCR also would like to congratulate the other finalists considered in the poetry category; they include Jenny Crews, Madison Green, David Iacob, Kristan Key, and Sujash Purna.

It was a great pleasure for everyone involved to sort out the students' work. We are proud to present the winning selections in the following pages.

Madison Green

The Housefly's Head, Thorax, and Abdomen

A thin piece of cloth covered Cynthia's fingers as she picked up a pan. The warm glow from the oven still lingered to the touch, but the oven mitts protected her soft skin. She moved from the kitchen to the dining room with quickened heels that clattered against the linoleum floor, then muted as she stepped onto the dining room's carpet. Platters of different foods covered the center of the grand table with one potholder open for the sweet potatoes in her hands. The glass lid rumbled as the dish was placed on the table next to the peaches encased in red gelatin. Cynthia smelled the sharpness of tuna mushroom casserole through its lid. Farthest from the kitchen doorway, her husband sat at the head of the table with one leg positioned on the other's knee and arms wide in order to turn the pages to the newspaper. The rustled movement of the newspaper caused the smoke at the end of his cigarette to flutter in the air as if it had wings, and the steam above the food danced beside it.

"Dinner's ready," Cynthia said to her husband.

She stepped a few feet back from the table, avoiding the china cabinet filled with expensive glassware. The man released a hand from the newspaper, the corner drooped sluggishly, and he extended his hand to tap the ash at the end of his cigarette into a tray. Cynthia then collected her apron and oven mitts, exposing her red-painted nails.

Between her arm and body, she folded the garments, keeping the warmth pressed against her breasts, and walked to the kitchen to set them down. At the kitchen counter, Cynthia turned to go back into the dining room but stopped herself as she laid her eyes on the window just above the sink. There, a fly was stuck between glass and screen. A whispered thud presented each time the fly came in contact with the four barriers that caged the insect. Seemingly, it played a game with itself as it collided against the window's glass again and again and again. The wings of the bug acted as a reflector of light beside the darkened outside. Cynthia stared at the insect, thinking how poor of a bug it had to be. To be trapped on its own accord, to have crawled into a slit where it will inevitably encounter a slow death. The fly stopped itself and landed on the bottom of the window. Motionless for a second, it stared out to freedom just beyond the window screen. Then the fly turned toward Cynthia, satisfied it had attained the attention of somebody. It rotated its head left and right as if introducing itself. Cynthia nodded gently back at the fly.

Cynthia broke out of her trance when a determined cough came from the dining room. Her husband's foot could be seen from her spot at the kitchen's sink, his foot bounced firmly on the hardwood floor.

"Have you heard from your mother?" Cynthia asked as she walked back into the dining room, stopping behind her chair.

"No," he said. "And if I did, you know what she would ask about, Cynthia."

Though she knew her husband was right. She couldn't help but raise her hands to the middle of her dress and feel the cushion that separated the palms of her hands to her bare, empty stomach. She dropped one hand to the back of her chair and glanced toward the hallway where a bedroom door remained closed. Cynthia shoved the thought away but stayed silent as she looked up at the deep cracks that surrounded the man's eyes. She smiled weakly, pulled out her chair, sat down, and began to serve the food to her husband.

"Go ahead and clean up. I have other matters," the husband said to his wife once he finished eating.

Her eyes followed the man's form as he took his cigarette, left the room, and walked in the opposite direction of the two bedrooms the house inhabited. When Cynthia heard the door close to his office, she pushed back in her chair and carried the dirty dishes to the kitchen. Cynthia made dreamy circles as she cleaned the plates and silverware in the sink. Her eyes focused on nothing but the fly still stranded in the window.

When the dishes were dried, food put away, and darkness filled the house, Cynthia went to her and her husband's bedroom to find it silent. The bed was still made, as it had been since the morning when she made it, with the corners of the comforter tucked in and pillows fluffed. Knowing her husband was in his office, she headed to the bathroom. Cynthia undressed and took off her pearl earrings to slip into a bath. She received the earrings and a matching necklace when she and her husband first got together. That was many years ago and seemed more like a faint memory than an event that had happened. The warmth surrounded Cynthia like the serenity of a blanket, and she felt safe. The water streamed in the spots her dress didn't seal to during the day, and her hair was relaxed just below her shoulders instead of being pinned up. She lay there, her body submerged in the murky water, the only sound coming from the insects outside and the water droplets as they fell from the spout until they pooled into the bath. Cynthia observed her body and the skin that has stretched from age. But it began to wrinkle and become almost translucent the longer she spent in the bath. She rose from the chilled water and put on her silk nightgown.

The texture of the bedroom carpet itched the bottom of Cynthia's feet until she removed the bed's blanket from its position and got into bed. Alone under the comforter, she suddenly felt restless. Cynthia placed her feet back onto the carpet and hugged her body with her arms. In the hallway, she saw the light of her husband's office peek through the door's crack. She began to walk toward the light and him, but stopped halfway, in the dining room, to hear the slightest thumb against glass, telling to her to go to bed. Cynthia knew it was the fly, still trapped within the window, and turned around to head back to the bedroom. On her way to the bedroom she passed the second bedroom's door. She halted in front of the room and just stood there. No sound came and no movement stirred on the other side of the door, and Cynthia knew that. She wished there to be giggling or sleeping feet that pushed their way out from under their blanket. That way she could walk in to coo them back to sleep or tuck them back to bed.

Cynthia extended her hand to open the wooden doorknob but hesitated as the knob lacked warmth.

Cynthia stood outside of Muscidae's Butcher & Market, just outside the suburbs. In front of the store's meat display and outside world, the lettering on the window obstructed her mirrored view.

As people scurried past behind her, Cynthia watched the images of those around. Women with proper pinned-up hair, along with dress suits and matching blazers, talked with their hands. White and blue cars with flat roofs rolled by on John W. Street. A couple of girls in apricot-patterned attire chatted about their favorite headbands. Men with frizzy hair, balding men, men that smoked, working men, and gay men, all wore fitted pants snug around each different-sized thigh and walked to the beat of no music.

A single bell rang above Cynthia as she was welcomed with nidor and the smell of smoked skin. She knew this place well and had gotten used to the stench years ago. Through the few steps of aisles, Cynthia passed the shelves of labeled cans and reached the stand.

"Ah! Welcome, Mrs. Cynthia," the man wearing a bloodied smock said as he stood behind the counter, wiping his hands with a rag. "What will you be getting on this fine Wednesday?"

"I am thinking I will cook Beef Bourguignon for my husband this evening."

"That sounds delightful," the man said. "Don't forget to add the carrots."

The two laughed in unison. Cynthia hovered over the glass that protected the animal products from her breath. Behind were piles of abbacchio, genoa salami, noisette, baron, and steak, all raw and damp, each muscle and bone touching the other. Forelimbs and femurs hung beyond the counter, exposed tissue and cream-pigmented fat.

Cynthia pointed to request a closer look at a particular beef cheekbone that lay next to a center cut. The man grabbed a piece of parchment paper with one hand and with a clutched, naked fist, dragged the tough meat into his prepared hand. He lifted the muscle and Cynthia nodded.

"So, have you heard the Horse of the Year, Kelso, retired recently? I think he won the Stymie Handicap back in sixty-two and again a few years ago. Wonder what he'll do now," the butcher said.

"Terrible to hear a horse with that much talent has to retire. But no, I haven't heard; I don't read much of the paper. My husband does enough of that."

They continued to exchange conversation before Cynthia's attention was captured by the luminous horizontal crevice that came from the back of a dark hallway behind the man. Small shadows jumped in the light from the outside and formed something like a show.

"What is back there?" Cynthia asked as she pointed to the slit of light.

"This door is usually closed; I apologize about that. That's just the back room though. It leads to the back alley, ma'am." The butcher stopped wrapping the beef cut into a paper envelope and turned to close the door behind him.

Cynthia stretched her neck to watch the sliver of peeking sunlight disappear from the closing door. When the butcher came back to the stand, he began the package process over again. As Cynthia waited for him to swaddle the beef, she imagined what could have made the shadows flicker in the light. Was it an eleven-year-old boy throwing pebbles at the building's bricks? Or was it a toddler just weaning off of diapers and his mother didn't want him to relieve himself in his pants, and this street had no public restrooms? Or was it a group of girls feeding wild pigeons with leftover rice from their lunch? Cynthia wanted to know the source, and this caused a hum to take over her mind.

The door chime rang again and Cynthia waved good-bye with her open hand, while the other carried a bag, the weight of the meat dragging her down. When Cynthia stepped out onto the sidewalk, the buzzing still remained in her head. She looked around and tried to make sense of it. Abruptly, her feet pulled her to follow the sound. Her ears took her to the side of Muscidae's Butcher & Market, and she drifted into the crack of the parallel buildings. In the alley, an odor was introduced to Cynthia that she had never smelled before, but she endured and advanced farther into the dim path.

Along the brick walls, trash cans lined in a chaotic manner. One stood out to Cynthia, and she quickly recognized the shop it belonged to. Written in white, "Muscidae" wrapped the metal can as ownership. Droppings of tender mammal and fish overfilled the bin and fell onto the concrete floor. The pile was overrun by flies and their young. Nephric ducts and pendulous veins leaked out of the garbage and hung to dry, ivory and black-colored portions of rotten partridge massacred by time and baby maggots.

Cynthia stared at the maggots that rummaged in the crevices of exposed muscle and at the flies that floated above, targeting a place to lay their eggs. She didn't gag, she didn't leave, she didn't move. She just stared. And that aroused a spark in her chest.

☾

"Dinner's ready," Cynthia said and put down the dish of meatballs.

Her husband rested in his seat with a cigarette and folded newspaper. He set both down beside his dinner plate and waited for Cynthia to serve the food. The two of them consumed their portions with the only sound of forks clanking against the porcelain dishes.

In the distance, Cynthia heard a new sound. It would hover over the silence, while also becoming the silence. Then a fly glided over the husband and Cynthia and out of the dining room. The fly soared back into the space like it was in a maze and landed on the table. It stayed for a second and looked around. It got up in an irregular pattern and darted toward the kitchen.

Cynthia could feel her husband becoming disturbed, and when she was about to speak up, the fly hummed past her ear. The man inched his hand to the newspaper, rolled the print, and stood to swing at the fly.

"Stop that," Cynthia said.

The husband stayed silent. He swatted with his batlike weapon as Cynthia watched him with a careful eye. After a moment, the man finally grazed the fly with the edge of the paper. Husband and wife watched the fly fall to the carpet and move no longer.

"No!" she said in a panic and stood from her chair. "Do not hurt it!"

"What are you spouting out? It is just a fly," her husband said, the grip on his newspaper becoming tighter.

"It is not just a fly. Leave it alone!"

Cynthia breathed heavily and sat back down in her chair, the legs of the chair struggling to push back under the table as they rubbed on the carpet's texture. Her husband kept his eyes on her, then jerked the plate from the table and left to eat his food in his office, while Cynthia stared straight ahead.

Once her husband was out of the room, the corner of Cynthia's eyes unlocked from the wall and moved to the insect on the ground. However, when she searched the peach-colored carpet, there was no indicator or trace of a fly.

☾

The sound of busy footsteps and conversation filled Cynthia's ears as she walked along John W. Street headed toward Muscidae's Butcher & Market. A caramel-colored car passed by Cynthia and the driver made friendly eye contact behind his wide steering wheel. The space between the man's eyes resembled the distance of the headlights. Cynthia recognized her own distorted reflection in the oval-sided mirrors, and then the car was gone.

Students with plaid skirts down to their ankle socks gossiped about the new miniskirts overseas in London, while young men in letterman jackets followed. A young boy stuttered, talking of portable calculators to his mom, while her tight restraint of his arm kept him two steps behind her. A lady then came into Cynthia's reflected vision. She passed Cynthia as she pushed a stroller into the butcher's shop, and a ring fell in suit. Inside the cart was perched a blond, rosy-cheeked toddler, playing with the faux hair of a doll that was too big for her fingers.

A bell signaled that Cynthia had walked into the butcher's shop, too and the same welcoming gamey scent of chuck, eye of round roasts, and fumet wrapped itself in the room.

"Welcome, Mrs. Cynthia. Glad you've come again," the smocked butcher said.

"Me as well," she greeted. "What would be the best complement with glazed ham?"

"That's a hard one, though I'd say potatoes myself."

"I was thinking that, too," she smiled.

"Let me grab the fillet steak for you," the man said and turned to grab the pre-cut parchment paper.

Cynthia knew the butcher would get the appropriate leg cut for her, so she wandered around, peering into the frosted glass. The rough bands of tissue that held the piece of meat together looked saturated in the noxious air. Each flesh scrap was situated in a haphazardly fashion, making the products look like one heap of a cruel mass.

The butcher set Cynthia's order on top of the counter and signaled to her that it was ready. She approved but dawdled in the aisles in the front of the store. In the lanes of canned and boxed merchandise, Cynthia saw the lady with the stroller on her knees next to her child. She caressed her daughter's jaw then leaned forward. Cynthia watched the lady's gentle mouth whisper into the ear of the pudgy toddler.

The daughter giggled while she lifted her small shoulder, trapping her mother's face in her neck. The lady then tenderly removed herself and embraced the child's face with the pads of her thumbs. Her right hand remained on her daughter's cheek and moved the other to lift a fallen piece of hair. The lady's fingers took the strand and lined it along the toddler's hairline, putting it back in place.

"I will be right back, ladies," the butcher said on the other side of the store. He gathered crates of gray and stale meats and left through the archway to the back room.

The two women stood and acknowledged each other in silence.

"I have two," Cynthia said.

"Excuse me?" the lady said but only saw Cynthia's eyes to her daughter. "Oh, you do? I have just this little one."

Cynthia didn't react to the words the lady said, though she continued looking at the child. She noticed the way the girl's hair had just begun to curl above her collared neck. How the girl's plump arms and legs looked restricted as the skin outpoured on itself. How the girl's nose, which matched her mother's, set scrunched as she played with her doll. Cynthia also noticed the girl's turquoise dress and every crumple and wrinkle and where each stitched flower would come next.

"There's talk of a new children's show. Are you going to allow yours to watch it?" the lady asked.

"Anything that may distract them while I cook dinner," the women laughed together.

"So where are your little ones?"

"Oh, them?" Cynthia hesitated for a moment. She looked down at the little girl in the stroller, innocence emitted as the girl frolicked her doll's limp body. Just then the butcher came into view from the back door. The outside light highlighted the man's figure. Cynthia heard faint humming from eager insects, now that a new rotten feast had been given to them. "I'm picking them up after I leave here. They're out and about."

"How old are they?" the lady asked.

"About the same as yours," Cynthia said and faced back to the butcher. "May I have some extra scraps? I must feed my growing children."

The lady was perplexed but didn't question fast enough. The butcher agreed to Cynthia's request then handed her a small, drooping envelope of meat.

A signal that Cynthia left rung in the air after she paid. She turned past the Muscidae's Butcher & Market lettering arranged on the window and walked into the alley. The callous stench of the deteriorating meat hit Cynthia's nose and made her heart jump. She didn't dodge the insects that swarmed around her head as she bent down onto her knees and leaned forward to the decomposing prosciutto and foul calf spleen. The maggots fed off of the oleic acid and tissue of gullets and kip meat below her eyes. Cynthia turned and set her bag of fillets on the alley's ground. She then took the envelope of extra scraps the butcher had given her and opened the paper flaps. Exposing the nude meat to the afternoon air, she took her chipped red-painted fingernails and elongated her reach. She picked up a handful of larva and maggots, feeling them squirm in the palm of her hand. Pieces of beef and moldy intestines made a home alongside the maggots in her hands. Cynthia calmly ladled the fly's young into the excess food pouch, got up, and left.

"Dinner's ready," Cynthia said.

In silence, the husband and wife ate. Shares of both asparagus and Beef Wellington on their plates. The man ate in a haste to get back to his readings and cigarettes; Cynthia cut every other bite into small portions, as if setting an additional plate for another, smaller mouth to feed. She ate one herself, then picked around at the breaded meat and placed the scraps gently on the outer rim of her plate.

She gawked at the blood that leaked from the beef. The pinkness of the meat and the maze of marble on each bite. Cynthia imagined her flies flooding over her arms and hands and fingers and onto her fork and finally on her food.

"I have always wanted kids," Cynthia said.

The man remained silent.

"Do you not hear the constant vibration in the air that is above us?" Cynthia asked.

"What has been wrong with you?" her husband said as he sat his silverware next to his plate.

"I don't know what you're talking about."

"Talk of kids. You know you cannot have children. Do I need to call the doctor?" he asked in a stoic tone, not having lifted his brow. "I have the money for you to have treatment again. Oh, what was it called?"

"Don't say it," Cynthia said with a pained twitch and shock as her husband smirked.

"Do you know how badly that would affect my appearance if I had to send you there again? But I will do it," he huffed. "And think if my mother ever heard about it."

Cynthia fled from her seat, the chair almost crashing into the China cabinet.

"I need to go. They need me."

"Who? Who needs you?"

"My children," Cynthia said. "I need to go to them right now."

"What are you going on about? You have no children. You've never had children and you never will."

"No, I do. I will show you." A smile curved around Cynthia's mouth.

The man rose from his chair in bewilderment. Cynthia turned and stepped toward the kitchen doorway, running away from the man. She continued through the house like a maze with sharp angles. Her head collided with the hallway walls and made paint chips fall like pollen. She hovered over the trashcan in the kitchen until she smacked her breast into it, whacking it to the ground. She jumped on the furniture in the living room and fluttered her arms about. She went in and out of her husband's office, their bedroom, and the hallway bathroom. She closed doors before her husband could reach, then let him in sweetly before swiftly dodging his reach. She fell into the fetal position in the hallway, her nose facing the peach-colored carpet.

"Cynthia, what are you doing?"

"I am trying to show you something," she sang.

Cynthia stood and opened her eyes, showing her husbands the whites under her eyelids. She stopped roaming the house and turned to her husband. The tendons in her neck stretched as Cynthia pointed her head to the hallway, her husband followed in suit.

The two of them walked down the house corridor until they reached a closed door, the room next to their bedroom. Cynthia reached for the wooden handle and turned it slowly. When the door was fully open, the man stood behind Cynthia but saw nothing different in the space. The same wardrobe tucked in the corner and a rocking chair, frozen in time. Dust hovered over the room, motionless, just like the crib that was set in the middle of the room. The sunlight peeked through the rose-colored curtains and landed on Cynthia's figure.

"Cynthia, I don't understand what's going on."

"Shh."

"What are we doing in this room? And what is that smell?" the man asked and scrunched his nose is disapproval.

"Shh," she warned. "You'll wake them up."

"What do you mean?"

At that moment, Cynthia got onto her hands and knees and opened the drawer of the wardrobe. A plethora of flies gasped for air and quickly darted out of their cage. The man raised his hand to his nose in shock and fell backwards. He tried to catch himself with the door frame but misplaced his step and began thrashing, limbs in the air. A thud marked the point in time when the man's head hit the carpet, and his limp body followed.

Cynthia cooed at what was inside the drawer. Her clothes were in a ratted mess as spoiled chitterlings, tissue-less bones, deteriorated liverwurst, and blacked aiguillette covered by larva and maggots of all different sizes corroded their food. The insects spasmed with their tails in the air, as if reaching for the light. Mold had not yet started to form, but the cartilage that held the decaying meat to its bone had transformed to a white web. In the lining of the drawer, a few lifeless flies lay decomposed. Their legs stiff and wings dehydrated.

"No, no, no," Cynthia wept. "I promised I would take care of you all."

Cynthia took her shaking hands and pressed them against the wardrobe's drawer. Her fingers curled around the edge and nails dug into the wooden material. The insects below jerked around in her piled clothes and watched as Cynthia fixated her eyes on what was in front of her. Her heart inflamed with the thought of holding the maggots to her breast, wanting to keep them alive, warm, and full, unlike the deceased flies below. With tentative hands, Cynthia removed herself from the wooden plank the separated her and the adolescent bugs. She descended her hands into the drawer, as if collecting cherished water. In her cradled hands, the maggots fidgeted in their place next to the vile bits of torn medallion. They rolled into the creases of Cynthia's palms and left damp trails as they grazed for veal to feast on. Cynthia took her thumb and caressed a single maggot that settled between the ring on her fourth finger and the folded skin beneath. She kneaded the maggot's skin, like the lady at the butcher shop who had pinched her daughter's cheeks.

The man on the floor lay silent in his place, his tailored shoes just inches away from Cynthia.

Cynthia got to her feet and backed away from the wardrobe.

"I need to go to my children," Cynthia said as she placed the maggots in her hand next to her husband's sleeping body, stepped over him, and left.

Cynthia picked up her feet and with each step left dainty heel imprints in the peach carpet. She abandoned her house with the door wide open and walked into the dimly lit streets.

She crossed Amber-Perkin Avenue, wandered by Becher Road, ran by Guillaume Duchenne Street, and finally reached John W. Street. She headed straight to Muscidae's Butcher & Market and ignored the few stares she got from nightly prowlers. On the window, the business' logo stamped on the glass adjoined Cynthia's reflection. Inside the room was dreary as the only distinguishable factors were the suspended cow humerus and hindquarters, a few lightly swaying. Cynthia's head began to buzz. She threw her hands over her ears in an attempt to make it stop. She became disoriented and lost her balance. Her ankle gave out and forced her heel to clatter against the sidewalk. Catching herself, she stumbled closer to the side of the butcher shop. Closer to the alley. She stood up tall and began to limp farther into the narrow path.

Beetles, flies, mosquitos, and moths soared through the twilight air as Cynthia walked deeper toward Muscidae's Butcher & Market's waste. The bugs landed on Cynthia's exposed arms and face, but she proceeded. She didn't shake off the insects, and they began to gather on her and around her. The more that massed onto Cynthia's skin, the quieter her mind got. She halted at the overflowing trash bins and rubble made from the slaughter that had been left by the butcher's shop. An exuberance of lust overwhelmed her.

"I am here, I am here," Cynthia said.

Her knees buckled, and she fell to the ground, her dress securing her fall onto the decrepitated Braunschweig sausage. The remains of used carcasses and pungent galantine lay next to spotless bones. There were places of moist bits that absorbed leftover liquids poured over each other, creating a new residue of broth. The fell of roasts and limbs tarnished as their color was lost. Maggots continued eating away as they left gaping holes in gizzards and kidneys.

Cynthia lay there in the butcher's filth like a bed. She felt safe and wanted the serenity of the flesh blanket beneath her to devour her whole body. In spots where her dress sealed to her sodden skin, she felt the core temperature of supraspinatus muscles and the spongy material of lard. She wanted to feed off the rotted smell that ran rampant through her nostrils. The parts of the decayed culatello that was stripped from the underside of a pig, left for maggots and for Cynthia to savor. Her mind rushed as the flies encircled her, giving a sense of arousal. Grabbing the moldy, sour flank steaks with a grip, she squeezed the bavette until a discolored extract ran down her wrists like a vein. Having the fluids flow alongside her protruded tendons provided an awakening in her chest. The darkened wall of waltzing insects encouraged Cynthia to recall being in her mother's womb. She trembled around in the womb and eventually released. She ate away at her surroundings and dug into the ground and waited to be birthed again. She crawled out of her own skin and became a hardened body of what she once was.

Amelia Fisher

There are seven or eight categories of phenomena
in the world that are worth talking about, and
one of them is the weather.
—Annie Dillard

July 19, 2018

A flashing arrow over a lit-up sign, a colored flag, hanging limp save for the promise of a breeze every now and then, and the word HOOTONTOWN stenciled in red, block letters on the side of the STORE (also stenciled in block letters, though in blue), that faces the road announces our arrival. We take a left into a gravel parking lot. Disturbed ground tornadoes outside the window, coating patches of grass in a layer of dust when it floats back down. We unload ourselves and our gear (SPF, meat-and-cheese sandwiches, a Bluetooth speaker, joints, beach towels, alcohol, wide-brimmed hats, more alcohol, etc.). It's around ten in the morning, and the six of us are already sweating under our swimsuits. There are a lot of trucks and minivans and families, and the sun has opened up above us like an invitation.

Out here, where you'll find yourself if you follow the curvy roads in the heart of the Bible Belt that snake in and out of the Mark Twain National Forest and small towns named after God's creations like Crane and Galena, there's no cell phone reception. I miss a call about my grandpa's test results. (Luckily, the news is good—no Alzheimer's, but still no answers.) Even if I had thought to check, the weather app's connection would be lost in the untrimmed trees that sprout vines as if they have adapted to their new technological predators by suffocating the telephones poles and wires. A dozen or so outbuildings surround us—wooden shacks, campers, RVs, sheds, mobile homes, covered patios, carports, garages. I can hear two blond ladies chatting, both of their voices informed by years' worth of cigarettes, a country song that echoes off the metal roofs of the concession stand and storage lockers, men tossing canoes onto trailers. Nothing about Hootentown (with an "E" according to the website and the address, an "O" according to the hand-painted sign and locals) is uniform except for its dinginess. Still, the river rushing down the hill, the fruitiness of this beer, and my friend, Bridgette, naming the birds after hearing their songs—a beltedkingfisher, tufted titmouse—adds color to the morning.

> *Whoever you are, no matter how lonely,*
> *the world offers itself to your imagination,*
> *calls to you like the wild geese, harsh and exciting—*
> *over and over announcing your place*
> *in the family of things.*
>
> —*Mary Oliver*

There's no need to paddle, and the crane seems to be our guide, waiting for us at the shore before flying away again under the branches. I break the surface of the James River with my toes and dunk my sun hat when it gets too hot. And we always take our time when we float, pulling up to a gravel bar every half mile or so to swim and eat. Our first stop is across from a cabin with a private dock and friendly mutts who paddle across to greet us. We give them pieces of cheese and bread and scratches behind their ears. At another stop, we take turns riding down a strong current shaped by a fallen tree. I float on my back and am carried downstream, and it spits me out in a foamy whirlpool. We stop to play monkey-in-the-middle; I'm consistently the one in the middle, struggling to get my hands on the ball, throwing my body against the water, switching techniques, trying to outsmart everyone. It turns into a wrestling match; either I tackle Ben, my boyfriend, or he tackles me, and my nose is burning from inhaling too early, my bikini is giving way to hands with determined grips, but I'm laughing, and so are all my friends. I think I eventually secured the ball.

But today, we have a reason to rush. Half of us had rented kayaks for the trip, and they have to be returned by five. Unlike many Missourians, I'm not sure if I can chalk this potentially life-saving circumstance up to anything. Luck, maybe. I've stopped myself from thinking too much about the *why*. As I research the details of the accident for this articulation, I watch videos of adolescents saved by strong-willed men struggling to respond to reporters' questions about fate and consequences and happiness. I would have crumbled in front of the television cameras then and there, unable to process what it means for everything to happen for a reason. Doesn't that go against everything science has to offer? Sometimes I have to close the tab. Interrogations lead to torture when you don't know the answers. And I don't. All I know is that since there's no time for another stop—the temperature is dropping, the sun lowering—we'll reach safety with a handful of minutes to spare, and I'll write an essay as a tribute to those less fortunate. Or, as a way to relieve the pressure of wasting precious time on earth, this opportunity to continue living when the dirty water could have claimed my body. We paddle straight into the heat for the last half-mile, a few of us lagging and wishing we could jump in one more time, like fools.

It's generally true that the worst part of good days and fulfilling activities is when they end. But the last hour of any float trip is especially brutal, because someone is always too fucked up to function, and the dehydration starts to settle in behind your eyes as a headache, and kayaks weigh, like, fifty pounds, so lugging them up boat ramps can be a struggle for listless stoners like me. Usually two people have to drive all the way to the launch site to get the other car, then turn around and come back to the pull-out spot. Which is the case today.

> *I go down to the shore in the morning*
> *and depending on the hour the waves*
> *are rolling in or moving out,*
> *and I say, oh, I am miserable,*
> *what shall—*
> *what should I do? And the sea says*
> *in its lovely voice:*
> *Excuse me, I have work to do.*
>
> —*Mary Oliver*

I sit in my stickered kayak with my knees pulled up to my chest and my towel wrapped around my shoulders, my hair darkened by the water that drips down my back. Unexpected clouds sneak up from behind a wall of cliffs and greenery. Ben and I wait for our friends to return with the cars. The exhaustion that comes with a day of swimming and sunburns settles in (and what is taking them so long, and it is getting dark a little early, isn't it? Because of the clouds, that's right). It starts to sprinkle. I join him beneath a leafy canopy and rest my head against his arm, shivering. He smells like bug spray.

The breeze that entered the day like a secret was beginning to raise its voice. I hope the kayak we pile to the top of Bridgette's car will withhold the strain. I see a loose tube barrel away from its stack in the distance. (Once, on my family's first vacation to Florida, my brother lost his tube to the Atlantic, and no matter how fast or far my dad swam to catch it, he couldn't win against the strength of the ocean. He would never swim a mile for me, I think, just like no one is chasing after this runaway tube that probably smells like mildew or has a leak.) A pebble in my cheap water shoe digs into my sole. The old school buses here along the shore of the campground look especially dangerous as the overcast sky dims their undeniable yellowness. The revving of an unfamiliar engine, the waiting, and soft, soft sounds of thunder in the distance have Ben on high alert. Suddenly, this isn't fun anymore. I wonder how I can be so close to a high school and a Walmart and still feel this isolated. I wonder how anyone survived before cell phones and GPS. I wonder if my friends and I are going to be safe or not.

But they come back after an hour or so, and the raindrops are still falling slowly like ghosts. Despite our gelatin limbs, we load our damp gear and plastic boats into the truck bed and onto the SUV with more urgency than we had earlier this morning. But it feels like it's been days since we met to carpool and smoked a bowl in my back yard, basking in the precious seconds of summer. My lime-green, sit-on-top kayak is the longest and the heaviest, so it lies on top of Ben's. Trials of different ways to secure them with different types of straps have led to our specific method of arranging and tying and cranking. (We'll never forget when the job wasn't done quite right, and the kayaks caught the highway wind like sails before breaking away and skidding across the blacktop and into the ditch. It could be a miracle that nobody got hurt if you believe in those.) When they're finally too tight to budge, we lift our tired selves up before sinking into bucket seats and stretching out across a bench in the back. It's after six o'clock when we pull out of Hootentown, Ben and I following Bridgette and the rest in her car. I'm in charge of warning them if her kayak loses its stability. We take a right onto Highway M. And as if the gates of a dam burst at its seams, as if a curtain of water falls before a stage we're driving on, as if we cross into a parallel universe where humans take their oxygen with two shots of hydrogen, the rain pours down.

July 19, 2018

☾

Stone County Sheriff's Office

July 20, 2018
Press Release

On 07-19-18, at approximately 7:09 p.m., the first 911 call came in reporting a "Duck" tour boat had sank near the Branson Belle in Stone County, MO. It was reported that people were in the water.

Stone County Sheriff's Office, Taney County Sheriff's Office, the MO Highway Patrol, Branson Police Department, Western Taney County Fire, Southern Stone Fire, TCAD ambulances, and Stone County Emergency Management responded to the scene.

There were 29 passengers and 2 crew members on the Duck. At this time, 11 people are confirmed fatalities. 14 survived and 6 are still missing.

The wind was worse than the rain. We cautiously drove through the outskirts of Nixa, the hail knocking against the glass like angry cops with batons. Ben and I acknowledge that if Bridgette's kayak gets blown away, it's heading right towards us. We keep as safe a distance as we can without losing sight of our friends. (The windshield wipers on this Ford Ranger are useless.) The storm propels walking sticks against our windshields and bumpers, flings debris across the road and sky ahead of us. It's nine miles to the first place that's safe to stop at—a Casey's General Store—but it doesn't take that long for my phone to reach its signal. I read about 75 mile-per-hour winds and a severe thunderstorm warning for a few counties in southwest Missouri, including Greene—where we are—and Taney, and when I look at the Doppler radar, we are right in the middle of it, right in the red.

Luckily, it's moving quickly. We make it to the gas station with our various vehicles still intact and wait for it to pass. I have goosebumps from sitting in a wet swimsuit and can't help but close my eyes for a minute. I think of a shower, a nap, fresh laundry, all waiting for me. Bridgette taps on my window, holding her wide-brimmed fishing hat against her head as it flaps in the wind. I roll the window down, and she says something like, *I'm going to use the bathroom, and then we'll be ready to go?* The weather has calmed, though not completely. We say yes and check the straps on our kayaks one more time. I scroll through Facebook while we wait in the truck with the heat on, and try to get dry, thankful for 4G LTE. The first article I see about the duck boat accident is from a local news station—KY3 or *The Springfield News-Leader*, maybe—shared by an acquaintance from my hometown. I grew up in the Branson area, went to school in Reeds Spring. The towns are connected through the tourism industry, specifically through Table Rock Lake, which flows through the Ozarks down to northern Arkansas. I spent a lot of time riding in golf carts to boat docks and cliffs and tanning on pontoons and partying during winters at empty lake houses. For five summers, starting when I was fourteen years old, I worked as a dock hand at Rock Lane Marina. (For the most part, I was the only girl who worked there. The boss made me a custom T-shirt that read "Sea Kitten" on the back. The boys' shirts read "Sea Dogs.") I learned about river rats and lake bums, how they drink rum-and-Cokes like water and aren't ashamed to flirt with a high-schooler. We worked for tips. I made a lot of money. Sometimes, when customers got too rowdy, I was sent to detail a speedboat or hose goose shit off the sidewalks.

We used to see the showboat *Branson Belle* from the marina, flamboyant with its red paddle wheels and two columns in the front. Later in the news I'll see some of its employees and even a tourist or two had jumped off, trying to pull people out of the choppy water after the duck boat's roof disappeared below the surface. Others chose to stay dry and watch. One woman caught the whole thing going under on camera, but I wouldn't see the low-quality cell phone footage until later in the night. Once it goes viral, though, I'll find that it's almost impossible to get away from. The still image of the canopied amphibious vehicle, white-top wake up to its windows and overcoming its nose, will pop up on my screen every time I scroll through Facebook for the next month or so. The boat seems to bob in slow motion. Those of us left to wonder in awe pointlessly beg to know about the lifejackets. *Were there any on the boat? Did the captain ask the tourists to secure the fluorescent orange around their waists? Why didn't the vests keep them afloat?* I wouldn't have to go searching to find the answers; any new information about the accident would be published every day for at least a month. And the answers are what manifest my nightmares into ghosts. A defense attorney for the victims of a *different* duck boat accident said, "People get trapped in the canopy; the life jackets force them up, but the canopy pulls them down. It's a Hobson's choice." Visions of mothers and babies and the elderly getting sucked deep into the lake's depths along with the boat, their cheeks and palms pressed against the windows, kicking and choking, trying to escape the metal sea monster, choosing between what is available and nothing at all, will regularly flash in my mind. This moment was captured and will be shared endlessly.

The article cites unofficial reports of a fatal boat accident on Table Rock Lake. We are about to leave Casey's and head back to the comfort of our homes when I ask everyone if they've heard about it yet. *No, are you serious? Six confirmed fatalities?* And that number just kept rising and rising: eleven, then fourteen, and finally seventeen total deaths. There were only thirty-one aboard. I'll see another article that quotes one of the survivor's mothers. She believes her daughter had been rescued for a reason, that God himself had reached down through the storm to save the chosen few, the ones who deserved it. Her daughter is special, and she knows this because it's all part of God's plan, and all the locals in the comments section agree. Everything happens for a reason, even the deaths of a grandmother and her granddaughter, of a pair of married couples from the Midwest, of a father and his soon, of Bob Williams, the boat's driver, and of a husband, three children, a sister, an uncle, a nephew, and the in-laws, all on the same evening, because of an accident that could have been avoided.

> *When the totality of the situation hit her, she told God, "If they don't make it, Lord, take me, too. There's no reason for me to be here." Asked whether she was happy to be alive, she told a reporter, "I don't know yet. Time will tell." She added: "The only thing I can think of is that God must have something for me. There's no way I should be here."*
>
> —*Christal Hayes*, USA Today

Nine victims of the accident belong to the same family. The Colemans had traveled from Indiana to Branson for a vacation that was cut short by tragedy. Only Tia and one of her teenaged nephews will return home to bury their loved ones. It won't take long for the news to break that Tia is filing a $100 million lawsuit on behalf of the victims, and it won't take long for Internet trolls and middle-aged white women to question her motives and her character below clickbait headlines. As if all the money in the world could replace the hole left in Tia's heart from the loss of her children, her husband—the people she held tightest against her chest and prayed for the most. I'll want to stoop to their levels, write bitchy but compelling responses to these strangers who believe they are holier than thou. I'll want to ask them what's the right way to grieve, and what will it take for them to empathize with a black woman in pain. But I bite my tongue and don't.

The purpose of a hashtag is to go viral, to bring attention to a particular issue, to raise awareness about something, etc. A hashtag is meant to be seen. It's a marketing tool. It's a way to brand an event or a concept. And #TableRockStrong provided space on multiple platforms for arbitrary bouts of finger-pointing, which makes sense; we believe that if we can understand something, we will suffer less, and if we can punish someone or some*thing* for these otherwise meaningless deaths, there's potential for closure, for peace. This misconception is one I've held tight to throughout this process. Anything to avoid the suffering. But if *surviving*—not only this deadly flash thunderstorm, but my childhood, sexual harassment, being a woman in Trump's America—has taught me anything, it's that suffering is worthwhile. After all, it's the only thing that all humans have in common. And if we can be honest in our suffering, if we can open up and listen and remain flexible, maybe we can connect. Maybe down-home, farmer's-tanned, Old Testament Midwesterners could finally understand a perspective outside their own. Maybe these deaths would matter a little more. Maybe this essay would feel more urgent. There are too many lives lost to unexplainable senselessness for us to dwell on one for much time at all, though. I know this very well.

But how can you blame the driver when he, too, fell prey to the water that Thursday; how can you blame the passengers for not thinking to check for pop-up storms on a day that had been so lovely; how can you blame the weather? Instead, some will choose to blame it on the company (or the entire duck boat industry itself), but most will give credit to a higher power. Like the survivor's mother, like Tia Coleman, the people who live in the heart of this country and grew up going to church three times a week and work hard and abuse drugs and cheat on their wives and float down rivers—people around here—will justify the senselessness of the Branson duck boat accident by chalking it up to God's plan. And even though their *thoughts and prayers* will get under my skin like splinters for the next few months, I envy them. I envy their faith in divine intervention. Because if I were able to believe, then maybe I would be able to feel as warm as I did on the day of July 19, 2018, every day, before we survived by the skins of our teeth.

Amelia Fisher

Why I Like Bad Boys
According to the PCL-5

He used to save   his empty lighters   in a shoebox, tagged   with
their death dates   in permanent marker.   He did this until   he
got arrested   with a white lighter   in the cupholder of his car.
Questions to be answered   on a scale   of *Not at all*   to *Extremely*
on the form   at my therapist's office: *Being superalert, watchful,*
or on guard?   He couldn't shake it,   the white lighter's presence
like a stranger's ghost.   The night the window   was broken,   the
white lighter lay   amongst the shards.   It stalked   him, hiding
in friends' pockets   and in the gutter.   The white lighter on the
coffee table   at a coworker's house party,   where we were   right
before our first   falling out, lives on   in the background   of this
Polaroid: Me   and my long hair draped   over his lap, both of
us   laughing. The picture   is on my fridge,   a reminder of our
potential. *Feeling distant or   cut off   from other   people?*   He
hated   the way I showed it off,   he said it's like having   an
upside-down cross   over the front door.   I like that idea, though,
the same way   I like   lightning storms   and snorting lines.
Taking too many risks   or doing things   that could cause   you harm?
We used to cruise around college towns   passing his piece   until
we burnt it all up, throwing   our heads back   as we released
smoke   like steam engines.   We did this until   he got arrested
with a white lighter   in the cupholder of his car—   *having*
negative beliefs   about yourself   or the world?—   and I prayed to
my rosary   as if I believed   the Holy Spirit lived there   and not
in empty lighters.

Jeannine Hall Gailey

Every Time I Take Another Cancer Test, I Feel the Universe

collapsing in on me like the special effects of a cheesy movie about
   dreams
or time travel, the walls of reality tilting in on themselves like glass
   panes

as doctors discuss tumor markers, scans and measurements in
   monotone.
Is this an MRI tube or perhaps an isolation chamber on a trip to Mars

because life has become scary like bad sci-fi; in fact I expect a villain
with a microscope and supergerms to jump out at any moment.

I would like to ignore any ignoble cells gone awry, avoid the needles
and radioactive machines, almost like avoiding the ending

of the story. I don't want to read the last page just yet, no spoilers,
I want the party scene with the band and the unicorns to keep going,

a magical garden opening up before me, each path eternal and
   symmetrical,
each footfall silent on grass that provides a green escape, a patient
   place to fall.

Jeannine Hall Gailey

Self-Portrait as Fifties Hygiene Film

Any art form can be made propaganda.
Wear your socks as straight as your hair,
as straight as your spine. A skirt twisted
or a lock out of place might unleash
a tornado of desire. You wear the same
white saddle shoes and white button-down blouse
in every film, unmussed and constrained.
What might erupt from a pair of red heels,
a smudge of lipstick too bright or eyeshadow
too dark? The screech of tires in the darkness
a reminder of what goes wrong.
Make sure to put your best foot forward
in a world that might instruct you on the proper
shoe, the proper handshake, the proper means
of washing your face. Be invisible, be part of
the blank, whitewashed landscape, fade into the background
until exactly the right time for the fatal bite,
the forbidden dance step, the shaking loose,
the hurricane of gold bared skin
and the flash of your sharp teeth.

Jeannine Hall Gailey

July 5, 2019

It rained on the Fourth on the capital.
The earth shrugged off a little of the continent,
causing earthquakes from California to Utah.
I myself didn't feel that great. America
is harder to celebrate than it was when I was
a child, and I was suspicious even then.
Patriotism didn't suit me, maybe it was
the men in black suits who haunted our neighborhood,
or the clicks on the phone line that meant
Big Brother was definitely listening. I was
seven when I learned about phone tapping.
I should have become an anarchist hacker,
but instead I went in for poetry, which really
leaves you no practical way forward except
to celebrate the bright goldfinch that landed
on your sunflowers, or mourn the way
the July air smells acrid for days until rain,
and no amount of lemonade takes the smoke
taste out of your mouth. A man brought a gun
to the fireworks at the beach, but he was shot.
The emergency room was full of food poisoning,
burns and people falling off ladders.
So happy birthday, America, wash your hands,
see your red-white-and-blue ideals
as what they always were—a shiny memory,

like the fireworks, always more destructive
than beautiful, apartment buildings still smoldering
in the aftermath, all burnt grass and singed fingers.

Amelia Morand

Wimpy

Her real name was Angela but everyone called her Wimpy. The
Garcias lived two doors down from us on Calle Contenta, nine of
them in a six-room house and our family six in a three. Her parents
had more kids than they could afford because they were Catholic and
mine because my dad couldn't keep his dick to himself, or that's what
I heard through the crumbling adobe walls one night before my latest
half-brother came to live with us on weekends. She never left him,
though.

Wimpy and I didn't like each other very much, but we were the
same age, and our mothers liked getting drunk in the abandoned lot
between our houses when our dads didn't make it home for dinner,
so we played together almost every day. I didn't mind. She had older
sisters to bother and spy on, and I only had the babies and a half-
brother older by three months who once lit a washcloth on fire and
dropped it in the bathtub while I was making a mohawk with shampoo
because his mom told him I was the reason she and our dad split up.

Besides, even then Wimpy seemed so comfortable in her own
skin, aware of who she was and resigned to it, and that was as alluring
to me as her sisters' makeup that we stole and applied in the arroyo
that ran beside our street. We'd kneel hidden among the towering
chamisa bushes that bloomed and flourished even in the driest years.
Our mothers hated the way the clouds of tacky yellow flowers made
everyone sneeze and never stopped trying to wipe them from our
street, but privately, we thought they were beautiful.

Wimpy would work carefully with serious eyes, saying she'd make
me look prettier than her sister who could have won Miss Teen New
Mexico if she hadn't gotten pregnant, and I would slash her cheeks
with green eyeshadow and whiten her thin lips with powder, make her

ugly because I knew she'd never see it. I just smiled and she believed me.

When our moms called, we'd spit into our hands and scrub at each other's faces until our palms turned purple. I would re-enter my house with tight, sticky skin and a weight in my chest from the lie and from swallowing the piece of Fruit Stripe gum Wimpy split with me when we said good-bye. I'd sit on my bed and worry about when they would catch up with me, these bad things I'd done. With every lie, every secret, I felt more alone in that crowded house. I hoped maybe it'd be easier as I got older, that I'd turn into a better kid soon, but more and more I wondered if this was as good as I was ever going to be. More than anything, I was scared because Wimpy told me gum took seven years to poop out, and I imagined eventually my butt would be so blocked with Fruit Stripe that nothing else would be able to squeeze by.

But Wimpy's spit was not as bad as the smell of other women on my dad's skin when he finally slunk back home, the gum healthier than the Tequila Rose my mother drank for dinner. The misery of my parents never seemed to lift or deepen much, regardless of what they did. I knew that I was probably made of the worst of both of them, but at some point I saw that I pooped more or less regularly every day and figured our actions have little weight on our realities.

Even so, I dreamed of escape, but Wimpy's sense of her future was flat, practical. When we discussed our plans in our spot in the arroyo, I'd say I wanted to be a race-car driver or a sky writer, and she'd say she'd probably be a waitress like her mom. As long as she didn't have to share a bed once she grew up, she said, that'd be OK. Fifteen years later, she was working breakfast beside three of her sisters at the Plaza Cafe, and I was driving a school bus and sometimes selling plasma between 8:30 a.m. and 3:00 p.m. when that wasn't enough to make rent on the one-bedroom we shared on the other side of the arroyo from our parents, still miserable on Contenta. We still didn't like each other much, but explaining all of it to someone new would take too long, and besides, anything was better than living with our siblings. She'd bring home cold chilaquiles from work and let me wear the designer sunglasses that tourists left in the sticky booths and wasn't even that mad when she found out that I'd used her Social Security number to sell plasma when I'd exhausted the first-timer bonuses at Christus St. Vincent's Hospital and La Familia, the low-income clinic.

I'd fall asleep to the sound of her high, whining voice as she told me about the customers she'd waited on that day, the bitchy things her sisters had said, and I'd wake up to her uneven snore. I guess she was better than being alone.

By the time Wimpy was made front of house manager, I'd been put on the special seeds bus, which came with a pretty good bonus. So both of us were busy, making enough money, and held the power in our relationships, her setting the schedule for her cunty older sisters and me with the guy I was seeing who was anxious to please after his mom shot herself one rainy night beneath an underpass. Nailing those three things is the closest I think anyone gets to being happy. Or at least that was how I thought it was for both of us. But while I settled into the fixed nature of my life, made the best of things, she was getting restless in a way I hadn't seen coming.

I think it was the babies thing that started it. Like the older she got without finding herself pregnant, the more she realized she had any choices at all. When we were twelve, Wimpy had caught me getting fingered by some neighborhood kid in our spot between the chamisa, which we'd heard the older boys calling pussy bushes because of the oversexed smell of the too-yellow flowers in bloom. I had only recently begun to stink that way myself, to realize that no matter how hard I scrubbed down there, I'd never again smell clean.

We'd been squirming in the dirt while he pinched me in all the wrong places, my eyes shut tight so I didn't have to look at him, and when I opened them, Wimpy's face hovered above the chamisa, sorrowful and scandalized. It took a while to convince her that I couldn't get pregnant that way, especially since my secondhand shirts had become stretched thin over tits that were blooming like tumors, my hips, ass, spreading like mold. When Wimpy finally got her period, her sisters taped tampons to the spokes of her bicycle, and she fled into the arroyo and cried for days.

Her favorite sister got pregnant that year, and I'd noticed how Wimpy had stopped looking at her when she started to show. I remember once sitting in their cramped kitchen, watching the two of them start dinner for their mother, still at work. Wimpy was standing at the sink, rubbing black skins off the roasted chiles, and Desirée came up behind, reached above her head to grab a dish from the high shelf. Her swollen stomach pressed against Wimpy's back. Wimpy pulled away so hard that Desirée went down, and even then, as we both helped her up, Wimpy wouldn't look at her. Later, I asked her what her problem was. She told me that she couldn't stand to be near it, that body. It's not hers anymore, she said. Or maybe she said, It's not her. I agreed that Desirée looked gross but didn't understand what the big deal was—we'd all be there someday. At least we could get fat together, I said.

She said it wasn't like it ended when you had them. She saw it with her nieces and nephews, the way they were always tugging at their mothers, climbing in their laps and pulling at their boobs, and when they couldn't get to those, stuffing hair and fingers into their mouths. You can never get away from them, she said. It might be nice, I thought, to be needed that way.

We were almost thirty when she first discovered there was a procedure that would make it so she couldn't have kids. I didn't get why she wanted to go through so much trouble when we had a drawerful of Plan B at home (the nurse practitioner always pressed several boxes at me to "keep in your back pocket," as I drank the apple juice and ate the stale cookie and asked if there was anything else I could do for cash while I was there). But once Wimpy had an idea in her head, it was all she talked about. She could be really boring that way. Finally I told her if she made the fucking appointment already, I'd loan her the rest. I always liked getting tangled up in her shit and further away from mine, and besides, I never really thought she'd do it.

She could have just gotten her tubes tied, but between the strength of her obsession and that stubborn, simplistic thinking she'd always had, Wimpy wanted it all out. She said it would be cleaner that way. It took a little while to find a doctor who was willing to do it to someone so young, but Wimpy had done her research. She told them that her mom had died from that kind of woman cancer, so she wanted to take every preventive measure possible. As she spoke this carefully rehearsed phrase, Wimpy would pretend to choke up and grab my hand, and I would grimace at the floor, the same bile green tiles everywhere we went. I wasn't as bothered by the lie so much that she was willing to tell it. It seemed more like something I would do.

I asked her after that first appointment if she wasn't worried about God, that he might really give her mom cancer to prove a point, especially since Wimpy was making me keep the whole thing a secret. We were sitting at our kitchen table, eating leftovers from her weekly family dinner. From our house you could just see the Garcias' flat gray adobe, surrounded by the blooming chamisa they'd never managed to kill. Wimpy's mother had hung laundry on the line, and it sagged with the weight of all the towels and sheets and clothing of the daughters who had returned home with their own children when waiting tables wasn't enough. The spring winds were blowing, and I knew that by the time she came home from her double shift to pull them off the lines the edges of her linens would be brown from sweeping back and forth across the cracked dirt.

I looked at Wimpy, guessing she, too, was thinking about the pointless work of our mothers, the sheets that would never be clean, but she was absently shredding the last tortilla, staring at the empty lot between our parents' houses, which no one had ever bothered to build on, or even to claim. She tore off a tiny piece, then another, dropping them in the pooled red chile on her plate. I was still hungry so I grabbed for the chunk she hadn't ruined, but she slapped my hand away. It's fucking mine, she said, drowning the tortilla in honey before she crammed it in her thin-lipped mouth. She'd never talked to me that way, so I didn't tell her that she had chile on her chin.

The night before the surgery, I was wide awake, but Wimpy was snoring loudly as usual from her side of the room. I pulled back the curtain that we'd hung down the middle and watched her chest rise and fall in a graceless rhythm. Her pinched face was lit a little by the bright stars that passed above our skylight, or I guess it was our room that moved beneath them while they lay fixed in their position through the years.

She couldn't eat, of course, but I made breakfast burritos with those homemade tortillas her mom sent home with her after church on Sundays, piled on eggs and chorizo and smothered them in green chile and cheese, the way Wimpy liked them. I set one in front of her as she sat rereading the pre-surgical instructions. She walked out of the room and didn't speak to me the whole drive to Albuquerque. As she was changing into her gown, I asked her if she remembered the plans we'd made in the chamisa.

Wimpy said she remembered the way I always made her share her gum, even if it was her last piece. How I'd tell her if she swallowed it it would stay inside of her forever.

I said that wasn't how it'd been. How I'd been. I lingered in the doorway, but I didn't know how to say what I meant about our hiding spot, how even in the only place we could be alone, we'd been together. It wasn't the kind of thing we said.

I thought I might as well sell some plasma while I was there. I'd been so distracted with everything that it'd been awhile. I'd always liked to watch my blood being sucked out of my arm through the little tubes, the way it was spun, separated from the murky yellow plasma and mixed with a bag of clear saline, dripped back into my vein. Afterwards, I'd feel clean, new, but that day it just made me sick. I returned to Wimpy's empty room, lay down on the extra cot, and listened to the hum of anxious families pacing up and down the hall.

I woke up as she was being wheeled in. The fluorescent light made her skin shine yellow and waxy, cast shadows beneath the sharp angles of her face, but her expression for once was not pinched but peaceful. The machines she was hooked up to didn't beep like I would have thought but towered quiet above her, whirring with low starts when the numbers reset. She looked young with her face so slack and clean, smaller and removed somehow, like part of her had fallen into the hole made from what they'd taken. I put my hand on her gown as though I could feel the emptiness beneath it.

I felt totally alone with her asleep beside me, her betrayal so much worse than all my years of small and shitty things. Part of me always thought that someday the world would shift while I wasn't looking, that eventually my life would just take off. Despite all my plans and pretending, I'd never really been able to imagine myself more than an arroyo away from Calle Contenta, from Wimpy. Now her private, stubborn choice had moved her beyond me, beyond the limited happiness I thought we'd both agreed to. I thought people couldn't really change, but Wimpy had remade herself entirely without even being awake.

And so I left her there.

I was her ride, obviously, and it was a really crappy move, but in that moment, I felt like just another piece she'd cut out and thrown away. Desirée came by a few days later to pack her things, told me Wimpy wouldn't say what happened, just that she'd gotten her appendix out and wanted me to stay away. She was pregnant again, and when she stood sideways in the doorway and said good-bye, her belly filled the frame.

Wimpy left not long after that, for Oregon, or maybe it was Virginia, my mom said with a shrug. Someplace too fucking green. I tore down the curtain that divided the room, but I never moved my bed toward the middle, beneath the skylight. She loved the brightness of the stars, but they always kept me awake.

I never told her family the truth about the operation, but I don't know if I was finally trying to do the right thing for Wimpy or I just didn't want to admit to helping her leave us all behind. At some point they quit inviting me to family dinners, and eventually I just stopped by when I went to see my own parents, and even that became only a nod and a wave when we saw each other across the lot, still empty after all those years.

She wrote me once, a few years after she took off. I was waiting tables by then because I'd failed a random drug test and couldn't drive the bus anymore. I wouldn't have thought I'd miss it, having to drive so slow and careful as the kids yelled and sang and cried behind me, but I did.

The envelope was full of cash. It was everything I'd given her for the surgery. It was stupid but classic Wimpy to trust the postal workers wouldn't steal it. On the front of the card was a picture of a small plane skywriting, "Go Fuck Yourself." She'd signed it Angela.

I always think of her when the chamisa starts to bloom, the smell making me gag and lonely all at once. I cut yellow clouds of it some days, fill my house with the sticky flowers and their inescapable ripeness. I can't say if I'd be able to do anything differently if Wimpy gave me another chance, but I'd like to think that this time I would stay there beside her, do all the things that people who love each other are supposed to do. I'd buy flowers, nice ones, and arrange them carefully by her bed, and I'd sit there, too, so she wouldn't have to wake up alone. I would hold her hand as the machines sputtered and sighed, watch her eyelids flutter, and wait.

Caroljean Gavin

Barren

The first time Suzy offered me one of her apples I was shy, confused, heart beating, beating, beating. We were squeezed together in a latched bathroom stall, sharing the toilet seat, both of us fully jeaned and sitting on the edge, cold bowl of water beneath us. I was sharing my cigarette with her. Grand adventure. High school theater restroom, during drama class. The rest of the class was practicing Shakespeare. Loudly. In British accents they learned from American actors. Suzy wasn't inhaling, but she was leaving a sticky ring of pink lip gloss on the filter that tasted like petroleum jelly and chemically simulated raspberries. Her giant cubic zirconia ring, prism, chandelier caught and flashed the bathroom lights over me every time she lifted her hand to her mouth. *You don't just pull the smoke into your mouth,* I told her. *Pull it all the way back, you know, breathe it in.* The way her body shook when she coughed, one of her apples fell off and splashed into the toilet bowl. We both got wet. I took the cigarette. *It's ok,* she said, pulling back her hair, revealing all the red, green, pink globes of apple fruit there. *You can have one if you want.* I pointed the cigarette toward one, pulling it closer in, laser pointer, glow stick, magical wand. She'd be beautiful as a lantern. *Not like that.* She took my other index finger, the bald thing, and rubbed it against the skin of an apple that hung just below the tongue of her earlobe like a bauble, trinket, orchard-picked heirloom earring. She closed her eyes, lids twitching, like a trance, dream, rapture. The bathroom door creaked a long open and exhaled, puffed out, and in a terrible, over-enunciated English accent, some girl said, "Hark, a smoke break! But where the weed at, bitches?"

☾

That lime-green backpack was always fit to burst. I never let it go. Slept with it behind my pillow. *What you got in that thing?* Mom would ask. *Don't those teachers think about your developing backs?* Mom would say thinking about doctor's bills. *You planning to run off somewhere? Where would you really go?* she'd ask. *Have you ever thought about that?* I thought about that every night, every early morning, every time I went to the bathroom, every time Mom left the room. Every time I was alone. Unzip just a little bit, just at the arch at the top of the backpack, just for the peek of the apples, heaped one on top of the other, soft, pulsing, blushing, the juice I knew pushed beneath them, that pushed up at the skin, that pushed up at my skin, that smelled just like the perfumes Suzy stole from the drugstores. I rubbed apples against my cheeks and thought of the places I could go: nightclub, beach chalet, top of a Ferris wheel, bottom of a waterfall, under hotel sheets crisp and fresh. I'd close my eyes, take a breath, and chance a bite, a taste, a changing. I asked mom for a new backpack, shoved the lime green one under the bed for safekeeping.

What happened was two of the stagecraft boys, Josh and Bryce caught us kissing outside behind the theater during class. They were just fetching wood for sets, unsupervised and horny, *Ho, ho, ho! What do we have here?* One of them might have said. *Rehearsing!* I blurted and broke away, let Josh share the rest of my menthol, and Suzy snatched her apple out of my hand and handed it to Bryce. Later she called me *ashamed* and I called her *slut*. I was Juliet that year, Ophelia the next. I heard Suzy actually dated Bryce for a while and I didn't care, but she cut her hair really short, dyed it black, and eventually disappeared. When I was packing for college, I found a lime green backpack full of rotten apples and just tossed them with the rest of the trash.

Rebecca Schumejda

Sweet Fruit

Peeling a mango with a paring knife
on a snowy April morning, allowing the
blade to meet my thumb, I think about
my brother; I always think about
my brother, especially when handling hope.
Somewhere sweet fruit grows year-round,
but not in the cell he is confined to.
Overripe mangoes smell and taste like fish
to me. The shape of the island we grew
up on, the shape of the shame for a horrendous
act I didn't commit. My daughters, at the
kitchen counter holding the slices up to
their hungry mouths like bait,
do not know how my brother haunts me
like that weakfish I pulled from the
Long Island sound, three hooks
dangling from its mouth, how against
my father's wishes, I cut the line, yes,
I cut the line and set it free.

Rebecca Schumejda

Peel

As I remove the skin from a clementine, you tell me
you may drop the civics class you're enrolled in
through the prison degree program because
it gets so loud on your block that you can't read.

I don't tell you my husband brings our daughters
outside whenever you call. There are only a few
dirty mounds of snow left. I watch my girls run
straight to them with their good sneakers on;

I don't tell you this, either; instead I suggest earplugs.

We once lived under the same roof in the same house
where the paint never peeled. I remember how quiet
it was there. You could feel the quiet like someone

holding your ungloved hand in snow until you begged:

Let go. While I listen to you talk about the noise
pinballing against your sanity. I feel sick. All these
orange slices in my hands, my girls burying themselves
in dirty snow as if it is beach sand, you asking me to look

out at an unbarred sunset and tell you there is no god.

William Palomo

The Coming of Your Firstborn Means Pupusas in Brooklyn

As Mama headed to the hospital,
Papi headed to the pupuseria to order
dos revueltas, una con loroco y queso,
y una ronda de cervezas y Kola Champan
for him and his coworkers, men celebrating
the miraculous agony of birth. My sister
received Mama's maiden name, Amaya,
so years later, as children, we knew
Mama and Papi weren't married
when my sister was born. Once, before
my brother and I knew anything
about what an appropriate question
was, we asked Papi if he loved Mama
or whether he just knocked her up
and got stuck. He shrugged and said
his father raised him not to leave
children thrown around, but that he fell
in love with Mama after he came home
from a graveyard shift to find her
rocking my sister and singing,
Unos inditos somos, hijos de Cuscatlán.
We asked Mama about giving birth,
and she said she called him to let him know
the child was born. My father howled
with joy and ordered another round.

G.H. Yamauchi

Coconuts Land on Sand; Buckeyes Fall Into Dirt

MY PARENTS WOULD REPEAT STOCK REMARKS ABOUT HOW THEY VIEWED OTHER ASIANS WHEN THEY WERE GROWING UP IN HAWAII.

WELL, WE ALWAYS THOUGHT THEY WERE "SHORT, DARK, AND HAIRY!"

OKINAWANS

HMM...

BUT THEN I MET YOUR DAD, AND HE WAS TALL!

I ALWAYS ENVIED THE OKINAWAN GIRLS' EYEBROWS. THEY WERE DARK AND BEAUTIFUL!

NAICHI DON'T REALLY HAVE EYEBROWS. THAT'S WHY I PENCIL MINE ON.

MY MOTHER USED TO WALK BY THE FILIPINO WORK CAMPS WHEN SHE WAS A CHILD. THEY WERE ALL SINGLE MEN, MIGRANTS WITHOUT FAMILIES, AND SHE WAS SCARED OF THEM. ...SHE ALWAYS RETAINED A NEGATIVE VIEW OF FILIPINOS, EVEN WHEN SHE LATER MOVED TO L.A.

FILIPINOS

IT WAS HARD TO DIG DEEPER THAN THE SAME OLD ANECDOTES.

KOREANS

WHEN MY SISTER TOLD US HER FIANCÉ WAS "ROBERT O.", WE FIGURED "O." STOOD FOR OSHIMA, OR SOMETHING. BUT IT WAS "OH". A KOREAN NAME!

SO, WAS THAT A PROBLEM?

WE WERE SURPRISED!

DID YOUR PARENTS OBJECT? DID IT BOTHER YOU?

WE'D JUST ASSUMED HE WAS NISEI, LIKE US!

THEIR AMBIGUOUS DISTINCTIONS AMONG ASIANS WERE HARD FOR MY BROTHER AND I TO PARSE, GROWING UP IN A MOSTLY WHITE TOWN IN S.W. OHIO. BUT WHITE PEOPLE SELDOM MADE AN APPEARANCE IN MY PARENTS' CHILDHOODS.

OH, THERE WERE JUST A FEW HAOLES IN OUR SCHOOL. WE THOUGHT THEY WERE — WELL, THEY USUALLY WEREN'T VERY BRIGHT.

MY OWN CHILDHOOD, HOWEVER, INCLINED ME TO NOTICE THE FEW STORIES THAT DID EXPLICITLY REFER TO WHITE PEOPLE.

GO HOME!

MY MOTHER'S BROTHER, KAORU, THE ONLY BOY AMONG SEVEN SIBLINGS.

HE SERVED IN THE ARMY CORPS OF ENGINEERS, IN VIETNAM.

HE BOARDED AN ABANDONED BUS, WITH SOME MEN UNDER HIS COMMAND—ONE OF WHOM SHOT HIM THROUGH HIS NECK.

THE ARMY SAID IT WAS AN "ACCIDENTAL HOMICIDE."

HER FATHER, BORN IN HAWAII IN 1900, SAID IT WAS NO ACCIDENT. SOME WHITE MEN WHO HATED TAKING ORDERS FROM AN ASIAN.

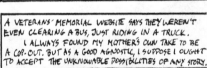

HEY, SPEC 5!

HER SISTERS SAID NO, HE MUST HAVE BOARDED THE BUS FIRST; THEY MADE HIM A HERO. AS FOR THE SHOT? MAYBE A NERVOUS DRAFTEE TRIPPED.

CHECK UNDER EVERY SEAT, MEN!

A VETERANS' MEMORIAL WEBSITE SAYS THEY WEREN'T EVEN CLEARING A BUS, JUST RIDING IN A TRUCK.

I ALWAYS FOUND MY MOTHER'S OWN TAKE TO BE A COP-OUT. BUT AS A GOOD AGNOSTIC, I SUPPOSE I OUGHT TO ACCEPT THE UNKNOWABLE POSSIBILITIES OF ANY STORY.

OKAY MOM, I'VE GOT TO GO NOW!...

HANG ON!

SHE ALWAYS SAID, "WELL, I WASN'T THERE. SO I DON'T THINK I CAN EVER KNOW WHAT REALLY HAPPENED THAT DAY."

AS YOU KNOW. MY WIDOWED MOTHER WORKED AS A MAID...

MY FATHER EMPLOYS A SIMILAR DISTANCE.

"WE LIVED IN MAIDS' QUARTERS, AND MOVED ALMOST EVERY YEAR."

"IN THE FORTIES, MOST WEALTHY CAUCASIANS DIDN'T MUCH CARE FOR JAPANESE AMERICANS."

NO, HARUKO, YOU CAN'T "TAKE LITTLE PIECE FOR EDDIE"!

"SHE TOLD ME OF COMING HOME ONE DAY TO FIND ME WITH THE BOSSES' SON WHEN I WAS PERHAPS SIX...

C'MON?

GIDDYUP JAP?!

I DON'T RECALL THE INCIDENT MYSELF, BUT SHE SAYS SHE QUIT THAT DAY.

HE USUALLY COUNTERBALANCES THAT STORY BY TELLING US:

"AT THE LAST FAMILY, WHERE SHE STAYED 8 YEARS, THE FATHER TAUGHT HER HOW TO DRIVE. HE EVEN LET HER USE THE CAR ON HER OFF DAYS.

"IT WAS UNHEARD OF. SOMETIMES HE EVEN DENIED USE OF THE CAR TO HIS OWN CHILDREN, AND TELL THEM, 'NO, ITS HARUKO'S DAY!"

-OR, AS MY GRANDMOTHER WOULD SAY:

BEFORE I WORK FOR HIM, I THINK ALL HAKUJIN SO CRUEL! I THINK WHITE PEOPLE, THEY ARE NOT PEOPLE, NOT HUMAN BEINGS! BUT HE WAS A KIND MAN. VERY KIND.

Kathryn M. Barber

Whiskey River Blues

They say if you sit on that swinging bridge out off Nottingham Road, lie on your back on those wooden planks, stare out at the sky, the river'll whisper to you. Smoke you a cigarette, swallow you some whiskey, wait for a shooting star. When you see it streak across that full, black Virginia sky, ask the river a question, and it'll answer you back—if you listen hard enough.

I been coming out here years and years, since before he was a part of me, part of anything. He always said he knew me better than I know me, but that's not true, and I know that—because he didn't know all the nights I came out here, drove all the way from Nashville and crossed this state line just to stand over this river that raised me up, river that held me all through high school, college too. Back before there was him, before there was him and me. When all there was was me, just me and this river. The air's sticky tonight, dogs barking somewhere off in the distance. If it was a Saturday night, there'd be banjos and guitars creeping through these woods, ghosts of Maybelle and June Carter humming through trees, but tonight, I can't hear anything but the water rushing over those rocks, singing something else, something sadder.

The bridge rocks with my weight, swings me back and forth, creaks soft. This bridge rebuilt me over and over, loved me back when I forgot to love me. When he forgot to love me, too. Back to them damp wooden boards, I kick my feet in front of me, face the heavens my daddy swears the Lord made all in one day. I know the voices of these currents better than I know my own voice, better than I know anything, know the whistles and whispers of these trees like I know these roads that curve around the back of this mountain, the ones that stretch from the Carter Fold all the way to the house I grew up in on top of that highest hill. I blow smoke over my head, tip the flask from my jean pocket up to those stars, feel the whiskey burn down my throat. Pray it'll burn out from my tongue every time I ever told him I loved him, every time his tongue was quiet, wouldn't, couldn't, just didn't, say it back.

For more than a year, I hugged his neck, kissed his whiskered jawline. More than two years after I left, I'm still singing sad love songs, not because I miss him, but because I miss who I was before him. Before he tipped me up, poured me up and out again. Emptied me out, and when I was gone, he sobbed there wasn't nothing left of me. Burned me up, and when I was gone, he sat in the smoke, lamented the ashes.

Four years ago, I stood on my Nashville porch, begged begged begged God for that man—don't care if he wrecks me, I said, don't care if he ruins me, let me have him let me have him let me have him. God obliged. I was sorry.

Two years ago, when I finally left that man out in Belle Meade I thought I loved so much, I found myself on a different porch, hollowed out and gone—like a stack of Russian dolls, and he pulled me apart and apart and apart, wanted to find what was at my core, who the smallest version of me was. My mama told me once after she left my daddy you can't always see how somebody's hurting somebody else with your eyes. That sometimes bruises get left on the inside. She said difference is nobody can see what's been done to you, not even you, and sometimes you convince yourself you're what's broken instead of him. I didn't know what she meant then, but I do now.

Three years ago, I came out here to this same bridge, that Thanksgiving he stood me up, and I tipped my head back to this same sky, same God, same river, and I cried out, let my hollering echo across this holler. I smoked until my lungs hurt and I drank until my throat ached, and I waited waited waited for that shooting star. It never came. But it didn't matter because the river whispered to me anyway—Run, it said. Run.

And now, now there's some man back in East Nashville who leaves trails of red- and purple-colored skin in the shape of his mouth when he kisses me, marks from loving, not wrecking, only he doesn't love me, either, but it doesn't matter. It doesn't matter because even if he did, even if he could, that man back in Belle Meade took all there was left of me, didn't leave nothing for nobody else.

If my childhood best friend were here, he'd hold my hand, say it doesn't matter who we love and who we don't and who doesn't love us, because we'll always have each other and we'll always come back here. Can't nobody take this bridge and this river and us from each other, and nothing else really matters, and I reckon he'd be right. We used to stand over this river, nights and mornings, too, sip whiskey, pour some in the river, sip, pour, sip, pour, watch the river mingle with the liquor we kept drowning ourselves in. Our own whiskey river, our own swinging bridge. And now, now feels like I'm all filled back up, and I'll be damned if I let somebody else pour me out into this river the way that man in Belle Meade did.

But just last week, I was sleeping on the chest of the man back in East Nashville, and I was dreaming about the man in Belle Meade, dreaming one was traded out for the other, the good one for the bad one, and I had to escape all over again. When I woke up in the arms of the man in East Nashville, he wrapped himself tighter around me, didn't know I'd been somewhere else in my head, all the way on the other side of the city, running running running, again, like the river told me to. Didn't know in my dreams he'd disappeared, and I couldn't feel him right there next to me in his bed. And I pushed my face deep into him, into all the pictures on his skin, only man I ever been with who had more tattoos than me. I wanted to tell him I'm only scared sometimes now, but I didn't because he isn't anything and neither are we, and so how come I felt safer there than I ever have anywhere else?

Tonight, I suck down more smoke, more whiskey, keep waiting on that shooting star, the one to tell me what to do, where to go, who to be. These stories, they end the same—me on this bridge, begging the sky and God and the river for answers that may never come.

Miles away, back in East Nashville, I bet he's at some bar laughing with somebody or other, bet he's sucking down whiskey, too, bet it don't occur to him, not for a second, that even if it was nothing, it was still everything. It was everything because he made me feel like there was still something left in me when I didn't think there was. And I bet he don't know there's a difference in feeling something and actually wishing you belonged to somebody.

I hold my lighter to the wire-squared fencing between the top and the bottom of the bridge. Spiderwebs climb between, one side to the other, but there aren't any spiders. They're all gone now, gone somewhere else, and maybe that's where I ought to go, too—

somewhere else, somewhere farther and farther away from the man in East Nashville and the man in Belle Meade. I burn those webs down, watch them light slow and slow and dissolve, and I wish I could dissolve with them. I sip that whiskey again, hold my breath.

A star streaks across the sky.

Be still, the river says. Be still.

Andy Smart

A Numbers Game

My symbol of soldier will always be my dad, but that of the Missouri Army National Guard is a militiaman with a musket at his hip. Beneath him is the credo: ALWAYS READY. ALWAYS THERE. The symbol of the 1138th Engineer Company is a mounted knight on a golden horse; his sword is pointing like Babe Ruth's bat into some outfield and victory.

At a writer's retreat somewhere in the Ozarks, a pot-smoking poetry proctor asked me, *What is the symbol of your people?* It's curious to me that I didn't say either the bronze man or the gold horse, either the gun or the sword; that I didn't claim the radar tower outside my father's barracks, or the F-16 with shark teeth that Dad said would provide air support if I was ever in trouble. I didn't pick the poppies Dad got from the bank every Veterans Day, or the First Sergeant's Major Achievement Award he had framed and hung in the living room. I didn't pick his boot knife, either, or anything violent.

I chose 1138 without thinking. It's one, two, three, or four numbers, depending on the day. But 1138 is also a shadow of my father standing on the tarmac of an airport telling me to take care of my mother. It's the cool underneath the branches of the dogwood tree where Dad laid down to die. The number is a time, a place, a sensation. It's a window through which I stare in at myself when I was undamaged. I sleep with and under 1138, I wear it in my night sweats like my father wore his dog tags and my mother wears her wedding ring.

In Roman numerals, 1138 looks like this: MCXXXVIII.

Under my eyes it looks like fatigue.

On the page it is a dragon in the uncharted seas of old maps.

Child Andy remembers:
The old man's unit in the National Guard was the 1138th Engineers. I remember the armory at Jefferson Barracks: the long white building where Staff Sergeant Daddy had his cubicle—the GI desk that looked stolen from the set of a low-budget documentary about public school principals or from a film noir detective's office, the bulletin board with fliers from recruiting and retention events three years before still push-pinned to it, the chair on casters that squeaked like a stepped-on kitten, magazines and Pepsi cans overflowing the trash basket, the smell of cigarettes and Mennen aftershave, young soldiers saluting as they became silhouettes in the doorway before moving out and leaving echoing footfalls, a tall black soldier the next spot over offering me root beer.

Adult Andy knows:
The old man's unit in the National Guard became the 1035th Maintenance Company several years before Dad died. The 1138th moved to Farmington, a Podunk outpost nearly an hour south of St. Louis. They were activated for duty in the Gulf; Dad and the 1035th were sent to Germany to repair old tanks. He brought me back a beer stein and some French cigarettes. He brought mom chocolate and kinderwein.

Pop deployed to Europe twice, for a month at a time, when I was in high school. Then 9/11 came. If war had ensued right away, he'd have fought and so would have I. Our rage was fresh, our patriotism dumb and raw. By the time the offensives in Afghanistan and Iraq began, Dad's political machinery had begun to work. He was old. Too old for that shit, for sure, and besides that, he couldn't back George W.

So my father retired from the service. I remember the ceremony: Pop standing tall before a general who was younger than him, receiving a handshake and a brass medal that, in military speak, read, "Congratulations, you can no longer hack it." His boots were shiny for their last inspection.

11:38 a.m., yesterday, almost four thousand days since Dad's death
I am sweating and my boxers are knotted around my nuts. My comforter is on the floor and the tower fan on the nightstand is blowing in my face. Mucus drains down my throat. I look at the time and wonder what I was dreaming before all this. I wonder what sorcery

or sleepytime voodoo jolts me awake at this time, exactly, at least three times a week. I wonder why I haven't found a job that makes me wake up before noon. Perhaps it would alleviate the ghost clock problem.

I do not believe this.

11:38 p.m., yesterday, the end of the almost-four-thousandth day since Dad's death

The lines on the highway are blurring together in the rain. I've got no windshield wipers, no driver's-side mirror, and a photosensitivity to oncoming headlights. Pop parallel-parked a Humvee once at the armory. He could manage this, now, better than me. He used to tell me, "Sometimes you've gotta say FIDO: Fuck It, Drive On." Fuck it, but I'd rather pull over and call my dad for help. I pray to the lesser gods of traffic instead.

1138

Eleven is a master number.

If ten is order in the universe, eleven is chaos. If ten is purity, eleven is sin.

1138th on Dec. 21, 1993

Again the white building, again the barracks, but this time the basement. A long room, a gymnasium. Buffet dinner in chafing dishes, paper plates sectioned into threes so Daddy's mashed potatoes don't contaminate his noodle salad or mostaccioli. I have a roll Mom buttered for me. After I eat, I chase Kirk Darling's daughter around the gym. She wants me to kiss her under the mistletoe, but there isn't any and we wouldn't know it anyway. We are eight years old.

When we leave the party, I am sweating in my short-sleeved dress shirt and I have cake on my tie. Daddy is angry with me about this, Mom is angry with him about something else. I am angry at Kirk Darling for having a daughter.

Mom throws an orange that I didn't know she had at the building. Daddy says she threw it at him. They scream outside the car in the cold. Inside the car they are quiet.

It will be Christmastime again soon, and my father is not here. My mother is eating an orange in the living room and watching a true crime program on TV.

135

1,138 days ago

You are standing in line at the grocery store, waiting to buy beer and toilet paper. A man behind you is pushing his cart into your ankles and you wish he were dead. In front of you, there's a newspaper on the endcap. The headline reads, "Police Chief Issues Apology to Michael Brown's Family." Michael Brown is a young black man shot by a young white cop last month, and the riots following his death have not yet cooled. The man pushing his cart into your heels mumbles that Mike Brown was a porch monkey. You wonder what your father would've said, or if he'd have stared at the rubber conveyor belt and waited in silence. The man pushes his cart again, and you remember you wished he was dead, like Mike Brown and your father. You don't wish they were dead, you don't think, but they are and you can't change it. The man is talking to himself as a way of talking to you.

"I wouldn't apologize to those niggers," he says. "Out there burning down their neighborhood. Don't see white folks pulling that crap when somebody dies."

The man is waiting. His cart wheels are full of potential energy. You want to tell him to back off. You want to make him back off. You wish you were your father, because you realize now what he would do. He would become Hartmann, the gunnery sergeant from Kubrick's *Full Metal Jacket*, your old man's favorite film. He would glare at the man after turning on him slowly, cinematically.

"To me, you are all equally worthless," your father would say.

You set your beer and Charmin Extra on the conveyor. You step away from the man and his cart.

He follows you.

1138

Eight is my life path number. I have added the digits in my birthdate and amalgamated them into a single digit. The sum is indicative of my destiny to make a big splash in the world of money, control, power, and influence. But I have authority issues and can, when out of alignment, be bullyish or blame others for the obstacles facing my eventual greatness. My life key is accepting that I am a born powerhouse.

I do not believe this.

The total number of words before this sentence is 1,138.

Eleven minutes, thirty-eight seconds into *Full Metal Jacket*.
I freeze the frame and watch electrofuzz bisect the screen.
Play.

Gomer Pyle whimpers, and his chipmunky cheeks puff out and collapse down, like little loaves of punched bread. He is smarting from being slapped across both sides of the face for confusing his left and his right. In another second, Hartmann will menace him:

"Don't fuck with me again, Pyle."

But for this lone instant, the camera is trained only on his pinked flesh and his bruised humanity. It is as close to a film cell of my father as there ever will be and eerily similar to the only photograph I have of him. For all the Hartmann bluster, Pop was still a fat, scared recruit underneath.

1138

Three means lucky, fortunate. Three means unity.

Pythagoreans consider three the first real number because there are three sides of a triangle. Three triangles interlocked are a Viking symbol for the slain dead. Three naked men and a Latin epithet appear on the Nobel Prize.

Three means trinity: father, son, holy ghost.

Which of these is the hypotenuse? What do I square to discover it? How is the ghost of my father holy? Three questions. If I answer one, the other two become obvious.

In tarot, three is the card of the empress—the creator, the benevolence.

Christians believe their savior was dead and in hell for three days before being resurrected. My father has been dead much longer. Three does not work for my father.

1Z39

When I cry these characters look like 1138. They are the coordinates to my father's grave—latitude is 1Z, longitude 39. His is the white marble headstone that looks like everything else.

1138th at the Bungalow

It's the oldest beer garden in St. Louis and is a tremendously beloved shithole. You have been drinking here for two years legally, four years total. You know the middle-aged prom queens who tend bar, the lechers and dotards and cirrhosis-livered who come here, the ice in the urinals that doesn't quell the stink of piss and vomit. You are as much a fixture as the barstools here.

You see a man with biceps the size of your waist. His girlfriend is stripper-pretty and they are both blackout drunk. On his right forearm is a tattoo of a lightning bolt and the letters TCB. Takin' care of business. He falls into you while slap-fighting his woman.

"Sorry, bro," he says. "Buy you a shot?"

"I'm all right, thanks," you say.

"Fuck that noise. Whiskeys! I'm still spending my Iraq money. Haji wants to buy me a whiskey!"

You are laughing and nervous. You are witnessing PTSD, you think.

"What branch of the service?" you ask.

"Army—1138th Engineers. Fuckin sappers. You know what they say? An engineer can be a grunt, but a grunt can't be an engineer! Twenty-one fuckin Bravo, best MOS on earth. You serve?"

"Not exactly. My old man was a drill sergeant in the 1138th when they were at JB."

"Fuckin-A! My fuckin bro!"

You toast your father, who is not dead yet, but alive and asleep. You stumble home from the tavern, buzzing with fermented fraternity. You have a new friend, a blood brother named Chance. You are trashed and you are happy. Streetlights have halos and you imagine they are grenades suspended in flight and just beginning to detonate. Everything is still except you, who barrels toward goodnight but not gently.

"Semper fi," you mutter to the Dumpsters. "Be all you can be! Aim high! Join the Navy, see the world!"

You are vast. You contain multitudes. Do you contradict yourself? Very well. You contradict yourself.

When your father dies, Chance will take you to a 3 a.m. bar and get you puking wasted. A frat brother from a Catholic college will bump into you and apologize profusely but it will not stop Chance from choke-slamming him through a high table.

You will never be far from violence again.

11:28 p.m., tonight

It'll come, whether I notice it or I don't, but I will because I'm waiting now. It's not always artificial, the noticing. My heart has an arrhythmia from alcoholism and smoking but it is tripped, too, by time. I have two cardiac events per day. Eventually that will stop and I will be honorably discharged from the strange and sentimental business of existing. But in seven minutes my chest will go tight and I will know. Six minutes.

My phone goes off.

"Are you OK?"

It is my Lisa, my best-friend-turned-common-law-wife from Kansas.

"Yes," I type back.

Four minutes.

"It's coming."

"I know."

"I know you do."

1,138 steps

You are dazed from want of sleep but not lack of fatigue. Your arms are goosebumped, your lower back tight. It is late, or it is early, or it is always. You leave the house and the air is an icicle overhead. The first breath stings, the second is mentholatum, the third you do not notice. You're moving without thinking, but you are thinking about something else; you are remembering your father's voice telling war stories he did not live. He is braggadocious, grandiose. He is in a bar called the Ashau Valley, after the battleground in Vietnam. You cannot see him or the other men who are staring at him in silence, but you can hear him. And you can hear them thinking, *This guy's full of shit.* Your father is Payback in *Full Metal Jacket*, talking about ops he wasn't in-country for. Where you are going now, there are dead who were killed living the life your father mythed about.

Proceed as you are, north. A long chain-link fence to your right, a sleeping German shepherd guarding a used car lot sleeping inside it. The tax attorney who called your father every day for a month to collect a past-due bill lives a block up on the left. You cross the street.

Turn left into St. Matthew cemetery and follow the road toward the mausoleum with a Buddhist swastika on each of the front columns. Resist the urge to spit and remember it is a symbol of unity in consciousness. Instead walk faster and feel the winter phlegm in your throat, hear a rattle in your lungs. Wheeze a bit in the brown grass as you veer off the road and toward the black marble bell marking your double-great-grandfather's grave.

Lean on the stone, feel its permanence and let it frighten you. You are in a field of cholera, consumption, tuberculosis, and simple despair.

But Ron Bozikis, who went to high school with your parents and was killed in Laos during Vietnam, is buried where you are walking, double-time, now. His headstone is still clean white, so many decades on. His photo is still that of a smiling boy whose belly does not push against his uniform. Ron was an Army Ranger and volunteered to fight.

He looks nothing like your father.

You kneel down and try to pray, or to say, *Thank you for your service*. But you are not grateful or penitent; you are sleepy and cold and alone. You were a child once, even younger than Ron, who is forever twenty-two, and you are not now. You are a pedestrian on a one-way street being surveilled by the inevitable and the unwanted.

You stand. You leave the grass blades and dust on the knees of your jeans.

You have traveled one-half of three-quarters of one mile. As you begin to work backwards, out of death and into its prelude, you are less nimble. You shorten your stride, square your shoulders, and know the wind will be at your face this time.

You walk anyway.

You go home.

End Credits

The numbers 1, 1, 3, and 8 add up to 13. But the symbol of my people is not that number, the upside-down horseshoe, or a "Born to Lose" tattoo. It is not 7.62, the size of the bullet that gives *Full Metal Jacket* its name. It's not 6, 15, or 7, though together they make up the date my father died. My symbol for soldier will always be my father. In my naivete, which comes and goes, Dad will always be standing in the doorway of our house in his BDUs, looking ready. Appearing there. The time on his GI wristwatch will always be 11:38. He will never die all the way; twice a day he lives for sixty seconds.

Jason Lee Brown

Fresh Stimulation

Along the plant's west wall, all day
I form sheet metal into complex shapes,
each within a thirty-second of an inch
or less from the blueprint's measurements.
I punch in numbers, each bend, each
angle, adjust adjust until perfect, until
I can control at least one aspect of life.

A box fan blows 110-degree air, dries hours
of sweat on top sweat until a sticky paste
numbs each day into the last and the next,
each without change or fresh stimulation,
same rhythmic hisses, thumps, and groans
from twenty-four-old hydraulics, each piece
of metal forming an inescapable melody

You can–do better than–this.
You can–do better than–this.
You can–do better than–this.

Jessica Mehta

Horn OK Please

I began to learn the language
of Indian horns. The wail of a rickshaw,
the trumpeting of cargo trucks. Buses, they pulse
like whales navigating overpopulated pods.
We don't talk like that here—

we're all anger, rapid-fire blastings,
fingers saluting the air like bloodied
full-mast flags. Remember: We understand
before we speak. Our parents urge us,
Say mama. Say papa. I love you. Open
your mouth, purge mistakes. We spend
our whole lives afraid of stumbling
while the lot of the world is desperate
to wire our jaws shut tight lest
truth and hard things tumble out.

Melissa Boston

Pastime: A narrative

Let me tell you a story of a girl
who worked in a field, growing organic tomatoes,
who later tried to tip a cow on her way home
in a neighboring field one afternoon: it mooed
and kept walking away and she followed it
still pressing her hand on its side.
The girl kept pressing harder and harder
until she lost her balance and fell in a puddle.

That night she cried. She began downloading videos
of boys trying to tip cows in the fields

where, late at night, they drank their parents' beer.
Eventually they started to throw the empty bottles
at the cows' heads and the boys would laugh
as the cows mooed and they all walked away as if nothing happened.
These boys were baseball players in Windsor, Illinois,
so they could throw hard, straight, and fast even when drunk.

She moved to Illinois where she tried to find the boys.
Let me call her Edna. Edna wasn't that great.

Sometimes I can almost understand how she must have felt,
that need to push, that need for aggression, that hard desire
for people like her. Understanding has its advantages.
You're in Seattle now, sitting in a hotel, watching TV,
drinking coffee, getting sober, and I'm wondering

if it's only rain blowing off the tops of buildings or if it's really raining.
The understanding of me and you, nearly giving way to the ground,

nearly feeling the give of losing balance by the hour.
It's April now and it's just too late for that feeling to stop.

Garrett Ashley

You Just Have to Know
They're Very Sensitive

And if only to put more strain on our marriage, we got this call from the elementary school saying Clark had just done something very inappropriate to some girl in his classroom; he'd been suspended and we had to come get him immediately. So we initially debated who was going to pick Clark up. I told Kate it was her job; she was the mom, after all. I was just kind of there. Clark hadn't gotten used to me anyway. I didn't feel like much of a dad. So I told her this, and she came back with the stuff of Clark just *needed* me, he just absolutely needed a father figure in his life. Clark's real dad fixed computers in New Orleans and hadn't popped up since Clark was born, as far as I knew. So I thought sure, a father figure was something I could maybe try to be. I've always been a little afraid of the commitment, but now I guess it's too late. It'd been a few months since Kate and I hitched, and I'd gotten to know Clark a little—the kind of toys he liked, for instance, plastic trains and collapsible houses that you could put little figurines in. He had a couple Wiffle bats in his closet he liked to play with, which reminded me of growing up in Lincoln, Nebraska, where I'd beat the crap out of my brother whenever Dad wasn't looking. Clark was pretty normal, I thought, a normal kid, and I wondered exactly why a normal kid would be acting inappropriately at such an early age for, anyway.

When we were finally let into the principal's office, Kate's son was sitting there with his little book bag in his lap. The building had the stuffy atmosphere of a hospital, all smells and enclosures. The principle, a tall, lanky woman, was having a laugh about something with Clark. Kate gave Clark an eye and we stood behind him. Then the principal told Clark to go wait outside the office on the bench. He got up and left and we sat down in his place. I hadn't been in an office like this in a long time, with red-and-blue school banners on the walls, a few trophies on top of a bookshelf which contained in itself a few pedagogical manuals. The air was thick, but that might have been the principle's aura, since she was kind of a stiff-looking woman, blue eyed, and perpetually irritated by young people, according to Kate.

"How are you anyway? How are things with you?"

Kate smiled and nodded. She smiled and nodded when she was nervous or angry. I guess in the grand scheme of things, everything must have been relatively OK. Sometimes when I came home from work I wanted to go straight to the back porch to smoke. The back porch was the only place I could smoke and really get away with smoking. Kate wouldn't go out there with me because it was too cold. Sometimes it was too hot. Anyway, it was a good moment for me, going out on the back porch to get away from everything, Kate's false-mood simulation technique—however she did it—included.

"Just tell me. Give it right to me," Kate said, blasting one hand off the other like a jet.

The principal had bony fingers. She also had curly blond hair and long teeth, which I noticed when she sort of rolled her head and inhaled. "OK, then. Well, it goes like this. There's a girl that sits next to Clark in the morning. She goes up to Miss Levine at her desk and asks to sharpen her pencil, and Miss Levine lets her sharpen her pencil, of course. Then she goes back, and when she goes back down the aisle Clark reaches out before she has the chance to sit and grabs her right on her crotch. You know what I mean?"

"No," I said. I didn't know what she meant. The way she'd said it indicated that I was supposed to know exactly what she meant by grabbing the crotch, which implied there was some additional meaning, but of course I had no idea if this meant one thing or multiple things.

Kate asked, "What's the suspension like? For how long?"

"Three days. The usual. But it's policy. We don't make exceptions. We run a tight ship. Even though he's pretty young. Nobody is using the words 'sexual harassment.' It's nothing spectacular. Just a policy. And we have to rotate his schedule so he won't be in … well, he's getting moved around, that's all. By request of the parents."

I asked, "Who was the girl?"

"We can't divulge her name. Why would I divulge her name?"

I didn't know why I asked. Kate seemed irritated by me, understandably.

Then she gave us some spiel about how kids are these days, what other parents are doing to handle behavior problems, and how the school system is intervening as early as possible with kids that are likely to cause trouble based on socioeconomical stuff and so forth. There was apparently a science to figuring out whether a kid was going to be a terror depending on what part of the city they lived in and what year they were born, whether they had lots of public amenities, how poorly their parents tended to judge situations like when to discipline their own children and when to let the school do the work, where to draw the line with sexuality, etc. Then she said, "You know, it's nothing new. Not really. You just have to know they're very sensitive at this time in their lives. It's a very abrupt time. Sometimes it's hard." The principal reached across the table and patted my hand.

Back in the main office Clark was sitting on a bench with his hands in his lap. He wore a big, puffy red jacket his grandmother had gotten him. He also had a little hat on his head with a puffball on a string. He looked like a cat toy. I offered him my hand and he took it.

"I was just wondering what she meant by sensitive," I said later in the car. "Didn't that seem a little weird to you? What do you think she meant by that?"

Kate was driving. I checked the back seat for Clark every now and then. His feet hung over the seat a little above floorboard. He kind of just looked out the window as we drove home.

"Kate?"

"I heard you. Yeah, I guess she kind of made it seem like it was our fault. I don't know, though. Was it? Is it? What did we do that would be, you know, our fault?"

I couldn't think of anything. Then I told Kate I didn't like it, the principal's insinuating that we were somehow bad parents who didn't know how to raise a kid the right way. A wad of birds flew out of some bushes a few feet from the road. Kate slammed on the brakes. Everything was quiet except the hum of the car's engine. I said, "It's kind of like she was pointing fingers. No kidding. I don't know what to do."

"Clark?" Kate glanced back at her son for a moment. She switched her head back immediately at the road. Then we were moving again.

"Mom?"

"Honey, do you want to talk about what happened at the school?"

Clark looked down at his lap and shook his head. Kate pushed him gently with her knuckles. I reached over and touched Kate's leg, which felt hard and warm, and then she grew quiet.

"Yeah," she said. "OK."

Kate started to feel that whatever we'd been up to in the house was practically on hold because we'd somehow managed to rub our sexual tendencies off on her five-year-old. I'd always thought we went about sexual intercourse in the most discreet way possible. I felt lucky we didn't have to leave the house to have sex. I didn't marry Kate because I knew we'd only have sex occasionally when Clark was incapacitated. But still. Clark would come through the house and make his way right into our bedroom without so much as knocking. He'd have one of his toys with him, like a yellow dump truck or something. He'd sit next to Kate on the bed and let her rub his back. Kate would also twist her hair with her free hand. I reminded myself that Clark was my son by right and Kate was right about me needing to be a better father figure. I tried not to let it bother me too much. If she didn't want to do it, she didn't have to do it, that's fine, but I didn't feel that was the case, and I tried to talk her out of our sexual hiatus.

"I want to. I do. But what if he comes in here?" she said. "What are we supposed to do if he sees us?"

Kate was doing her hair in the vanity mirror. I was picking strips of plastic off my running shoes and sprinkling it on the carpet. "Well all we need to do is lock the door more often." We didn't normally lock doors in the house because Clark would cry if he encountered a door he couldn't just walk through. It was just as bad as not keeping a door locked at all.

"Well, then, he'll stand outside the door and listen to us. You know. The way he'll knock and just stand there like forever. We won't hear the doorknob jiggle, then he'll just stand there and think all kinds of things if he hears us. You know how he doesn't knock or anything."

I started to suspect that Kate had simply lost her sense of intimacy and she was using her son as a scapegoat to get out of sex. If this were true, I wished she'd just say it. I told myself it was a phase what we were going through, which was fine, because marriages had phases. I've had phases. Phases could get you through rough patches. So I told myself that was fine, nothing time can't work out on its own.

Clark and I went to the park on Saturday. Going to the park was something I did with Clark when we had free time and he was feeling bored. He was like a little pet following me around. We watched the ducks in the pond. We ate chips on the bench and looked out at the water. He couldn't sit still so we started walking around again. I got the feeling I needed to bring up everything that had happened, that it would somehow help things at home if we could just get him talking about where he'd seen someone do what he'd done.

"Hey, Clark. Hey, you want to talk about what happened at the school? Are things OK now?"

He looked at me. I realized I'd asked him two questions at once, which probably wasn't a good thing. I just reverted back to the former: "How has school been, man?"

"Good," he said. He looked out at the ducks in the pond.

"Do you want to talk about the girl? Why you touched that girl? Why did you do that?"

Clark shook his head.

"But you know that's her personal space? You know it was wrong to do?"

He affirmed this, the way five-year-olds do. I didn't know what it was like living with his real father. I wondered if his real father ever took drugs and Kate just wasn't telling me. Clark was a naturally quiet kid, and everyone thought there was something wrong with him. He had this blank stare with a half-smile that I didn't know how to read. You never knew what was on his mind. Sometimes he'd show signs of advanced color coordination, which felt like a good thing. You never knew whether he was happy or sad or both, if you could be both. I wondered whether his emotional bouts were more instinctive than genuine. I'd read somewhere that people with autism have something called alexithymia, or vice versa, which makes having real emotions difficult. I didn't know the extent of anything. And Clark was just a little kid, anyway: Why should it matter, if there was anything wrong? I thought there was a world of difference between my definition of "wrong" and another person's, anyway.

"What do you want to talk about?"

He shook his head.

"There's gotta be something going on in your noggin."

"I don't want to play baseball."

"Who's playing baseball? You're not playing baseball, are you?"

"The school is starting baseball."

"And you don't want to play?" He shook his head.

"Well, then, don't play," I said. "You don't have to play if you don't want to." I'd never thought of baseball and didn't know what else to tell him.

"But."

"But what?"

He shook his head. He either didn't know or didn't want to tell me.

One night I touched Kate's left knee and proposed maybe just wringing the truth out of Clark about why he'd touched that girl. We lay in bed sort of half-curled up, and Kate shook her head. Then she rolled her shoulders like she does when she doesn't know what to say, or doesn't want to say it, or something.

"No one is wringing anything out of him."

"Why the hell not?"

"Because. He's a little kid. He doesn't know what he's doing. He doesn't know what universe he's in. Probably all it was is he realized he had a penis and he figured somehow there was something different about girls and he was just making sure. You know how he's sort of compulsive like that sometimes, good or bad. You talked to him about it didn't you? You told him not to do it again?"

"I don't know what's already ingrained in him," I said. Which I know was wrong to say.

Kate had told me before that Clark's father was compulsive, which is why he worked at a computer shop in New Orleans and never called to check on his kid. I tried to steer us back in the direction of whether Clark really knew what world he was in sometimes.

"I didn't really know what I was doing when I was a kid. Like everything is sort of a fog now. You ever just sit and stare at the wall and think about the way you used to be growing up? Like how I used to cry a lot in class, up until the sixth grade? What do you think made me like that? You think I'd have cried if I knew how people were there watching me?"

Which was a lie, I guess. I remembered knowing what I was doing when I locked my brother in a closet at one of his birthday parties because he kept getting his friends to stick their tongues out at me. Or sometimes we'd go to the pond and I'd pluck up a blanket of snotty tadpoles and stick them in his pants. And then he'd cry pretty much the rest of the way home because he could feel things wiggling around down there and he was too scared to reach in and pull them out.

Then she offered to do something in the bathroom, which I was all for—we locked the bedroom door and put a towel down on the crack to keep sound from escaping, then we locked the bathroom door behind us, put some towels in the bathtub, tried to make it as comfortable as possible. Then we started to get kind of loud, so I got out of the tub and turned the sink on. By the time I was back at the tub, which was like a second, I'd already lost some of my energy. When I reached down to tease Kate she grabbed my wrist and told me she didn't want me to do that.

"It's gross," she said.

"OK," I said.

We put things on hold again. The bathroom had been a good idea though, I liked the idea of doing stuff in places that wasn't intended for sex. Even though my knees hurt a little after knobbling back and forth against the hard ceramic. The bathroom had been a pretty good effort, but I can also see why she might have given up early, how the thought of us influencing Clark in some way must have been turning over in her head. She told me, later, that she didn't like the idea of living life like under scrutiny like that, locking the doors and putting towels on the carpet to keep the sound out, she didn't even like the idea of beginning it, even to try it out, because it made her feel like a teenager. So I agreed with her because why not? As I said before, it all seemed a lot like a phase to me at the time. I wanted to be reasonable about it.

Clark wanted to go to the park the next Saturday where there was this particular sand pit he liked to jump down in and play with his Star Wars toys. I walked around the sand pit with my hands in my pockets. I asked him if he knew what the sarlacc pit looked like originally, before they added the beak-snake to it with digital CGI, and he asked what?, and I said it looked a lot like a vagina, and Clark had no idea what I was talking about. Which wasn't true anyway, the pit looked more like a wounded butthole, but for the sake of making a point I said it looked like a vagina.

"You know, kind of like a woman. You don't have one. It's something women have. You didn't know that?"

"Yeah."

"You did know?"

He nodded. He stuck his toys' feet in the sand.

"Well, how'd you know?"

"A library book," he said.

I told him that was fine. I was just glad he hadn't heard it from us. The weather was nice, and I looked forward to relaying what I'd just learned back to Kate. I felt a little restless standing there at the sand pit over Clark, and I decided it might be good to have a drink of coffee. There was this stand a block down on the edge of the park. I could see a small line of people there now. So I told Clark I'd be right back; I was going to go get some coffee, and I'd get him an icy if they had anything he liked. He ignored me, and I walked over there with my hands in my pockets thinking about what I was going to say to Kate about the whole library book thing. Then I thought it might be possible that Clark had just made it up because he was tired of us asking questions about it. I'd been embarrassed to talk about these sorts of things when I was his age, too, so I didn't blame him for just wanting the whole thing to blow over. He was old enough to lie. I'd probably been younger. Five, I think, is a very profitable age for lying. The guy selling the coffee was like eighteen and had a tiny beard. I was maybe thirteen before I knew anything about the opposite sex, much less what I was supposed to do with my penis when I had the opportunity to use it. The stand didn't have an icy or anything like that so I just got a coffee and decided I'd let Clark try some if he wanted. I took the coffee back to the sandpit and looked in for Clark, who'd gone off somewhere. I stood there for a moment, and took the lid off my coffee so it'd cool down faster. I looked around for Clark. There was the duck pond, a few kids there, and a woman with two dogs on a leash. I went over to the woman with the dogs and asked if she'd seen a kid with a bunch of Star Wars toys. She said she hadn't seen any other fucking kids. She said this kind of angrily, like I wasn't supposed to be there asking about somebody else's fucking kid. I told her sorry for fucking bothering her, went off towards the woods where there was a trail and stood by the empty bike rack with my hands on my hips. I felt nervous. Clark wandered off sometimes, it wasn't unusual, but he never really went out of sight. The park was big. So this is to say I was freaking out pretty bad. I called his name towards the woods, and some runner that was coming through stopped to check on me.

"Nothing's wrong. Just looking for my fucking kid."

"I haven't seen any kids in the woods," he said.

"Alright. I'm going to fucking look anyway."

"But I haven't seen any kids in the woods. It would be hard to miss a kid in these woods."

He was right. The woods were perfectly manicured to reflect the overall aesthetic of the park, which sometimes resembled a golf course. The woods, when Clark and I had gone in there, were always trimmed, had grassy patches, trash barrels, disc golf nets, and purple flower beds beneath some of the pines.

"Have you checked the bathroom? Maybe he went to the bathroom."

I started to walk into the woods.

"Hey, did you hear me? There's nobody in the woods."

He grabbed my elbow, and I stopped and looked at him. He was bald, had a sharp chin, and I could see a nicotine patch poking out from beneath his left shirt sleeve.

"What?"

"You heard me. You don't need to go in there and waste your time. Your kid's missing and you're going to be looking in the wrong place."

"I just thought he'd be in the woods. He likes the woods."

"Well, fuck off then," the guy said.

I swung at his face, dropping the coffee midswing; he dodged the swing and ran off. It was a good moment, having swung at the guy, and I really wished I'd actually hit the guy, but at the same time I'm glad I didn't because he definitely seemed like the kind of guy who would call the police or something. I took a run through the woods, even ran off the track to check around some of the flowerbeds. I came out and looked towards the water and the dock. I stood on a bench and looked around the dirty slope leading into the water. There were kids who were kidnapped all the time around here. I thought I could maybe just tell Kate that it'd seemed like a good idea to leave him in the sand pit because no one was going to know he was fucking there anyway. And the idea did make me feel better; I felt like maybe he really had just gone to the bathroom, all this was just a big misunderstanding, and I'd go to the bathroom and find him in there with his toys on the sink reaching up to wash his hands, which he always had trouble with because he was so small.

At the bathroom the running guy I'd taken a swing at was in there taking a leak. He turned back to me and said, "You found your kid yet?"

I left the bathroom without saying anything.

The wind came at me, cold, lifting the hair from my forehead, lined with sweat.

I looked towards the lake and saw Clark standing next to the water, throwing something in towards the ducks. When I got there I saw his knees had grass stains and his chin was scraped. His hands were also bloody. He looked like a mess.

"Hey? Where were you? What happened?"

"Some kid pushed me."

"Fucking shit," I said. "Who pushed you?"

He shook his head.

"You won't tell me?"

"He left."

"An older kid?"

"I guess."

"Why'd he push you?"

"Because I was playing with toys."

"Is that what he said?"

Clark nodded.

"Where are your toys?"

"I threw them in the pond."

"What?"

"I threw them in the pond."

"Why?"

Clark rolled his shoulders. I asked him if he wanted to go and he said sure. We got back to the car and he said he could see the kid that pushed him walking into the pottery store across the street. I'd started to calm down but now here I was in this fucking stupor again. The kid, who was wearing a thick red coat, walked behind an older woman who must have been his grandmother. She had big legs like hams, meaty ankles. The kid was tall, not very big, and I couldn't get a good look at his face, but I knew this might get ugly if I went in there.

"Clark?"

"Yeah."

"Can you wait in the car and not unlock it for anybody but me?"

"OK," he said.

I got out and went over to the pottery store and looked through the window. The kid was in there, standing with his hands in his pockets, looking at a blue pot on a shelf. I went inside. The grandmother was telling him not to touch anything or walk into anything. She told him to just stand there and be still. It reminded me of how my mother used to talk to me in public when we'd go into places like this. I almost walked away; it would have been a good thing to walk away, just go back to the car, tell Clark I'd take him home and put some Neosporin on his legs. Instead I picked the kid up by the shoulders and shook him, not seven feet from his meaty grandmother.

The grandmother just looked at me like she couldn't believe what was happening, and she just stood there. The kid was light as a briefcase. He started to drool. Then I put him down, and the grandmother came at me with a barrage of questions. Her face was red. She had skin like wax paper pulled tightly over the bone, except for her legs, of course. I kept staring at her legs while she was talking to me. I could have stomped her into the pottery store's carpeted floor, but she gave me a look that reminded me of my little grandma and I immediately felt bad even though I was still doing that threat posture with my shoulders I tend to do with guys my own size.

"He shoved my son," I told her.

"I'm calling the police. Stand right there, OK?"

So I left the store in a hurry. When I returned to the car though Clark was sitting there looking at his hands. He began to cry silently.

"What's wrong?"

"I threw my toys into the pond."

"Yeah I know, that was dumb. You shouldn't have done that."

"That kid told me I was dumb for having toys."

"You shouldn't listen to what other people tell you. You do whatever the hell you want. You know?"

I drove us home. I figured I wouldn't mention anything about losing Clark momentarily, but I'd have to explain what had happened

155

to his knees and hands, that some kid pushed him down in the grass. I'd turned to throw a Coke bottle away, and when I'd turned back Clark was sitting there crying and looking at his hands. The kid got away; we never saw him again. So the story goes. Clark wouldn't say anything about it. I'd tell Kate it'd hurt his feelings mostly, and she'd avoid saying much to him about it aside from the usual stuff of don't play with kids you don't know, especially the bigger ones.

I kind of enjoyed being here with Clark in the car on the way home. I'd felt something when I was looking for him earlier, and when I was shaking that other kid. Now I thought he looked like me. A product of an overstimulated brain, I thought. He stared quietly out the window at the passing traffic and the water at the edge of the bridge. I told him I'd get him more toys, not to worry about throwing his toys in the pond because there were more toys to be got and I'd get them as soon as I went to the store. He stopped crying after a while. I let the idea of new toys absorb into his head until I thought everything would be right.

Christen Noel Kauffman

They Took the First Photo
of a Black Hole

and I remember
how you held the rabbit
behind the ears,
an arrow clean
behind the left eye
and right jaw,
the way its body pulsed,
as you lifted it above
rows of young corn.
How you put
your hand on my
back, the blood dried
black around your nails.
How it took
ten years to pull
the tip from my skull,
carry these flooding
wounds into night,
a red dappled trail
from my bed
to the Mackinac bridge.
I was never the rabbit
for you, soft fur stiff

with death, your shirt
tucked around its legs.
How you mourned
your grip on the bow,
breathed into the
open mouth,
cradled its body
for years
after I was gone.

Hasan Alizadeh

Letter

Here
in this bright room in the inn
I'm happy you're not here with me anymore.

The landscape of the sea
is bluer than
your earrings
& the forest
is an emerald wave
& the air's skin
is moist & fragile
& a seagull sits
every morning at the window.
There is no anxiety
& your eyes
fade in my mind
like boats receding
perpetually from the dark beach—
slowly
coldly
lightly.
Without scuffle,
without bloodshed.
Everything is fine, fresh & tired
& it's so sweet to sleep

until morning
when again the shadow of a seagull hovers at the window,
like the moth-eaten cypress in that scene in *Ithaca*—
I was kidding:

                    I'm happy you're not here with me anymore.

Translated from the Persian by Rebecca Ruth Gould
and Kayvan Tahmasebian

Hanna Bartels

One, Two

There are steps that must be taken before selling a home: First, clear it of you. Your real estate agent tells you this. She is red all over. Face scrubbed to flush with blush dusted on razor cheekbones.

A buyer needs to see herself living in your home, your agent tells you.

You think of a miniature jade dragon on your bookshelf from an alley market in Beijing, your husband armed with broken Mandarin and a honeymoon glow, bartering down the already-low price; your son's Pop Warner flag football jersey hung in a shadow box on the wall; a picture of your daughter, bubblegum dress and LED fairy wand, in a silver frame on your bedside. These things, windows to the life you've lived here, now belong in a box under the stairs.

Buyers need to visualize their own furniture, their family photos on the wall, their toothbrushes in the cup next to the sink, the real estate agent explains. Best to scrub the home of memories, she says. Show them a blank canvas.

A house, your husband says, taking your hand. Not a home.

There's a difference, sure, the agent says. She pouts her red lips, her eyes narrow. She is sympathetic but uncomfortable.

Do we have to disclose the—. Your husband looks down at his lap.

Oh, no, the agent says quickly but not quickly enough.

Your husband's hand slips out of yours. It hovers in the air, like he doesn't know where it should land.

The real estate agent clears her throat, shuffles her papers. Well, then, she says, I'll have my photographer stop by on Saturday.

You nod, look at your husband, his eyes still focused on his lap where his drifting hand has now fallen.

You'll have the house ready by Saturday? And you'll clear the yard? she asks.

She watches your husband, careful. Your husband doesn't respond and too much time has passed.

Yes, you tell her.

Letting go can be difficult, she says, sliding the signed, dated listing agreement into her leather binder. Of a home, she adds.

The house is full, but also empty. Your husband stands on an upholstered chair in the dining room to remove the screw from the chandelier escutcheon. The chandelier belonged to your grandfather, an heirloom. You want to keep it, but you are annoyed that your husband hasn't removed his shoes before attempting the takedown. Your husband is annoyed that you are annoyed.

Do it yourself, he says, throwing a shoe at the doorframe where you are standing so leaves come unstuck from the sole and pepper the hardwood. Shoes removed, he continues spinning screws with one hand as the other cups the glass bowl.

Did you flip the circuit breaker first? you say.

Did I flip the circuit breaker, he says.

You start to respond, something barbed, but through the arch-top French doors to the formal living room, you notice your son. His eyes are wide and slippery-smooth, watching you both. He is sitting on the plush carpet in his orange scrimmage vest, a pile of sticks sorted by length in front of him.

He has started counting things. First days, then months. Sometimes Tuesdays. Marking time on the other side, the clean chasm of your lives. Before and then after. When he ran out of days, he began collecting things inside and outside. Pebbles, twigs, socks, old pacifiers from the drawer next to the sink. Organizing them and reorganizing them in his own perfect order.

Your husband doesn't like it. You argue about it after tucking your son in at night, door cracked an inch so you can still hear the rustle of sheets, the ghostly vibrations of his breath. Your husband's voice is strained in whisper. He needs to stop, he says over and over. It makes me uncomfortable, he says.

He'll grow out of it, you say.

He's old enough to understand, your husband argues. Nine is old enough.

None of us will ever be old enough, you said, once, and your husband's face hollowed.

Your husband looks down from the dining room table, holds the chandelier out to you so the drop crystals clap against each other from sweeping silver arms.

Ready for football, bud? he says, his face suddenly bright, a fluorescent lamp.

Without looking up from his sticks, your son nods.

You drive and your husband sits in the passenger seat beside you. Your son counts trees from the back seat, forty-two in total, spaced evenly along the road between your neighborhood and the practice field. He counts them out loud and your husband's face twists into itself.

When you pull up perpendicular to the practice field, your son opens the door and leaps out.

Shoelaces tied? your husband calls, window rolled down.

Yep, your son says, running without looking back to the scrum of boys in the center of the field.

You watch him run. He is sinewy, like your husband, stretched thin and tall for his age. His hair is platinum and shock-straight, like yours, so you keep it shorn close to his crown. He'll be a good tight end, your husband says often. His position in football is important. Your husband thinks it gives him purpose. He is comfortable with football but not with counting.

When the coach separates the boys into position on the field, your husband rolls the window back up. You slide the car into reverse, check behind you, and pull away from the field.

The support group meets twice a week in a church basement, conveniently aligning with your son's flag football practice schedule. The group is run by a man with the beginnings of a fleshy paunch that sometimes peeks from below his shirt hem when he reaches toward the heavens, which is often. His hair is long and white and tied into a low ponytail. He lost his son seventeen years ago to an overdose. He is both zen and frantic, the kind of instability that causes a tornado. You wait for the downdraft at every meeting, prepare to batten down the hatches, just in case.

You sit to the left of the group leader; your husband pushes his plastic chair back a few inches so he isn't visible to the rest of the group.

The group leader starts the meeting as he always does. He welcomes newcomers, acknowledges old-timers, points to the coffeepot in the corner. He says that the dues to belong to this group are more than any person should ever have to pay.

At the group leader's urging, the people in the circle begin to talk one at a time: candid narrators of stories that should be fiction, but aren't. Their stories are full of seemingly insignificant detail: the television show set to record that night, the color of the sky, black or blue or yellow, the clothing they were wearing. They apologize often for sharing too much, or too little. And their stories don't end because they are here, where there is no coda, no satisfactory finish.

The group leader always nods deliberately. When the people in the circle finish their stories, he volunteers a comment about how unfathomable it is, how immense, and every time he does this, the group mutters their agreement.

You look at your husband. You know him, but you don't—not since your daughter died suddenly four months before. He snorts, then, and you follow his gaze to a wooden pallet washed white and hung over an empty wall. The blue letters, hand-painted over it, read: GOD HAS PERFECT TIMING; NEVER EARLY, NEVER LATE.

There's no name for us, one man says when everyone has shared their stories.

Not you, though. Never you. In the circle, you only listen. To feel a part of it, of other people's grief, of their anger, to stay moored to land by your sameness.

The speaking man is gray and wrinkled and his hands are full of veins.

When my parents died, he says, my mother then my father, I was an orphan. When my wife died, I was a widow. My losses had a name. Then my son died, and there's no name for me.

You feel overlooked by this void in our language, the group leader offers. He is more zen than frantic today, which is helpful.

The old man considers this. Yes, I suppose, he says. I just feel like I need a solid word. Something no one will question when they ask me if I have children and I tell them yes, but no.

The people in the circle hum and nod and you realize he is right. There is no word precise enough to explain that once you had two children, a boy and a girl, but now your daughter has died and your house is full of things to count, but also empty.

Another woman whose baby was born still a year before begins to explain the story of an orca mother, buoying the body of her dead calf as she swims through the Salish Sea.

They are calling it a Tour of Grief, the woman explains through sobs, green snot beads under her nose. Fifteen days, she's carried it, she says. Draped over her nose, or by the flipper with her teeth, sometimes diving down into the deep to retrieve the calf's body when it slips away. All day and all night.

You stick your finger into your husband's rib. Time to go, you whisper, and he stands so quickly his chair tips backward.

So sorry, you say to the group leader. The sobbing woman looks up at you, her mouth a black grotto of surprise. We have to pick up our son, you explain.

The group leader nods as you gesture toward your husband: we, you said, and it feels foreign on your tongue.

Your husband doesn't drive anymore, not since your daughter died, so you have to chauffeur him to work, to your son's football practice when he says he wants to watch, but really to call out corrections from the sideline. This makes it easy for you to bring him along to places he doesn't want to go. He is quiet in the car after support group, so you sing along to the country song on the radio. You turn it up loud, and the warbling voice of the female country star makes the windows tremble.

Your son is sweaty and red, already waiting when you pull up to the practice field, his orange vest crumpled in his fist. He waves to the coach as he opens the car door and climbs in.

Your husband's face has a glow again. How was practice? he asks, turning in his seat to face your son.

One of the guys said we're moving, your son says, his eyes on his muddy cleats.

Your husband doesn't turn to look at you, doesn't have to; you can see his neck tense, his shoulders rise slightly.

Well, buddy, he says, that's true. We have to sell the house first so we didn't want to tell you until it was a done deal.

Your husband turns to face you. You can tell from the way his eyes narrow that he knows now: You told people after you agreed you wouldn't.

But not far, he says to your son. We just want to move to a new house, start fresh, you know? You can still play for the same team, even.

Because of Stella? your son asks, face still parallel to the car floor.

You don't like to lie to your children. To your son. It is one of the fundamentals of parenthood that you and your husband decided on when you were first pregnant with him, together, newlyweds tangled across the king-sized bed. When you would talk dreamily about the future.

Your husband is silent, staring out the window again.

Yes, you say. It's hard for us to live there now, since Stella.

You don't say since we lost Stella. You don't say since Stella died.

Your son doesn't say anything for a long time. He turns back to the window, back to counting the long line of fat trees.

Will Stella still have a room in the new house? he asks finally.

You hit a pothole too quickly and the car jerks into the air. Your husband's body stiffens.

Christ, he says.

I'm sorry, you say, I'm sorry.

His eyes are tight slits. He holds his breath. Your son counts fifteen, sixteen, seventeen. Your husband exhales.

I'm sorry, you say again, and he shakes his head.

You take a wide turn around the blue pickup truck, skewed sideways over your driveway, one wheel still in the grass. Parked and abandoned for months.

What's for dinner? your son asks as you pull into the garage, turn the key, kill the ignition.

Leftovers, you say, thankful for once for his short attention span. You shut the car door, gently. Your husband's eyes are still closed, seat belt still buckled.

After you tuck your son into bed, kiss his forehead, stand at his door until his breathing slows to a rolling cadence, you start to take photographs off the wall. There are so many. Faces blown wide and tall, framed in uniform silver, many of them gifts from your mother-in-law who has a penchant for Hobby Lobby's custom framing services.

Your husband has poured himself a glass of bourbon, neat. He sits on the stairs leading up to your master bedroom as you pull nails out of the wall.

Curb appeal is important, you say, finally.

Your husband doesn't say anything, sips his bourbon.

We'll have to take care of everything outside, too, before Saturday, you say. Even the truck.

The silence has become familiar. Your husband is untethered, set adrift. For a moment, you think of reaching out, knocking his bourbon from his hand. You imagine his face, stunned, focused only on yours. He might yell and you might yell back, and then you might cry and he might hold you. Or he might stand and walk out of the house. Walk to the edge of town, past the trees. You aren't sure anymore.

OK? you say, instead.

OK, he says.

You pass one of the frames to him and he balances it on his knee. It is a picture of Stella, the first from the hospital, taken almost three years ago. Your husband doesn't look down at the glass.

Your daughter was born en caul, like a slippery alien egg. Her nose had been smashed against the gauzy membrane so the doctor cut a tiny slit under her nostrils so she could breathe. You had cried, terrified, as the doctor peeled the film back from her skin. She was so pink, rubbed raw, and loud, shrouded from the wide world for a moment like almost nothing else. Her newness, when you held her, stunned you. She was a strange and beautiful thing: in and out in a rush, a shock.

Sometimes, in the days after she died, you would drive without knowing where. Your son anchored you to Earth, asking again and again where you were going. You would turn around, then, drive toward home. When your son saw the practice field, and the line of trees just beyond it, he would begin counting backward.

Thirty-six trees until home, he would say. Twenty-two trees until home. Four trees until home.

You never told your husband.

Do you have to take them all down? your husband asks. All the pictures?

Anything personal, you say.

No sign of life, your husband says and sips his bourbon long and soft.

☾

An early-morning shelf cloud has brought turbulent rain that whips against the church at support group on Friday. The group leader flails as he tells the newcomers where to find the coffee, and he pushes his long hair back against his scalp too often, a nervous tic.

The orca woman is back, talking about the mother again.

After seventeen days, she says, the orca mother finally let go of her dead calf.

Thank God, the gray man says, and a few others applaud.

The researchers who have been tracking the whole ordeal say the mother is alive and well, the woman says, looking around the circle purposefully.

Well? your husband says. You turn to face him. His voice in this room is a bullhorn, unfamiliar and severe. She's alive, he says. She's not well.

The group leader leans forward in his seat. Would you like to share? he asks your husband.

No, you say, and slam your palm on your husband's knee beside you. You feel the panic, hot and tight, rising in your throat, constricting your chest. Not you, never you. Always listening, never speaking. No one, not even the wide-open faces of the support group, could understand. Your husband suddenly wants to be a part of it, he wants to share his story, and he will change the way they look at him, at you. Your husband, who has already taken everything, all the anger, all the pain; who doesn't believe in support group, who doesn't believe in counting, who doesn't believe in anyone's grief but his own. He will take this, too. He will ruin this one place, this space you have to listen, to feel for twice a week, every week, that you aren't the saddest person in the room.

No, he says, and you fight tears, relief, as you force the panic back down deep.

The group leader sighs, and his lips purse together in the shape of a meditative Om. Maybe, he says, she has just moved on from this phase of her grief.

Your husband focuses on his hands in his lap.

After a moment, the woman looks at the group leader who nods for her to continue.

Yesterday, she says, the pod of orcas formed this circle with the mother. They kept it centered on a moonbeam, shifting with the current as the light moved. Like some kind of ritual or funeral or something. Isn't that crazy? She stops to invite reaction, a few shake their heads, the gray man places his veiny hand over his heart. But it was too dim to see if the calf was still being kept afloat, she says. It was only this morning that the researchers realized the calf had probably sunk to the bottom of the sea. So, she says and shrugs her shoulders.

Finally, a coda.

There's a catch in the throat, an intake of breath from your husband beside you. You close your eyes tight.

You would have held her forever. Seventeen days, one hundred and four, two thousand, ten million; counting without end, on and on until they pried her from you.

You remember her dress spangled with stars, you remember her running, singing. Stella was a comet, orderless and free, hurtling toward tires as they moved backward in your driveway.

He never saw her.

This room is a vacuum and all the air has left it. You are rocking, back and forth, in the plastic chair.

The group leader thanks the woman for sharing. Always forward, he says, pulling himself up, every vertebra uncoiled in perfect alignment. The world doesn't stop, he says. It intensifies.

The group nods and you nod with them, and the white walls of the church basement are luminous, blinding.

Your husband reaches over to you, slips his hand under yours. It is warm and whole. You don't recognize it at all.

Your real estate agent stands in the driveway, face puckered. Your husband is still in bed, where he has been since returning home from support group the night before; your son is collecting sticks, placing them, tender, in the hammock of his shirt.

You didn't move the truck, your agent says. She props a hand on her hip, sweeps her bangs out of her right eye, blows a curl away. Your husband's blue pickup is still skewed across the lawn, a muddy track to the pavement has welled with rain and leaves.

You watch your son kneel in the grass next to the truck, wet from last night's storm. His fingers slide through the blades, searching. You want to run to him, yank him away from the wheel, but the real estate agent keeps talking.

You're going to need to move it, the real estate agent says. Before my photographer gets here, she adds. We need to move forward with the listing today or I'm afraid we'll run into issues in the slow season.

Yes, you say. You understand that curb appeal is important.

Your son digs into the rubber tire tread with his finger, uses his nail to loose a pebble. He examines it for a moment then turns toward you, his face smudged with morning light. His hand cocoons his prize, raised high up into the sky.

Your agent considers you, her lips crushed in a pout, a look you recognize. Pitying and pitiful. You do still want to go ahead with this? she asks, sweeping her arm across the face of the house.

Your son adds the pebble to his collection, wedged between the tire and a leaf still attached to its branch. No one has touched the truck in four months.

The real estate agent shifts foot to foot.

The night before, after your husband turned off the light and closed the bedroom door, after you stood alone in the dark hall, gathering yourself again, you packed your son's room into boxes. He touched everything, his footballs, his jerseys, each individual twig, collected and counted over and over for all the days the truck stood still. When your son finally slipped off to sleep, you stuffed the sticks into a garbage bag and you set the bag by the back door so you could empty it into the creek near the practice field. Then, you stood in the doorway of Stella's room, taking inventory of her things, those you would carry with you, those you would leave behind: dolls and dresses, fairy wands, books about stars.

When Stella was born, the doctor warned you that she might have permanent scars; the caul could leave open wounds on her skin at the attachment points. The doctor had offered to preserve it, the gauzy membrane, after it had broken over her face and left her smooth. There are superstitions about it, he said, protections for the child. But you didn't want it.

Your son reorganizes two sticks in front of him so they straddle the stones.

Yes, you say, finally.

Sometimes, you think of the day your husband drove to the edge of the sea.

Stella toddled along the shoreline, chasing kelp that had tangled into a crown. Your husband built castles in the sand, and your son knocked them down, laughing, and you counted your children: one, two.

You remember that you waded out into the water, Stella held to your chest. Her fingers wound in your hair and a swell broke over you both, soaked her dress through.

And on the shore, your husband waved, frantic, took a few steps toward you.

Terin Weinberg

Sonnet (1)

We've made violence a home—
gathered it in silver boxes
and tied starlings to the ribbons.
Invasive birds tend to sing
louder when they're held down.
Violence likes it here. It hums
and drones on into the cold silence
we were never comfortable with.
A portable radio does the singing now
as the motel room moves states
and tells the birds to fly, to fly north.
Their wings hum—engines of loss.
Home: It's the direction you face
the opposite of when you're leaving.

Marcia LeBeau

Training

My skin is a soft snow
coat that shields me from hurricanes
and hatred. Too short to cover my thighs,
it beckons the man to sit

next to me in an empty New Jersey Transit car. I cannot
hear what he's saying, his salt and vinegar
breath so close. I'm trained to sit and smile and nod
and cannot

(yes, believe this), cannot think of any other way to stop
the talk beside a fake yawn, a turn
toward the window, my temple cold
on glass. Minutes later he is rubbing

his finger up the side of my thigh, light as meringue, I can almost
pretend it is not there. I am ice. Who knew blood could
stop while napping. Slow breath fools no one. The finger
extends its length. I tunnel inwards. His pressure

gets heavier. My eyes snap open like a broken
shade. I stand, turn so he will let me out. I do not look
at his face. As I squeeze by, enticed by the mouth
of the next car, he yells, "What's wrong?"

"Need more space," I whisper back. He doesn't hear me. He can't. I have flown away. A species of bird never named.

Liz Marlow

Elegy for the Orphans in Minsk

Mud splashes onto my daughter's
satin sequined princess dress
as she runs from house to
house on Halloween. It has
rained so much, neighbors
have started pouring sand
into their yards' low spaces.
Desert sand, rounded,
useless for this job, floats
away in breezes, but river sand,
with jagged edges, settles.
After imprinting green and tan
patched yards with rainboots
as her appetite for jawbreakers
and chocolate grows, neighbors
drop handfuls of cuboids
and cones into her jagged tooth
bucket. Her sweet tooth developed
in infancy as I bribed her to latch
with sugary water on my breasts.
Though she ate many vegetables
before tasting pears or apples,
she never forgot sugar. I imagine
parents in ancient Egypt toiling
over recipes, inventing honey

and raisin candies to bribe children
into finishing their salads as I do.
Did the Minsk orphanage staff,
void of their own children,
bribe orphans into cleaning
their plates with lollipops?
With guns pointed at their backs,
the staff led orphans down
Ratokmskaya Street through rain,
letting girls stain shoes and dresses
with mud, letting them laugh
one last time enroute to sand pits,
where Nazis threw handfuls
of gum and candy bars, bribing
girls into quiet with sweet
breath as sand filled their mouths.

Catherine Uroff

Connecticut Was Closing

Our last day of work was on Halloween, and that was why we didn't notice Stuart coming into the office with a machete. A lot of us were dressed up for the day. Tammy King from Accounting was wearing a saggy Donald Trump face mask and what looked to be a big, cloth diaper pinned to her jeans. Johnny MacDonald in Receiving came as the Cowardly Lion. Our receptionist, Tricia, dressed up as Cruella de Vil. I was a nun in a long, black habit.

We were just doing what we'd done every year: showing up in costume for the lunchtime parade, where we'd weave around the tables in the cafeteria to be judged by a group of executives in categories like Most Creative, Best Overall, Scariest. Our prizes were always something with the company logo on it. Emergency car kits. Mini-flashlights. Mouse pads.

But that day, there was no contest because the office was closing for good. Everything was moving to the new headquarters in Huntsville, Alabama. There were tax benefits, that was how it was explained to us. Alabama was providing an incentive package worth millions in exchange for the company making capital investments in the state. None of us were getting any severance. If you wanted to work in Alabama, you still had a job. But Connecticut was closing.

On that last day, there were workshops on resume writing and networking, but some of us skipped out early and went to the Chinese buffet across the street for lunch. There were Bob, Sue from the mailroom, Danny, and Heather, who was younger than the rest of us and thought that living in the South would be fun. She was the only one of us who still had a job. Bob couldn't move because he'd just gotten married and all of his wife's family lived in the Hartford area and they'd be damned if they were going to let Bob move her anywhere. It was Bob's second marriage and he wanted to do right by his wife. "I won't fuck this one up," he'd told me the day he came back from his honeymoon on the Cape. Sue had just moved her mother into a home for Alzheimer's patients, so Alabama wasn't even a consideration for her. She'd gained twenty pounds in six months after her mother was lost for twelve hours before being found behind the McDonald's on Clifton Avenue, trying to lift herself up and into the garbage dumpster. Danny wasn't moving, either. "I'm not a dog and I won't be chasing my tail," he'd said to me when we first heard the news.

At the Chinese restaurant, we had second helpings at the buffet, gorging ourselves on slimy noodles, dry chunks of sesame chicken, greasy eggrolls. We didn't talk to each other too much and, right before the check came, Sue started to cry and Bob offered to get her meal. She dabbed her eyes with her paper napkin and thanked him. She'd worked for the company for twenty-three years.

"You're a good man, Bob," I said. He was wearing a cowboy hat and leather chaps and he'd kept his hat on throughout the meal.

"We're all good people. That's why this shouldn't be happening to us," Sue said.

"Since when has that ever mattered?" Danny asked.

"I feel uncomfortable," Heather said, "with all this sadness. I feel like I don't belong."

"It'll happen to you, too, someday. Don't think it won't," Bob said.

"Let's not turn on each other. Not today," I said.

"Always the peacemaker," Danny said, looking at me. We had a history together but I couldn't always tell what he was thinking.

Bob threw his napkin on his plate and we watched it get dark, soaked by the soy sauce that was pooled on his plate.

"I think this is over," he said.

After lunch, I caught Stuart coming out of the third-floor men's bathroom. He was wearing a pinstriped three-piece suit and a hockey mask that looked to be smeared with fake blood. I could see him smile at me through the mask's birdcage. Even though his pants legs were too short and his tie was clown-shaped wide, I thought he looked great. I assumed he was making a statement about how corporate America was really just a horror show. I was actually going to congratulate him on his creativity. *If we were having a contest, you'd definitely place.* But then I noticed the machete dangling down from his right hand—how could I have missed it in the first place, the deadliness and danger in its long, curved black blade? It clearly wasn't some prop that he'd gotten from Party City. It was the real thing and he looked to have a comfortable grip on it as he let it swing a little in his hand.

"Hey, Stuart," I said, trying to sound casual. "What's up?"

Stuart worked in another department. Maybe Billing? I wasn't sure. Sometimes I'd run into him in the break room and we'd grouse about traffic while waiting for a fresh pot of coffee to finish percolating. His father had died unexpectedly a few years back, and a lot of people from work went to the funeral home in Essex to pay their respects. I didn't go. I had a date with Danny that night.

"Hello. How are you? Don't worry. This won't involve you."

His tone was very pleasant. He could've been talking to me about the weather, his plans for the weekend, a car he was thinking of buying.

"Now, Stuart, this isn't a good idea."

I wanted to be calm and soothing, like the therapist I saw after Danny and I broke up, after I cried so loudly one night that my landlord, Mr. Doucette, banged on my door because he thought I was being raped. The therapist advised me to quit my job. She said that I needed to find another place to work, away from Danny. "Begin the healing process," she suggested. I did try to follow her advice. I interviewed for a job with Cigna and they offered me a position as an underwriter, but when it came time to quit, I just couldn't. Instead, I skipped my next two therapy appointments and then stopped going altogether.

Stuart just flashed me a grim smile and brushed right by me. He headed towards the east wing, a corner of the floor that was reserved for the executives and was nicer than the rest of the building with its wood-paneled walls, spacious offices with built-ins, boardrooms with all the latest video conferencing technology.

I ducked into the Major Accounts department and rushed towards some people who were standing by the copier. "Help," I whispered because I didn't want Stuart to hear me. "We need to leave now." Everyone reacted very quickly. They didn't act surprised at all, as if they'd just been waiting for some kind of crisis to unfold.

We swarmed out of the department. One of the women—Sheila, who handled Operations—shrieked because Stuart was at the far end of the hallway by that time, and he was using his machete to neatly slice off the top of a snake plant in the corner. Then he swung at one of the posters hanging on the wall, the one with the company motto on it—LET US HELP YOU SECURE YOUR FUTURE—and also knocked off the TV monitor next to it, the one that was used to advertise the cafeteria's lunch menu and the names of employees who were celebrating milestone anniversaries. Just the month before, my name had been displayed for having fifteen years.

After I guided the Major Accounts people towards the stairwell, I tried to round up other people on the floor. I found Danny in the break room, standing in front of the empty vending machine, staring at all the bare shelves, where the snack-sized bags of potato chips and Fritos used to be. When I told him that Stuart had lost his shit and had brought a knife to work and that I needed his help in getting people out, he didn't hesitate. He said that he'd handle the second floor.

By that time, other people on the floor had heard the news and were streaming out of their departments to leave. I rushed down the hallway and saw some of the women from the Global Client Services Team waiting at the elevator. They had their jackets on and purses hooked over their arms, like it was any other day. By this time, we couldn't see Stuart anymore but we could hear crashing sounds coming from the executive area. I screamed at the GCS women to take the stairs. One lady wobbled and I had to cradle her so that she wouldn't fall. Her pale tongue slipped out of her mouth and I tried to think of her name because she was a woman whom I'd seen every day for years in the ladies' room, washing her hands at the sinks after stepping out of a stall, but I'd never really spoken to her. "Please, we have to go," I said to her now, and she stiffened up in my arms and was able to stand again.

On the first floor, I slammed my hands on cubicle walls. I put my fingers in my mouth and whistled. I flicked overhead lights off and on. One fellow was actually sleeping at his desk. His monitor had gone into screensaver mode: three primary-colored balls morphing into each other. I shook him by the shoulder until he snapped awake. "What now?" He asked. Then I saw the red fire alarm box on the wall next to the light switch and I grabbed it so hard that my nails broke as I pulled down.

☾

Everyone got out safely. The only person working in the executive area that day was our Human Resources Manager, Judith, and she'd taken a long lunch. By the time she came back from it, everyone was already outside. The TV news trucks and cop cars were there, too. Stuart was the only one left inside.

I was trying to comfort Heather because this episode was reminding her of the time her uncle got drunk at a family picnic at Ocean Beach Park and took a swing at her father with a beer bottle in his hand. Both men ended up fighting for a long time, spilling blood on the sand castle that she'd just finished.

Danny was talking with one of the police officers. His father had been on the police force in town, retiring early after getting shot in the back. He'd told me about it once, when we were lying in bed together late at night at his house. It'd been such a shocking event, this almost deadly robbery, that the whole town had rallied to support his family. Casseroles showed up at their doorstep every day. Envelopes with hundred-dollar bills in them were slipped through their mail slot. "He never felt sorry for himself, though. He always said, 'It comes with the territory,'" Danny told me. I nestled closely next to him as he spoke, my head bumping up against the underside of his chin, and it felt like his words were just going down through me.

Most people didn't have time to take their coats with them on their way out, and as the sun moved lower in the sky, it got cooler. Steph Sherman pulled a blanket from her car trunk and gave it to Tim Mulberry, who was bare chested because of his caveman costume. Angela Murphy, who was wearing fishnet stockings underneath black athletic shorts, hopped around from foot to foot to stay warm. It reminded me of my grade school, where all the kids would parade around the town green on Halloween, dressed up like zombies or ghosts or fairy princesses. My parents usually got me something to wear from the seasonal section at Kmart: itchy polyester gowns, thin plastic masks. But one year, they forgot. They were always preoccupied about something: their work, their anger with each other. On that Halloween morning, before school, my mother was flicking the ashes from her cigarette into the sink when I asked her what my costume was going to be. I was hopeful that she had something planned and just hadn't told me about it. She looked at me and said, "Oh, shit."

Her mascara from the night before was still on her eyes, and some of it had smeared during the night. She looked as frightful as any scary kid was going to be that day.

I marched in the parade anyway. I was wearing jeans and Converse sneakers and a dark pink sweater with three-quarter sleeves. I told anyone who asked, "I've come as a little girl in third grade." But I was humiliated.

While we were waiting for Stuart to come outside, a black-and-white police car raced up the driveway with its lights flashing and its siren on. I thought it was carrying some kind of dignitary. The mayor. The police chief. Instead, a short woman wearing a rumpled raincoat stepped out of the car. She was bald and that was how I knew who it was. I overheard Amanda Worthington from the Call Center say to Chip McDaniel, "Poor lady. As if she hasn't been through enough," and Chip nodded because everyone knew that Stuart's wife was going through round two with breast cancer. There'd been a collection taken up at work to help with her medical expenses. Now a police officer handed her a megaphone.

"Stu," she said in a shaky voice, "what do you think you're doing now?"

At one point, Danny moved back, away from the crowd, and stood on the kidney-shaped landscaping island that separated the visitor parking spaces from the rest of the parking lot. I left Heather to be with him.

"You OK?"

"My heart's still racing," I said.

"You did good."

"So did you. We were a team."

I wanted to go on. I wanted to say something like, "I knew I could depend on you," even though that wasn't quite true. He'd broken up with me at an Applebee's by West Farms Mall. At a sticky-topped table, right after he'd ordered a side of mozzarella sticks, he told me about Dawn, an old girlfriend with a substance-abuse problem who'd recently gotten sober. "I hate like hell to do this to you, but I've got to see this through," he'd said. Dawn and Danny got engaged just long enough for Dawn to get pregnant. Then she moved to Phoenix because she felt herself slipping back to old ways and she needed a fresh start. His daughter was four years old now. He tried to see her whenever he could, typically during the summertime months and around New Year's and Easter. I'd never met her but her face was imprinted on my mind because he'd plastered his cubicle's nubby walls with photos of her. There was Sissy on a swing. Sissy kicking a soccer ball. Sissy just staring at me with her chin propped on her hands.

But before I could say anything to Danny, the front doors of our office building slid open and Stuart slipped outside. He was still holding onto the machete but the hockey mask was gone. He looked small with the three-story office building as his backdrop. One of the police officers took the megaphone from Stuart's wife. "OK, now," the cop said, "you're doing good. Drop your weapon and then everyone can go home."

And that was when it came over me. It was the oddest feeling, this absolute belief I had that the worse thing Stuart could do at that possible moment was to drop his machete. The only bit of power he had and would ever have involved him holding onto that machete for dear life. The second he let go? Everything would end, and not just for Stuart, but for all of us.

So I stepped away from Danny and started towards him. Danny grabbed for my arm, but I shook him off easily. I hopped the curb, shouting out Stuart's name, yelling "No. Don't." I wanted to breach the line of cops and rush to him, making my plea directly. *Don't listen to a word they say, Stu. Whatever you do, don't let go.* But before I got too far, I fell. I tripped on my own habit and landed hard, chin down, on the concrete drive.

A day later, Stuart's wife came to see me. I was home, watching the local news, which was still reporting on the event, playing videos of it on what seemed to be an endless loop. They put my fall in slow motion. You could see the moment when the tip of my toe connected with my costume's bottom hem, my arms flailing as I tried to keep my balance, the awkward tilt of my torso before I fell flat. I didn't like the way I looked on camera. The wimple I was wearing made my face look fat, for one. Then the camera switched over to Stuart as he dropped to his knees. He hadn't ended up doing much damage after all. Chopped up some office furniture: a desk, some chairs, a few filing cabinets. That was about it. I learned from the local ABC affiliate station's anchor, a tired-looking blond woman with a smooth forehead, that Stuart had been taken to Rushford Psychiatric Hospital for evaluation.

I'd missed Stuart's surrender because after I fell, a police officer put me in the back seat of his car. I was stuck there, staring at the steel mesh cage in front of me, while everything else unfolded outside, but I'd heard from Heather, later, that they'd pinned Stuart down to the ground, handcuffed his hands behind him so tightly that he'd yelped. I was let out after it was all over. "I don't know what you were thinking, lady," the police officer said as he glared at me. Then he pointed at Danny who just shrugged. "But he vouched for you."

"Hello. Thank you for coming. I'm sorry, but it just occurred to me. I don't even know your name," I said to Stuart's wife.

"Beth."

"Beth, it's good to see you."

I let her into my apartment. The living room was messy with used tissues scattered on the floor, a stack of newspapers using up most of the sofa, chipped mugs and soup bowls on the coffee table. I tried to pick up.

"Can I get you something to drink? Tea? Coffee?"

"No, nothing," Beth said. "Don't bother. I won't be staying long."

"How is Stuart? I'd like to see him if I could."

"Why in the world would you want to do that?"

"Well, because, I'm concerned about him."

"What do you know about Stuart?"

"Well—."

"I offered to move to Alabama, by the way. I didn't mind. One place is as good as any for me. Do you know what he said to me about it? He said, 'Don't be silly, Beth,' as if I'd just suggested we move to the moon."

She adjusted the paisley scarf that was wrapped around her head. It had slipped down low on her forehead, almost covering where her eyebrows should've been.

"Look, I'm not saying what he did was right, but what *they* did, just closing the office the way *they* did, like *they* had no care at all for any of us, well, that wasn't right, either."

"You're defending a man who came to work with a machete."

"I know that."

"I didn't even know we had one, by the way. They won't let me visit him at the hospital yet, but that's one of the first things I'm going to ask him. Where in hell he got that machete."

"I can see how this would be very upsetting to you."

She'd been holding her sweater closed with her hands. Now she opened up her arms, stretching them wide, and her sweater fell open. I saw the sharp bones of her clavicle, her thin, strained neck. She was wearing an off-white, tight camisole that clung to her ribs. I kept my eyes away from her chest.

"I have cancer."

I bowed my head.

"Yes, I know."

"I was alone when the doctor told me. She was saying all these words and I just couldn't hear anything. It's like I went deaf. When Stuart came home from work, he asked me how my appointment had gone. "Any news?" he said while he looked down at the day's mail. And I couldn't tell him because I didn't quite know myself. Because I hadn't been able to hear the doctor. All I'd been able to do was watch her lips move. So he picked up his *Rolling Stone* magazine, the one with Stevie Nicks on the cover that had just come in that day, and went to the bathroom, which is what he does every day when he comes home from work."

"So," I said slowly, hoping that she'd help me out, stop me from having to respond. "I guess what you're saying is …."

"The cops said I should get a lawyer for Stuart. A lawyer? We don't have the money for something like that. When Stuart's father died, he left us a little bit of money, and I cried when I found out. Stuart thought I was crying because his father was gone, but I was crying because finally, finally, I thought we could get out from under the debt we've been in since practically the second we got married. But do you know what we did with that money? We went to Mohegan with it. Brilliant idea, right? Bet it big. Stuart said it'd be the best way to grow our fortunes. That's how he described it. Our fortunes. He said the stock market's too volatile. Well, you can imagine what happened to that money. He's a damned fool."

"But at least he tried. I mean, look at the rest of us. We dressed up for Halloween, for God's sake. Look, I'm sorry. I know what it's like to love someone who, well, who doesn't do right by you. I have this coworker, see, but he's more than a coworker to me. His name is Danny and I've loved him for a long time—."

I would've gone on. Confessing my deepest thoughts to her. Maybe Beth would be the one to understand. I'd tried to explain it to my mother once on one of my rare visits home. She'd just come from the gym because she'd quit cigarettes and had taken up exercise as fanatically as she'd once smoked. She was wearing yoga pants and a V-neck T-shirt that exposed her crinkly cleavage. I told her that I was still positive that Danny was the one for me, despite what had happened with Dawn. I was just waiting for him to see that too. My mother frowned as she listened to me, and when I was done she put her hands on her waist and twisted from side to side. "You've always been so stubborn," she said.

But Beth stopped me before I could get too far. She knocked me on my arm with her fist, shoved me backwards so that I stumbled into the coffee table. She was a frail woman but she still had a lot of strength.

"You idiot," she hissed. "You don't know a thing about it."

After Beth's visit, I stayed in bed. I didn't answer my phone or any texts. Someone from corporate kept calling me, but I didn't listen to the messages. I didn't eat. Barely slept. Every time I closed my eyes, I saw our office building, its dark hallways and empty cubicle farms.

Danny eventually came to see me. He got Mr. Doucette to let him in because I wasn't coming to the door. When I heard them come in, I sat up in bed. I thought about rushing to the bathroom to check my hair in the mirror, but I just didn't have the energy.

Both men stood in my bedroom doorway. Mr. Doucette, who had a florid face and a big gut that pillowed out over his waistband, cleared his throat. "Always something with her," he said. After he left, Danny pulled a chair from the corner of the room and set it by my bed.

"Beth was here."

"Who's Beth?"

"Stuart's wife."

He stretched out his legs so that they were underneath my bed.

"What did she want?"

"She thinks I'm a fool."

"You did a lot of good that day. You got everyone out. In a lot of people's eyes, you're a hero."

"I didn't want him to let go of his knife. I wanted him to hold onto it until the bitter end."

He shifted in his seat.

"Well, I'm not sure that was clear to everyone. So you can always deny it, you know, if it comes to that. And, also, a lot of people are feeling bad for Stuart. You're not the only one. Someone started a GoFundMe campaign, and it's already raised four thousand dollars for his legal defense."

I struggled to sit up straighter.

"What happened to us, Danny? Why didn't we ever give it another go? We could have, you know. But we didn't. We just kept seeing each other day in and day out at work. And that was enough, right? But we didn't plan for something like this at all."

"Hey, now, don't. Don't cry."

"I'm not," I said even as I felt the tears burning my eyes before they escaped.

He leaned forward until he was very close to me. I saw the burst capillaries on his cheeks, the short whiskers on his chin and cheeks that he'd missed during his morning shave, his dark, thick, wavy hair that I used to touch, grab onto when he was inside of me.

"Get out of bed," he said.

He drove me past the Enfield Mall, which had just lost its Sears anchor store, and then we got onto the highway, crossing over the dull Connecticut River, passing underneath green signs for the Bradley-Windsor Airport. We didn't talk very much and I thought of the time we went to Mystic, calling in sick because it was the first warm day after a long, chilly spring and we wanted to celebrate. This was a few months before Dawn. I had no idea what was ahead of me. In the car, we sang along to songs on the radio. We put the car windows down and the air blew our hair back from our faces. When we got there, we took a short steamboat ride on the Mystic River and, afterwards, sat outside at a brewery downtown. I'd never been so happy, and when I told him that, he looked startled so I laughed. I tried to pretend like I was joking.

This time, Danny got off at Exit 48, that long ramp that curved to the right and poured into Mountain Hill Road. I could have driven this part with my eyes closed. Here we were passing the five-story Marriott Hotel with its long porte cochere. At the next light, the sprawling Amazon warehouse was on the right. Go a little bit farther and there was the rundown barn with the collapsed roof, the only indication that all of this had once been farmland. Then we were at the office.

The company name had already been stripped from the monument sign that sat flush with the lawn at the front entrance. The tall flagpole was bare. Danny parked in a space right in front of the building, in a spot that was usually reserved for the vice president, although that sign had been removed also.

We stood behind his car, leaning against the back bumper, and stared at the building's curtain wall of polished plate glass, its louvered aluminum trellis. Despite the snarl of yellow crime scene ribbon that was crumpled on the ground in front of the sliding glass door, it looked completely ordinary, just another vacant building.

"Here we are. We can say good-bye to it properly one last time," Danny said.

"I wonder how long it'll stay empty."

"Someone else's problem now."

"Strange to think we won't see it again."

"If you need me to spot you, I've got some money saved up. Also, you need to make sure you apply for COBRA. It's important, you know, to think of all these details."

"Thank you for taking me here."

"So we can go now?"

"I'd like to stay a little longer."

"Look, whether we like it or not, whether we want to stay in bed or chop up office furniture, it's all the same. This place is closed."

He sounded discouraged, sadder than I'd ever heard him before, even when he broke up with me at Applebee's or the day he came to my cubicle to tell me that Dawn was gone.

I turned away from him then. I just didn't want to see him like that. I looked at the office building again and, suddenly, I felt like I was back inside there, on Halloween, with Stuart. But this time, I didn't leave. I stayed with him during his entire rampage, listening to his breath, muffled behind his mask, hearing the swish of his sharp blade slashing the air, shaking along with his sobs that got louder and deeper the longer he looked for people who were no longer there.

"Danny," I said, gasping a little. "Alabama."

Walter Bargen

Swing of Things

After midnight, after the movie, in the parking lot
the air after a week of rain is dank, dripping.
He unlocks the door and winds down the window
to let the night in. He backs out and swings round,
headed for the highway, driving the car through

the wall of its own lights that don't seem to end
but thicken and harden the farther he goes. He's
not alone. They've gone to a movie to ease the pain,
to delay the truth, that now at seventy-something
she wants something more, but not really, and he's

not sure it's possible. As he turns the windshield
wipers on, she asks if he saw the movie *Swing*
something. She'd been interviewed over the phone,
and though she'd not seen the movie, she did live
through that time, and she said she'd danced "swing"

in the thirties in Europe, everybody did, it was like dope
today, it was just rebellion, and it was outlawed because

it was too sexy. He said he'd heard the movie reviewed.
It was *Swing Kids*, and the consequence of being caught
was a death camp. He's lost control of the evening.

Now she wants to know why they built
that thing in Washington, D.C., and he knows she's
referring to the Holocaust Museum, and doesn't
answer, and he knows there's one coming, and it does ...
because the Jews need so much money and that's

an easy way to get it, and she's seen proof that it wasn't
six million, it was only three, and every country
and nationality was involved, and did he know that
a reporter was at Dachau and nobody was burned up
there, at liberation they shipped in the bodies from

other places? And now it's just like it was before the war,
they control the banks and the government and the movies.
He pulls into her driveway, beside the immaculate
lawn. The automated garage doors trigger open.
The dachshund runs out yapping. It's Mother's Day.

Daryl Sznyter

Over Coffee

before putting my grandma's hearing aids in
my mother told me a girl was raped
in the alley behind her house
except she said molested   not raped
in order to avoid questions about the girl's age
girls get molested   women get raped
only woman mouths make hard A's
when they scream

my mother spoke like a meteorologist
when she told me the girl was molested
because although her hearing aids weren't in
my grandma didn't miss much   in order to avoid
a question about my grandmother's safety
my mom told me my uncles kept watch
in the daytime   what she didn't need to say
was the rape happened in the daytime

what i'm not saying is that the alley
behind my grandma's house where the girl
was molested was also behind a church

& the church was so tall it blocked the sun
from the alley   & my grandma's hearing aids
never worked too well   so nobody saw or heard
the girl be molested in the alley behind
my grandma's house until it was too late

& she became a woman who was raped
& what i'm not saying is that i grew up playing
in the alley behind my grandma's house before
my grandma ever needed my mom to put her hearing
aids in & i played with my brother & the neighbor's
kid   & i don't know how it happened but one day
i became a woman & my A's went hard & finally
these stories over coffee began to make sense

Elizabeth Leo

A Method to Push Back, Hard

We hoof it, Route Seven to Sabraton, then through to Preston County
where the trees close in and the breath comes clear.
It's better, brothers, just to measure the change: the silphium
    scratching out
the shale, and at the slope, all the green clinging and still.
And still, just for now, children's voices doing what they do—
we know their song, out of the forest. The ferns lean, the storm cloud's
edges trace a path. Pass the fallen ash, the paw prints.
Go past to where the moss curdles at the creek-bed stone. There
where we three meet and meet again, the gold water blooms
and muffles our demented mother's keen, and colors
blue gentian dull. Gentian's cover: blue and at our father's grave.
Palm me a skipping stone, we say, and we all do. Let's count
how far it goes, how fast it slides away.

Melissa Benton Barker

Tomorrow Morning

We don't sleep anymore. We wait until hidden light tugs the sky to blue. That's when he takes me by the wrist and we go down to the old horseshoe-shaped pier, the city behind us, winking in the hills like glitter spilled. The sand is ash and there are remnants everywhere—paper plates and plastic bags, clear ones for groceries and loud ones for chips and things, and all of them blowing like the living. There are seagulls with red-dipped beaks and crabs, too. Did you ever see a crab make a home from a bottle cap, doll's head, thimble? They'll take anything broken up to hide their tender belly. They'll take even what they don't belong to.

When I pull my wrist from his fingers, his knuckles are rocks in my hand. This place is empty. Everyone has fallen back. A bus clanks and glides behind us, tethered to wires. Did you ever see a bus come loose from wires and hiss on the side of the road? I did, and if a bus were stuck like that I might have time to catch it. I would climb to the almost-back, I would watch him through the smeared glass, I would go back to where I came from if I knew how to have a home.

Rebecca Fishow

As if in Prayer

My sister did not know what to do with her hands, or what to call her husband. He was three people, at least, and he ought to have had three names. He woke early, fed the cat, hiked the mountains when fog rose from the ferns. Once, he found his ghost there, carried it to the house in a jar, packed it in a pipe, and smoked. She trusted him when he predicted that the world would soon end, but not before they passed. "Your ghost was there, too. Look," he said, then packed it in his pipe. "You don't want any part of you to around at the world's annihilation, not even your ghost." She drew a puff, exhaled slowly, made a smile he'd never seen. He thought there must still be things he did not know about her, looked at the sun's leaving, then at his wife, who was beautiful and as old as mountains. She picked wildflowers, arranged them in bunches. She placed one on the bookshelf by the stairs, opened a curtain, slid up the window. The petals pulsed in light. My sister thought that each flower had a face, and anything that had a face must have a soul.

My sister stirred, remembering in the middle of the night. Our dead father, in the room and holding her hand. She was a littler girl again, long before she knew her husband. It was her birthday, the year our father couldn't be reached by phone. Our mother went to search, found him dead, wrapped in a blanket on his couch. He had been a secret hoarder all these years since our parent's divorce. Rotten meat under the unused bed, stacks of yellowed newspapers papers all around, maggots slithering in the toilet bowl.

When my sister finally fell asleep she had two sons in her dream. They fashioned weapons out of scrap wood and old nails. They dragged her to the front lawn, beat her through the the night. At dawn, they carried her to the bathroom, took turns washing her wounds. When my sister woke, she felt a void. She had always wanted children, but had none.

My sister remembered going to the war, where she was always surrounded by men. She worked in intelligence, threat-detection. All day she analyzed real-time maps. When a threat crossed a border, she alerted her bosses, who were all men. The alerted the ground troops, also men, who marched out with rifles, made kills. Later, she was surrounded by a single man. Her husband waltzed with her through the living room, manic, played old-time music through a bluetooth speaker. Their neighbors prepared for the end of the world in other ways. They built bunkers, stocked water and cans, put their hands together, as if in prayer.

One night, my sister could not sleep. Her husband had died, and she forgot to take her sleeping pills. She went outside, sat on the porch. The warm Southern heat, the big white moon, the air conditioners humming all around. She was the most alone. Just as alone as you are now. She wanted to complete herself before the end, so she reached her hands under her nightdress, touched herself in a place she owned. She closed her eyes and thought of ocean waves, a gentle breeze. That's were she went all by herself, her husband gone, and she did not bring him back.

My sister lost control of her hands, her husband, her ghost. I lost track of my sister. I do not know where she has been all these years, but I have faith. I imagine what comes next for her and me is better, spectacular. It's like she used to say to me when we were young: Every story in your bones can be loosed in the world. Anything you can imagine may be so.

Jennifer Wortman

Not the Kind of Girl

She's never been to his dorm because he always came to the restaurant to get away from Rousseau and then they always went to her place and she thought he was different and she thought she was different and she never said I love you but she felt it and he stopped coming around and she's not the kind of girl who shows up drunk on doorsteps anymore but last night she dreamed he died and once she dreamed her grandma died and when she woke up her grandma had died so after her dinner shift she drives to Rousseau and now the students stroll the street like it's their own private sidewalk and she wants to run them down but she doesn't and she passes old stone buildings and enormous trees and the big modern library and the pocket-sized downtown and once she told him she loved Bukowski and he winced and said you should read so-and-so and she said who says I haven't but she hadn't and maybe he stopped coming around because she loved Bukowski or maybe because she said who says I haven't or maybe because he was just another fucker who fucked girls over and the students don't seem freaked out like someone has died but maybe Rousseau students don't freak out or maybe they're good at hiding their freak-outs or maybe no one has found his body yet because in her dream he died in the forest so maybe he killed himself in the woods because he had cancer and left her to save her from watching him die but then the pain of cancer and losing her was too much to bear or maybe she's an idiot and the kind of girl who deserves whatever she gets and she parks her clunker and tries the café and it's packed and smells like sugary coffee and unwashed hair and she spots him up front leaning back in his chair and his profile is prettier and smarter than hers and an old guy on stage reads poems into a mic and she can tell by just looking the guy's not a professor just like anyone can see that she's not a student and her heart beats in her head and she should turn around and leave but she sucks in her stomach and pushes past students with tall steaming drinks and in her dream she climbed a tree to save him though the branches kept breaking and now her legs speed up and the students make way and it's so easy to go to him and it's so easy to see he's not happy to see her and it's so easy to see that something has died but she's not the kind of girl to stand there and cry so she slaps him so she can touch him one last time.

Rosetta Young

Delinquent Palaces

Three weeks before I was born, Aunt Trish called Dad and said, "Ona wants a namesake."

"Why the hell should I care?" he responded, gripping the plastic receiver, a landline, attached to the wall by a long ringlet jumbled in loose knots. Mom sat at the kitchen table, voluminous in maternity floral, as my sisters finger-ate Cheerios and put their ears to her stomach.

"She said she didn't have your number," said Aunt Trish, who couldn't have children, in a flat voice.

"Good," Dad said. "You think I want to get caught up in that circus? You think I want to go and pay admission and wait in line and get thrown around on the topsy-turvy and vomit on the teacups and lose my pocket money on the ring toss?"

"Well, you know how Ona is," she said, a phrase that only ever meant one thing in our family: *You know how much money she has.*

Maybe Trish changed his mind, or maybe it was Mom, who had only met my great-grandmother ten years before at her own wedding. On that occasion, the old woman had worn an exquisite pair of butter-yellow pumps. When Mom complimented the shoes, her husband's grandmother had replied, "I got them for nothing—*four thousand.*"

After that, Mom would only call her Four Thousand. She couldn't comprehend such expenditure. To her, the 4000, in its looping numerical form, had seemed to float in the air, before its half-arrow and three zeros—three perfect promises—popped like bubbles.

Either way, on the day of my birth, Four Thousand landed on the roof of the hospital, propeller blades whipping her short white hair across her face.

☽

When I was seven, Four Thousand came north for my birthday, arriving in a limousine with Raphael, one in a series of indistinguishable male companions. We were at Schwirley's Diner, my favorite restaurant in Albany, with its red pleather booths and Formica tabletops. She gave me a strand of pearls so long that I could wrap it around my neck and have the ends touch the floor.

"*Bon Anniversaire*, darling namesake," Four Thousand had said, her pan-European accent making even her words feel costly—every syllable and article an outrageous purchase.

That's how it was—we wouldn't hear from her for years, and then an Easter card addressed to me would arrive in June with a check for ten thousand dollars. She would phone occasionally, giving a date for a visit, and then never show up, until, one day, there the black limousine would be in the driveway, and she would stay for forty-five minutes, making stilted conversation while looking out the window.

From Aunt Trish we knew the story: Four Thousand had met my great-grandfather in Zurich, when she was seventeen and he was forty-five. On an evening stroll with his fiancée, my great-grandfather had glanced through an ice cream parlor's glass window and seen Four Thousand. Licking her spoon free of chocolate syrup, she looked him in the eye.

They married a week later in an Alpine village—the original fiancée ditched somewhere—and soon had my Grandma Abeline. My great-grandfather died a few years after the wedding—a heart attack—and Four Thousand deposited Abeline in a staffed Parisian townhouse and never really came back.

Aunt Trish tended to end the story by lighting a Camel Red and saying of her mother, "I don't think she ever got over it." Abeline died young herself—a brain aneurysm—when she and Dad were still kids.

The summer after my freshman year of college, the limousine pulled up in driveway. On the front porch, my oldest sister, Betty, was putting a braid in my hair while Miriam painted her toenails with a design from an ancient *Seventeen Magazine*. Our college summers in Albany were so long and quiet that all three of us seemed to go back in time, getting progressively younger with each passing day. By the end, we were sucking on ice-pops and reading decade-old issues of *Tiger Beat* and talking speculatively, sweetly, about boys we knew on campus who, during the academic year, we mouthed off to with confidence, brusque and dismissive. We would wake in September, surprised to find we were women in our late teens and early twenties, and look back at the past three months with bemusement. The limousine seemed like an early awakening.

We all looked over the porch railing, expecting to see Four Thousand. Instead a suited man opened the back door, stepped out and adjusted his tie on the sidewalk.

"Hello, girls," he said. "Are any of you ...?"

He said my name and then the news: Four Thousand had died; the limousine had come for me. Mom made me put on my high school graduation dress and a hint of Betty's Rev-Rev-Revlon Red lipstick.

In midtown Manhattan, where I had only been a dozen times in my life, three men sat like chess-piece royalty—the bishop, the knight, the rook—in a shining conference room.

The knight told me that everything had been set up, situated, for me. The money, the bonds, the stocks, they said, had passed from the moment of Four Thousand's death into accounts under my name. There was only one problem.

"This is all of them," the knight said, pushing a list towards me. "Or at least we think." He laughed nervously.

She had nearly a hundred homes, bought at different times, often under different names, all over the world, some of which hadn't been visited since before Dad was born.

Then, they introduced me to Jonas—tall, dark-haired, extremely handsome, not far over thirty. He was the last, I realized, of Four Thousand's male companions.

It took years, flying around the world, hiking through jungles, waiting for town cars, walking through streets counting numbers—Jonas and I, hunting houses. The manses and penthouses often had exquisite architecture: indoor waterfalls, spiral staircases, slides, ocean views, bay windows, ballrooms with mantles and chandeliers hidden under white sheets. Of course, there were flooded rooms, molded walls, broken floorboards, cracked ceilings, patchy roofs, clogged plumbing, electrical systems ancient, blown, potentially hazardous. The homes themselves had bloomed happily in an opulent rebellion: They were delinquent palaces, rambling and forsaken circuses of wealth overflowed. The teardowns were ecstatic, joyful ruins.

Some, of course, were in pretty good shape. In a few, staffs were still running, waiting for the return of Four Thousand. Once, I walked through a door in Brazil, and a butler cried, "Enfin à la maison!" and the servants swooped into a ludicrous formation, like something from *The Sound of Music*.

I called home, but every time I heard their voices again—Mom, Dad, Betty and Miriam especially—they all seemed more and more surprised. After a while, they started putting my name like a question into the telephone, as if they weren't sure who was calling. Between every call and visit, time swallowed itself faster and faster.

Finally, it was finished. I bought a triplex apartment in SoHo, a mansion in the Arizona desert, but time did not resume its normal speed. Now, I would call and hear things that seemed impossible—Mom dead, Dad quiet and sick in a home, Aunt Trish lost to the same thing that had killed her mother. I tried to focus when my sisters told me these things, to keep track of these events in my mind—births, deaths, illnesses, weddings, husbands, children—but I felt as if they were in another reality entirely, like they were on a television show I had long stopped watching and was now only hearing about secondhand. I started to understand why Four Thousand had always been late.

The last time Jonas and I went to visit, my sisters had identical husbands, indistinguishable children, houses built so like the one from our childhood that I said at Miriam's, "Remember how Mom used to stand right here...?" and she replied, hard and angry, "What are you talking about?"

Later, I overheard my sisters whispering in the kitchen. I had told Betty how much it cost to replace my aquarium, after all the fish had died while I was in Barbados.

Five Thousand, she said to Miriam across the table, *Five Thousand*.

Owen Neace

Holding Back Elegy

My grandmother would not be a ghost
        if I did not see her feet
    when trying not to come.

Say *slow* through their stepping in between.
      Long before our first time
      I saw them uncovered on a porch
in a slow nightmare named Tennessee:

Nails the color of earwax, wide as a cigarette,
      serrated & curved & jagged.
Too-bright veins & too-long toes,
    so much contortion:
When I learned some skin is see-through.
Ever since as specters of seeing through it.

When a body is cremated,
on which end does the burning start?
Or is it more like engulfing
      pronounced like release?

I'd never read this or say her name aloud,
      if I summon it is only to leave myself &
were her feet the last part of her to burn
          isn't a question to be answered, here

          with her rings I wear
     & skinsick bones
& last burst of words
     I'd kill myself if I could

me closer than very near, trying to hold back
     another little death, inevitable.

Its arrival, I mean, my surrender, I mean
I lie when I say this haunting is for you.

John Gallaher

Elegy for the Oil Industry

Pa Ingles is driving a wagon of nitroglycerine across rugged landscape
with his neighbor and friend Bobo the Clown. This is how it is
because I don't want to look it up. I want my memory, the Michael
Landon memory next to the grizzled befuddlement of his neighbor
and friend whose name I don't remember, to remain, to be the only
story. This life strategy is deeply flawed I know, but it's all I've got
if I don't want to ask. And I don't want to ask. You used to have
to really want to know something to ask. Now asking is a whim,
and the answers are as whimsical as the questions. As in, "Oil
is measured in barrels, which is equal to 42 U.S. gallons or 159 liters."
Thank you, do something dot org. But for now, I'm not thinking
about oil; I'm thinking about Pa Ingles, and I'm not even caring
if I spell his name correctly, because I'm sitting at a green turn signal
in Hannibal, Missouri, behind an eighteen-wheeler composed
of odd-looking canisters, vertical and sci-fi-looking. It's turning
slow, and I'm thinking, yeah, that's how Pa Ingles did it, too.
That's how I do it when carrying my morning coffee. That's how
God does it with our sacred souls. So I'm guessing it's something
to do with oil or hazmat, which makes me think, how quaint.
They're being careful. As if there were something left to ruin.
Here I am, being optimistic again. Can anyone be happy here?

Just look at this place. Even at a green light. I know I'm supposed
to love that. A forest of green lights! Happy herd of green lights
all the way to California! I like to imagine Amelia Earhart, whose
middle name was Mary (I looked it up because I spelled it Emelia
with an E and that looked weird, so now I know her middle name, too,
as a whimsical bonus), I like to imagine her content, crashing
into the sea, a kind of understanding that surpasses knowledge,
having been so close to the sun and nowhere else to go. I like
to imagine that because the sudden jolt and onrush of glass
and ocean likely tore her to shreds. The mad rush is hopeless
as we yearn for the transcendent final drift beneath the credits,
the ellipses, like the Tesla spaceman shot into space as a marketing
strategy. Say hello to the future, we've come for you, we dream,
lucky star, skipping past Mars, a dwindling dot in the night sky.

Nancy Takacs

Making Up

is like the first pickle from a mason jar,
raspberry jam in the tapioca. My husband
speaks to me for the first time after our
argument that shimmered with hooves.
Now his voice is all hallowed and velour.
Now my voice is hazy and mango. We halt
our sorrows for now. We go out to the tulips
and have a cookie. I put on my magenta
sweater. The dusky sky has one tamp of bitter.
Holding a hand can be like a hornet in a balloon.
It takes two hours for our toes to get drowsy.

Danielle Burnette

Collections

When I was young, I spent many days at my aunt's house while my parents worked. Auntie kept Beanie Babies at the top of a black lacquer cabinet with glass-paneled doors. A pristine army of doe-eyed plushness, their swing heart tags stuck out like badges of honor, signifying their virginity. I coveted them as much as any little girl would, gazing up at them from the moat of mossy-colored carpet cushioning my cross-legged position below. So, I dragged a dining room chair over to the cabinet and freed a black bear to attack my Barbies' camper.

Auntie threw a fit when she caught me. "Don't you know what it means to respect other people's things? They're a valuable collection, not toys. That's why I keep them together." When I protested again, she crossed her arms and said, "Why don't you go play somewhere less likely to get you in trouble?"

But porcelain dogs frolicked on every end table. Gnome cookie jars—not a single crumb inside—squatted on all the available kitchen counterspace (and I realize now why Auntie prepared all my snacks at the dining room table). She scolded me when I tried drawing with the floaty pens, afraid too many bubbles would obscure the smooth glide of bridges, trains, animals, and even an astronaut through the water-filled barrels. I told her there were no safe places.

She marched me to her bedroom, opened the closet, and pulled out four hard-shelled suitcases. I remember everything inside them: shoes too fantastical to imagine my aunt ever wearing; scarves in every fabric and hue; wigs with a frightening realness; jewelry with royal sparkle. I asked if these were collections.

"Ones I don't mind you playing with," she said and left the room.

I put on a fashion show for the hallway mirror, swishing my hips like my mother in her high heels. But one of the really short wigs wouldn't stay on my head. Atop a shoebox on the shelf in Auntie's closet, I spotted the solution: velvety black, wide brimmed, curtained with fishnet lace. I stacked the suitcases and climbed them to that beautiful hat. Just as my hand grasped it, my ladder shifted and the hat and shoebox followed me to the floor. I don't remember feeling hurt by the fall. I was probably too enthralled by the spilled contents of the shoebox littering the floor around me.

A gold watch, thick-banded and too big for my wrist. Ticket stubs to movies I'd never heard of. A crinkled picture of a man I'd never seen. Plastic bracelets, all snapped in half, with Auntie's last name printed on them. A yellowed handkerchief, stitched with initials I can't remember and wrapped around a couple of tiny brown bits—little raisins, all stretched out of shape. They squirmed in my mouth like baby worms and tasted like fried rubber bands, chewy but bitter. I was spitting them into the shoebox just as Auntie came into the room.

She rushed over and slapped me so hard I didn't feel it. So hard I still can't remember what she screamed at me afterwards.

My parents sent me to a babysitter after that. They said Auntie didn't understand children. As I grew older and asked why we never visited her, they blamed her hoarding. In horrifying detail, they described towers of old newspapers, piles of clothes, and other junk clogging every inch of space in her house. They said she'd become crazy and developed a fear of letting go. By the time I graduated college, we called her 'Fraidy Phyllis because she refused to leave her house. Not even my wedding could coax her outside.

Yet when I was eight months along with my firstborn, Aunt Phyllis sent me a package through the mail. I could smell the zucchini raisin bread before even opening it, and I remembered running through Auntie's house, pretending to be crazed with hunger, while it baked. As much as I ran, I'm certain I never bumped into anything. The bread tasted just as moist and sweet as I remembered, too.

Separate from the bread was a smaller gift box wrapped in glossy paper with blue rattles and pacifiers all over it. Inside was the gold watch, the picture of the man, and a note in Auntie's loopy cursive that said, "For my grandson."

I imagined what my parents would say, how my mother's sister wasn't right in the head. I wondered if I could still run through my aunt's house, if it was ever as crowded as I was told. Then I peered closer at the faded picture, at the stranger's face, and searched for signs of my own.

Danielle Burnette

Clean

Some smells never leave you. Like the acidic stench of sunbaked apple cider on old leather seats. I only managed one swallow from the half-gallon jug before it slipped from my hands and spilled all over me, my car, everything. My blue moon splurge, gone, gone, gone. Can't even describe how pissed I was. So pissed, I reveled in the stink, the only thing left.

Until this pimply manager guy kicked me out of the Paradise Buffet's all-you-can-eat hour. "Sir, your odor is offending the other customers," he said loudly enough for the dead to hear. Wouldn't even let me move to a more out-of-the-way table, and I'd just sat down with my second plate. Felt like I'd dumped another jug of cider in my car.

So I left and went to a Wash 'n' Dry—the one next door to Vito's Pizza Palace—to defunk my floor mats.

I know most of the people there now. Flannel Girl curls up on her dryer with coverless paperbacks. And Mikey slouches in a corner, calls his lovers, and tells every one, "C'mon, you know you're Mikey's only girl." They both bathe in cheap, candy cane cologne. I used to bum quarters off of them when I was short. They don't have extra change anymore. I get it. I'm tired of me being short, too.

My favorites are Papi and Mamacita. They show up every Friday night at seven with hangers, a white plastic basket, and a huge garbage bag of clothes. They snag a laundry cart (Papi rolls it back and forth to make sure it's not the one with the chase-your-tail wheel) and organize their laundry: Dickies and flowery scrubs on the bottom, girly hoodies in the middle, tiny dinosaur tees on top. Mamacita sprays something heavenly—I swear, it smells like fresh-squeezed orange juice—on the folding table and wipes it shiny clean before placing her clothes there. During the wash cycle, they eat—always burritos, stuffed with *frijoles, pollo,* and other goodies I can almost taste when I gulp the aromas out of the air. They caught me once. The next week, they brought me chips and a titanic Tupperware container of guacamole. I was so embarrassed, I almost walked out of the Wash 'n' Dry forever without my clothes. Almost. Glad I didn't, otherwise I'd be missing my weekly burrito.

Granny used to come on Wednesdays. Said I reminded her of her grandson, that he's a free spirit like me. She usually smelled like the good kind of skunky, the kind that goes good with late-night burgers and fudge brownies. When she smelled like that, she'd pretend the washing machine suds were ocean waves, and sing and dance to hula music from her cell phone. Her one regret, she said, was that her toes would never touch the beach in Hawaii. I tried to make her feel better by confessing my many mistakes. She shared her detergent and made me separate the lights from the darks—told me hard times will pass, long as I stay clean.

I listened. I swear I did. Then she stopped coming and I ran out of detergent. And I realized it doesn't matter anymore if my whites turn pink. Everything will stink again tomorrow. Despite all my washing, my home still reeks of spoiled apple cider.

I lean against the brick wall between the Wash 'n' Dry and Vito's as I jiggle the last few coins in my pocket. An old man wipes pizza sauce from his mouth. What a waste of a napkin. My whole body growls, asks me why it's so important to be clean.

Danielle Burnette

Rear View

She takes the yellow saucer eyes for headlights, the antlers for errant branches. Cars sometimes cross lanes on this blackened stretch of Route 21 to dodge potholes and dead tree bits. Then his brown body rolls up the hood of her hatchback, the antlers thrust toward her face. *Steer right*, her boyfriend says. She does and the car jumps off the shoulder. Glass rains like hail, pitting her skin. The airbag burns her arm; she fears losing her half of their winged-heart tattoo.

She calls her sister, her cousin, her parents. No one answers. Bathed in high-beams, the buck heaves and bewails her insomnia. She has no business driving this late at night, no destination except the empty home she left, but retracing well-worn roads provides a strange comfort. Her boyfriend reminds her of the gas station a mile or so back. She nods; she can walk it. Until she looks in the rearview mirror.

Red and blue lights shoot inside the car. The lights run circles around her head, blinding her, trapping her. Her mouth dries as the air turns to water and every breath drowns her. The steering wheel slips from her hands—no, her hands and arms have faded to something impalpable. She is puddling.

In the driver's side window appears a face, etched with familiar suspicion. "You okay?" he asks.

Keep your hands visible, her boyfriend whispers but his arms stay crossed over his stomach. Her liquefied limbs take forever to solidify. Finally, she white-knuckles the wheel and tries to speak. All she can do is cough up water.

Without waiting for an answer, the cop strides ahead to where the buck has crawled, inches from the safety of the woods. The cop plants both feet and fires. Antlers crunch onto asphalt. The brown body stills. Three more shots ring out, and she shuts her eyes.

Her boyfriend reaches into her lap, squeezes her hand, says, *Don't worry.* The bullet hole in his belly, now exposed, spouts blood. When she re-covers the wound, blood pours from his side, gushes from his chest, sprays her like a sprinkler. He is a fountain of death, a fate she cannot stop, yet again he says, *Don't worry.*

Hard knocks shake her window. "Roll it down," the cop orders.

She glances around the car, struggles to remember the color of her wallet, where she stashed it, so she can tell him. Life depends on certainty. She implores her boyfriend for help, but the passenger's seat is vacant. His brown eyes stare back from the rearview mirror.

A.R. Robins

When I Need It

There's a crack in my living room baseboard, an inch to the right of my bedroom door. Jason kicked it.

Maybe it was there when we moved in.

The deposit was $700 dollars, split between Kelley and me. If she sees the crack, she'll blame me—Jason is my boyfriend, and he stays the night almost every night without paying rent—and then I'll owe her $350 if we lose the deposit.

My phone pings. Mom.[1]

I text her back[2] and then sit for a second, thinking about the crack.

I could make Jason pay it. It's his fault it's there. He always kicks and punches things when he's angry. It's always my stuff that gets broken.

If I bring it up, he might change his mind about letting me move in with him.

Maybe Mom would let me move back with her.

Maybe Mom could lend me the money for the deposit.

I debate texting Kelley about it. I need to stop lying to her, but if I play dumb, I might get out of paying it.

I'm terrible at playing dumb.

I take a picture of the crack with my phone and send it to Mom.[3]

My stomach rumbles, but I'm afraid to start cooking.

I might get distracted. I have three solid hours to myself, no Jason, no Kelley, no urgent work projects, no pressing errands. I can work on my poetry collection, really work on it.

My eyes move back to my computer screen, my fingers landing briefly on the ASDF JKL; home base.

---

1   What do you put in your alfredo? Is it peas?

2   yea and a little red pepper

3   is this something i need to worry about will i lose my deposit

My phone pings. Mom.[4]

I sigh, sit for two minutes, and then study the picture. The lighting makes the baseboard more of an off-white, hiding the crack. Plus, my mom's eyes are basically worthless. She can't read most signs when she drives someplace new, and she is always asking me to read all the close-up text in the romantic comedies we watch together. Even in movie theaters, when the text is as big as her face, she'll pop off, "What's it say?" and I will shrink with embarrassment.

I send her a new photo, this time circling in red the more clearly visible crack.[5]

A warm pain radiates up my right side, from the top of my right knee up to my lowest rib bone. The pain pauses and then decides to sit below the rib bone and pulsate. I press three fingers into the ache and sit with it.

It's good to be present. Just sit and be present.

Think about the pain. Don't try to make it go away.

Just sit.

Last month, I went to the emergency room because the pain was so intense that I started vomiting. At first I thought I was having period cramps or gas, so I ran a hot bath. After two hours of wriggling in hot water, I yelled for Kelley to pull me out of the tub.

"I don't think I can walk."

On the way to the hospital, she pulled over twice to let me vomit.

"Are you drunk?"

"Are you kidding?"

About an hour later, a nurse watches me shake in front of her over her clipboard.

"When was your last period?"

I couldn't think.

I couldn't remember what day of the week it was.

I had sex with Jason.

Two weeks ago.

I was on my period then. He likes to finish inside me.

No.

It was sooner than that.

"Like 10 days ago?"

"On a scale of 1-10, with 10 being the worst pain you can imagine, what level of pain are you experiencing?"

4   What am I looking at?

5   theres a crack in my baseboard will I lose my deposit?

How much pain can I imagine?

When I see men stranded on the side of the road, I sometimes imagine pulling over to help them. Once I imagined that the man I was helping started hitting me in the face with a crowbar until I drowned in my blood.

"Seven.."

The nurse barely responded.

"I mean, the pain is really intense." I added, "I think I need some medication."

When the nurse left, Kelley scolded me. "You can't just ask for pain medication at three in the morning"

She was right. I was given nothing for the pain, just something for the nausea. I writhed all morning until about 9 a.m., when my body finally sank with exhaustion, and I slept. They woke me up at 10 a.m. for a transvaginal ultrasound.

Despite there being no blood, I still suspected what I assumed they likely suspected, that I was having a miscarriage. While the technician pushed the cold, jellied covered probe inside me, I thought about what losing Jason's child would mean to me.

I thought maybe it was an ectopic pregnancy. I had just read about them in a book about reproductive rights. In El Salvador, doctors wait until the fallopian tubes burst to perform surgery so that they can avoid being arrested for performing an abortion.

I was diagnosed with functional abominable pain.

No discernable cause.

That was about 2 months ago. Yesterday I got the bill for the emergency room stay.

It was $1,238.62. With insurance.

I should be grateful that nothing is wrong with me. I should be grateful to live in a country with doctors that won't watch my fallopian tubes burst. I should be grateful for transvaginal ultrasounds. I should be grateful that no one got me hooked on pain medication.

My side still hurts.

Every day.

My phone pings. Jason.[6] I don't know what to say to him. I'll think of something later.

When I told him about the hospital stay, he listened without asking any questions.

---

6   sorry about last night i was drunk.

When I was finished, he started crying. He held me and we cried together. His body shook with mine. I think about that shaking and breathe through my pain.

The pain dissipates; my fingers find their home base again. They softly tap the keys without actually typing.

Think.

Think of something clever.

ASDF JKL;

The only thing I picked up from typing classes in middle school was where to put my fingers. I could never concentrate. Regan, a boy with green eyes and sharp cheekbones, would whisper dumb jokes to me all hour. Outside of that classroom, he called me "Cum Stain," but for whatever reason, in that classroom he would whisper with me, and I adored him for it.

I stop tapping the keys to check my Facebook, scrolling through some old albums. Photos of me and Jason.

In one photo he is wearing one of my T-shirts. His pudgy stomach spills out of the bottom of the shit. I'm hanging off of him, clearly drunk.

I can't believe we put this photo online.

We look happy.

My stomach growls.

I need something salty.

Focus.

I read the first two stanzas of my poem, hoping it will bring me some inspiration for the stanza I'm supposed to be working on.

I called two men daddy before they stepped on my throat
I kissed their mud boots until my tongue withered dry
Your name on my tombstone I wrote and rewrote

Mother married a criminal who grasped the garrote
Then married another clutching a rope necktie
I called them both daddy, then presented my throat

My back shivers with shame. Daddy. It's so sexual. Was that what I was going for? Am I trying to be Plath? Which is worse?

I delete a comma.

I put it back.

My phone pings.[7]
No one ever gives me a straight answer when I need it.
I pull up Facebook again and type in the name "Dan Simmons."
Same results as always.
People You May Know.
I'm not looking for someone I know.
I type in the name "Daniel B. Simmons."
I click on the profile of the man with a snowy Santa Claus beard. For some reason, his is the one I always come back to, despite the fact that he is from West Virginia.
Mom says that my dad is from Florida.
I scroll through his posts. Same as last time. A post about a stove he is selling. A few profile picture changes. A review of a store where he bought some fancy chess set. Some publications at some very small magazines. Some self-publications. A political cartoon making fun of Trump. A picture album of an air show he attended in 2012.
I text Mom.[8]
This probably isn't him. I've been telling myself this for three years. But it could be. Maybe he moved to West Virginia. Maybe Mom got mixed up. They were just friends with benefits. Barely even friends.
He's a writer with some publications.
Like me.
He has my nose.
I click on the messenger icon. There sits the message I typed to him three years ago.[9]
No response.
I sound like a catfisher.
I sound pathetic.
I close my laptop.
I call Kelley. Voicemail.[10]

---

7   I don't know. It depends on your landlord.
8   what was my dad's middle name
9   Hello, I know this is a strange message to receive out of the blue. I promise I am not a robot or a scammer or anything like that. I've been trying to locate someone for about 15 years. I think you might be him. The man I'm looking for served in the army sometime around 1987 or 1988. He also went to prison for a few years at Fort Leavenworth. I think he was released in 1992, but I'm not sure. Does any of this information apply to you?
10   Hey, this is Kelley. Text me.

I hang up before the beep and send her a text.[11]

There is only one place within walking distance that sells decent vegan food. Kelley and I love it. The breading on their country-fried seitan is light and crunchy. Each particle of golden breading holds a tiny ocean of grease so that every bite explodes with little bursts of fat. I have no idea what is in the gravy, but it's better than the bacon-grease gravy my mom makes on Christmas.

Why did I text Mom about my dad?

She's going to think I'm losing it again.

While I walk, I trail a girl with pink hair walking her bulldog. I can see a red-brown spot on the dog's back that looks like a heart. The dog sniffs a green mailbox growing from the asphalt.

I want a dog, but I don't have one because I don't want to walk it. I watched this documentary about a guy who was accused of a murder he didn't commit. The whole point of the documentary was that you were supposed to feel sorry for him, but I couldn't do it. He was always harassing women in his town and he used to torture cats as a teenager. The whole thing made me anxious, especially the part about the murder.

The story goes that this woman—pretty, blond, the mayor's wife—is walking her dog on a beach in the middle of the day. Hours later, her dog shows up at a farm, chasing chickens, and she is found under a dock, raped and half dead. She died in the hospital three days later. Her body pulverized. Her face like hamburger.

It wasn't nighttime. It wasn't an isolated beach. She wasn't in her bathing suit or some skimpy summer outfit. She even had her dog with her, which wasn't one of those small ones but like a golden retriever mix. What's the point of having a dog if it can't protect you?

The girl stops walking, and the bulldog hunkers down in position. I'm feeling awkward now because I'm very close behind her. If I keep walking forward, I might step over her dog while it poops, and that seems—I don't want to do that. If I stop walking and wait for them to finish, she'll think I'm following her.

I pull out my phone and pretend to dial, then hold it next to my ear and face the side of the building beside me.

There's a bit of graffiti at eye level.

---

11   im going to get some country fried seitan do you want anything choco-late croissant?

A phone number: for a great night

Maybe I should actually call Jason.

My side starts to ache a little, so I stop and stretch out my back, pressing my left palm onto the sidewalk, my right hand still holding the phone to my ear.

Breathing is good. You are breathing. Just keep breathing.

Is she watching me?

I glance over in her direction. She's across the street. Thank god.

My phone pings as I press it into the back pocket of my jeans. I pull it out again. Jason.[12]

I text him back.[13]

Kelley wants me to get some medicine. She thinks the pain is some manifestation of my anxiety. Maybe it is, but I've survived this long without medication. No need to pay any more medical bills.

I walk past the green mailbox, then pause.

On the lip of the mailbox hangs a blue-iridescent bag of poop.

Dog poop.

There is a trash can maybe five feet away from the mailbox, but this girl, with her beautiful little dog with hearts on his back decided to hang a bag of shit off a stranger's mailbox.

Maybe it wasn't a stranger.

My phone pings. Mom.[14]

I text back, swallowing guilt.[15]

I leave the bag of poop to hang on the mailbox. I can't let myself touch someone else's garbage because I feel guilty.

From outside the restaurant, I can see the place is packed. I debate going inside.

My stomach grumbles.

I want this seitan.

I enter the door and look around. This restaurant is the kind of place with those long communal cafeteria tables, so all I need to do is find an empty space.

Nothing.

I'll be fine. I can wait.

12   are you not talking to me

13   im talking to you i just don't know what to say

14   I didn't realize you were still thinking about him. Are you still looking?

15   a little

I stand in line and fumble around the pockets of my laptop bag.

Keys.

Wallet.

Phone.

I pull out my phone and check Twitter. My notifications alert me to a recent tweet from "my cat is a refugee."[16]

I read the replies.[17]

The man in front of me smells familiar. Toothpaste. Aftershave. Something green?

I read more replies.[18]

"Hello."

I look up to a bright face. She's gorgeous, embarrassingly gorgeous. Dark hair with bangs. One of those manic-pixie types, I guess. I'm suddenly very aware of my outfit: black sweatpants and a university T-shirt. I haven't combed my hair. I come here all the time. Who is this girl?

"Yeah, I'd like a bottomless coffee."

"Would you like to purchase one of our new biodegradable cups?"

Those cups will eventually be in a landfill with the plastic, where the weight of the trash is so heavy that even the organic materials are cut off from the air, no oxygen, no way to break down. These supposedly biodegradable cups are just capitalism's way of profiting from our society's collective angst about the mounds of trash being swallowed by fish in the ocean.

"I'm eating here."

She swings her arms in front of her like Vanna White, referring to the crowd of people around us.

She's right, but I don't want to leave.

I'm already here.

Serendipitously, a couple stands up to leave. I point at them and smile triumphantly.

"I'll sit there."

The couple sees my pointing.

The man stops.

"What's going on?" he asks me.

16   What's your hottest Seinfeld hot take?

17   Elaine was a whore.

18   I really found all of the characters to be pretty flat. The show is appealing to the masses because the plot and characters are simplistic.

"What? Nothing."

"Why were you pointing at me and my sister?"

My sister and me. I bite my lip.

"I wasn't pointing at you."

The cashier chimes in. "Yes, you were."

"What is it?" the man smiles. He looks like someone who enjoys hurting people. "Do I have something on my face?"

Seriously. Just drop it.

"I was just pointing at your table. It's really busy."

"How was your food?" the cashier asks them.

"It was great," the man replies, still grinning at me. The awkwardness makes my throat close up, as if I were breathing in smoke. I can't tell if this conversation is my fault or his. My mom told me never to point. I guess this is why.

My phone pings. Kelley.[19] The man leaves with his sister while my head is down. I wait until they are gone before looking back up at the cashier.

"So a bottomless coffee, the country-fried seitan and two chocolate croissants. I'll need one to-go container. Also, do you guys have a strawberry avocado drink?"

"What do you mean?"

"My roommate just texted me about this strawberry avocado drink. Is it like a smoothie? Do you guys have something like that?"

"I don't know. I'm kind of new. Do you want me to ask my manager?"

I can feel the line groaning behind me.

"No. It's fine. That's all."

"That's $38.51"

I have $157.48 in my bank account. What am I doing here?

She hands me a number. Twenty-three.

I grab a white porcelain cup and head to the row of coffees lining the wall to my left.

All fair trade with quirky, stupid names.

Not Your Grandma's Coffee.

It's a Brew-tiful Day.

The Perks of Being a Wallflower.

I read in an article that fair trade doesn't actually help poor indigenous

---

19   YEEEEEES PLLLEaaaase! And one of those strawberry avocado drink things. I'll be home in less than an hour. Leaving early! Tell you about it when I get home.

people and that the market actually attracts the lowest-quality beans. I didn't understand the article, and I don't really understand how fair trade is supposed to work. I thought that the whole point was that you were getting beans that weren't picked by slave children. I guess there's more to it. There always is.

I pour myself a cup of "Cool Beans" and top it off with half-and-half. I look over at the empty seats and see the dirty plates still on the table.

I look down at my phone. A message from Jason.[20]

Shit. I text him back.[21]

The man beside me smells familiar. Gum? Tea? A sweet kind of green. He's waiting too. He's looking where I'm looking.

I'm already embarrassed. We're going to be sitting beside each other, and here we are standing next to each other, holding our coffees. How very meet-cute. I haven't really looked at his face, but from the corner of my eye I can see he has on dark framed glasses, and he's wearing a pale blue button-up shirt.

Clean cut. Not the kind of guy who would date me, but the kind of guy I might obsess about for six months.

But I'm still with Jason, and if he knew I was sniffing guys at restaurants, he would be super pissed. I avert my eyes.

My phone pings. Mom.[22]

I text her back. [23] I'm not going to feel guilty about bringing him up.

Once the busboy clears the section of the table, the clean cut and I make our way to the empty space at the table, our bodies in tandem. I slow down my pace, letting him take the lead so he can sit where he wants. I don't want us trying to take the same seat, fumbling around, touching each other all giggly.

We're both too slow. A different couple sits down.

I spill some coffee on my sandals. My toe screams in pain.

Now what?

I turn around and scan the room. Two girls are sitting at the solo café table outside. Plates are empty. Drinking coffee. Maybe they'll leave soon.

I rub my toe on the back of my sweatpants.

"Excuse me. You took our seats."

---

20 so your starting these games again why are you acting like a cunt?

21 im talking to you i was just distracted im not mad don't call me a cunt

22 Why do you want to know his middle name?

23 i looked up the prison records and found a guy named dan simmons who was released in 1990 his middle initial was b

I turn around. The clean-cut guy is standing over the couple who took our seats.

Our seats?

My side begins to ache. It feels like a small beetle is digging a little hole in my uterus.

This is what they called hysteria. If this were the 1900s, they would have removed my uterus by now and made me walk in a hamster wheel for exercise.

The couple look up at him with in awkward confusion.

"What are you talking about, dude?"

"First of all, do not call me dude."

Holy Jesus, what is happening?

"Twenty-three!" the manic-pixie girl shouts.

"That's me. You can have my seat. I mean, it's not my seat. It's your seat. It's fine."

Sweet relief. It's over.

The manic pixie girl holds up a bag of food behind her register.

I leave the clean-cut guy behind me.

I'm grateful.

I'm confused.

"I said this wasn't to-go. I want to eat here. I need to use your Wi-Fi."

"Ma'am, it is really busy today. I don't think there is any place you can sit."

Ma'am? I'm twenty-seven.

I see an empty seat in the back of the restaurant. On the edge of the table. Perfect. No one in front of the seat. Perfect. A woman in a pink sweater on the left side of the seat. Perfect. Jason is never jealous of women, even after I admitted some of my past relationships. He says they don't count as real relationships. Girls always get with girls. No big deal.

"There. I'm sitting there. I have my coffee already. I'm just going to sit back there. Thank you." I grab the bag of food and sprint toward the seat.

The clean cut guy is still talking to the couple. He points at me again, and I put my face down on the table.

Please, just go away.

I open my laptop.[24] I look around for an electrical socket. None. Of course there aren't any. They don't want dipshits like me stringing cords across the floor.

---

24   Battery at 15%

It's fine. I can just work until my battery dies.
I pull up my poem.

> *I dug around your castle a fine six-foot moat*
> *Dropping here a rib cage and there a thigh*
> *Your name on my tombstone I wrote and rewrote*

I sigh.

This poem is so fucking stupid. Why did I choose villanelle? No one reads villanelles. Villanelles aren't pretty on Instagram.

You murdered the child but left the zygote

That's the line that started this poem, and eventually this collection, something I wrote at the office during a working lunch meeting about work safety.

Zygote.

So fucking clever.

And now this fucking thing. It's so goddamned stupid. Another poem about daddy issues.

I feel the air shift beside me. I look out the corner of my eye at the woman in the pink sweater beside me. Did she read my poem?

I close my laptop to save what little battery is left and pull out the container of seitan. It smells exactly the way it needs to smell, salty, warm, a hint of grease.

No fork.

Of course.

I gather my laptop into its case and swing it over my shoulder. I make my way toward the pile of forks by the coffee decanters.

My phone pings again. Jason.[25]

Shit. I check my notifications. Seven missed calls, all Jason. I turned of the ringer so I could work.

I turn my ringer back on.

I text him back.[26]

I rummage through the forks, looking for a clean one. I used to work in a restaurant when I was still in school. I know that no one actually washes these forks. They get rinsed and then sanitized. Usually there's still food stuck between the prongs. I can't stand it.

25   If your not playing games then why are you ignoring me ive tried to call like 5 times

26   im not ignoring you I was just trying to write please calm down

My phone pings. Jason.[27]

I text him back.[28]

I go back to the forks, searching for something clean to eat with.

"Excuse me, ma'am, you can't touch all the silverware. It's unsanitary."

It's the manic pixie. Why does she hate me?

"Oh, sorry ...."

I'm searching for something to say, something that is neither insulting nor incriminating.

For reasons I can't put words to, I want her to like me.

My eyes dart, avoiding her face. Her beauty makes me blush. I look over her shoulders.

I see the woman in the pink sweater.

I see her take the container of my country fried seitan into her hands.

I watch her remove the lid of the to-go container.

I watch as a little puff of steam billows from the bowl and borders her face.

I watch her begin eating.

What the actual fuck?

My phone rings.

Jason. I can't.

I look at the manic-pixie girl. Her chin is speckled with acne scars where her foundation has been rubbed away. Her bangs cling to her forehead from sweat. Her eyes are dark against her pale Zooey Deschanel skin. She is so exhausted. I want to pull her into me, to let her rest her head on my shoulder.

I want to scream at her.

I don't want to cry in a restaurant.

My side starts to pulse now, a wave of heat throbs up and down my body, from my right abdomen to my upper thigh.

My legs feel empty.

Not right now.

I push through the hoard of people and leave the restaurant.

A breeze.

There are people out here, too.

They are staring at me.

Focus.

---

27   Bullshit you always do this you are being a major fucking bitch right now

28   dont call me a bitch

Breathe.

It's the golden hour. The sidewalk glows in a medium amber. The air clings to every particle of bright dust and pollen. I turn away from the sun, away from the restaurant.

My phone pings. Mom.[29]

I can't.

Breathe.

I pull my arms up into the sky above me. My chest feels full and heavy.

Breathe.

The pain is deeper now.

On a scale of 1-10.

6?

8?

What is the right answer?

My phone rings. Kelley.

Oh god. The crack in the baseboard.

"Hello?"

"Lacey. Your psycho boyfriend is downstairs."

Jason.

"Holy shit. Kelley. I'm sorry."

"He's like screaming right now. I think he's drunk again."

"Why is he screaming?" I feel like laughing. What is wrong with me?

"I don't know. He's your boyfriend. I'm not letting him come up. If he doesn't leave, I'm calling the police."

"Don't call the police. I'll talk to him."

How does this happen?

"I can't believe you're moving in with him."

How do we love the people who hurt us?

"I feel so bad." My voice shakes.

Kelley pauses. I hold the phone away from my face so she can't hear me breathing in pain. After a few seconds, she says, "Why do you feel bad?"

"I left your croissant at the restaurant."

"What are you talking about?"

"Your croissant. It's still at my table."

Silence.

---

29   Call me please.

The day breathes in.

The day breathes out.

"You're a fucking dipshit."

I laugh, tears welling in my eyes.

"I'll get you another one, I promise."

"Just come home. But not yet. I'll text you when he's gone."

"If you call the police, he'll go to jail."

"OK, bye."

She hangs up. My chest feels lighter.

Hollow.

People walk together in pairs. No one is walking alone today. I notice them, their nearness to each other, their intimacy, but I don't feel lonely.

My side.

Six.

Five.

I need to call Mom.

Five.

I dial her number. Three rings.

"Hi, honey," she sighs.

"Hi." I can't hide the pain in my voice.

Five.

Four.

"What's wrong?"

Four.

Four.

I can handle this.

I press my fingers into the ache and arch my back.

Breathe.

"I'm fine."

"You sound awful. Talk to me."

I want someone to tell me what to do.

"Mom. Someone ate my food."

"I don't know what you are saying."

"This lady. She took my food and started eating it."

"Like at a food truck?"

"No, at a restaurant. She was sitting beside me. She had her own food, but then she started eating mine."

"I guess she was hungry."

"I guess."

Someday I'll know what to do. When the world destroys itself, I won't be a part of it. I'll be somewhere else. I'll make art, and I'll be somewhere else. I'll only love the people who love me back, and I'll turn that love into art.

"I'm sorry I brought up Dad."

Four.

Four.

Three.

"Honey, it's fine. I get it. I still think about him sometimes."

"I shouldn't have brought him up."

"You're fine."

People together walk on the amber asphalt. I am alone.

I lean against a building and close my eyes.

"How was your day?" I ask.

Please tell me what to do.

The night after my stay in the hospital, Jason filled a bottle with hot water and pulled out every blanket in my apartment.

"If it's my appendix, heat might make it rupture."

"It's not your appendix."

He spread the blankets over me, one by one my while I pressed the bottle into my stomach.

I felt warm and grounded, and the weight of all the blankets made it difficult to move, which was oddly comforting.

He turned off the lights and lay next to me in bed.

"You should have called me when you were in the hospital. I would have come to see you."

"I wish I had. I was so scared."

"Listen, you are the only good thing in my life. You are the only reason I'm still alive. If something were to happen to you."

I let his words sit in the air between us and thought about the dark, how quickly it eats up everything in the room. I turned to face him, but my eyes hadn't adjusted. His face was a shadow, an abstract blur.

"Don't ever leave me."

"I never will."

Mary Christine Delea

John Steinbeck Delivers My Mail

and he is a noun, mastering sea shanties,
as I verb around all day, drifting without direction.
He slides letters to me like a small wave breaking—
a sharp smack on my back. Then caresses.

We are landlocked, both missing
a coast—he his West Coast tidal pools,
me the miracle of East Coast seaglass and shells—
and we ache for mail that
smells of salt and seaweed. People ship
me boxes of nautical adverbs,
but it's not enough. Only Steinbeck pausing

at my front door, smelling of Old Spice
and burning whale oil lamps, as he maneuvers
mail through the slot, every day,
as consistently as the tides. Then he crosses
southerly to the house next door.

I stare at his thinning sandy hair,
its spacing an adjective,
and our sorrow, an exclamation, washes over me.
This man of letters understands my need
for nautical grammar and how I stay
unmoored, even with an address.
I am a dependent clause:
dry, alone, fragmented.

Gale Acuff

Let Me Call You

In Sunday School today I fell asleep
and Jesus came to me in my quick dream
and told me that I won't be going to
hell because He knows how hard it will be
for me to miss Miss Hooker there, she'll be
up in heaven of course, she's my Sunday
school teacher, so as I was thanking Him
Miss Hooker woke me up, she had one hand
on my shoulder and shrugging it for me
as I was saying *I love you, sweetheart*,
not quite knowing where I was but knowing
all the same, the way dreams can do, and my
classmates were laughing and laughed me alert
and Miss Hooker was smiling like the full
moon, I mean, and I'd like to be him
but with Miss Hooker's smile or she could be
the moon and her smile actually mine
but anyway Miss Hooker answered me
I think that you're a sweetheart, too, Gale, and
my classmates laughed louder and louder 'til
they rattled the aluminum blinds and
metal ceiling or maybe it's plastic
of our mobile-home classroom, our church is
poor and somehow proud of it and somehow
it's OK, so then she dismissed class did

Miss Hooker and after everyone had
gone it was just the two of us just like
it will be one day in our own home, then
I asked her *What's for lunch, baby?* and then
she frowned but that's OK. My lips are sealed.

Justin Jannise

What I'm Into

Adam's apples, beards, brains.
A certain type of man you see on trains
between Connecticut and New York:
solid muscle, a starched white shirt.

Dilfs. Doctors. Dimples. Every man I've seen
offer his arm to someone crossing the street.
Fags—those who've reclaimed the word
with piercings, tattoos, unruly curls

sprouting from their heads, pits, chests, thighs.
Ghosts of long-dead poets, the sad eyes
of young Robert (Frost, Hayden, Lowell)
appearing, now, beneath the charcoal

brow of the barista. Men who make coffee, hummus, bread.
The weight of a body on the edge of the bed.
Megawatt smiles, goldspinning hips.
Intellectuals, lifeguards, motorcyclists with ripped

jeans, flabby abs, a bone to pick with the capitalist
regime. No mansplainers. No racists.
Nobody already romantically attached.
Anyone reading who thinks there's a chance.

Clayton Adam Clark

Algal Bloom

Lake of the Ozarks, Missouri

The planktonic algae in hot water
      rich in runoff bred then died and took

the dissolved oxygen with them, surfacing
      the larger crappie and walleye in record

fish kills, including in the next cove over,
      which summoned possums and raccoons, the heedful

turkey vultures down to the water's edge,
      so everyone's advised to keep their dogs

indoors where the AC runs on hydroelectric
      since all of this was river before the dam,

but it's still so hot and the conservation
      department called the asphyxiated fish

a natural phenomenon, although
      the die-off came early this summer, so

down on the dock we put on sunscreen even
      if we don't burn like we used to, and maybe

because we want to believe this backed-up river
      isn't just anyone's, when a thirty-footer

Algal Bloom

roars past, channel bound and far too near
   the buoys, sploshing green water on our dock,

we rise from pressure-treated planks and just
   how our fathers used to, we are yelling

No wake, No wake, and the driver, he waves back.

John McNally

Catch and Release

With the morning's sour breath still ripe in his mouth, Jason thought he could taste a certain cheese sandwich he'd eaten as a child, but the memory, like a dying bulb, flickered and then blinked out before he could remember what kind of sandwich it had been or where he'd eaten it. Lately, cryptic memories swam up to him through senses he normally paid little attention to, as when he touched the folded tablecloth at a garage sale last weekend and remembered standing in an aisle of fabrics with his mother at So-Fro while she examined a bolt with geometric designs, so bored he thought he might start crying at the sight of all the triangles and circles and squares, until he discovered the display of plastic eyes, the kind you'd find on a teddy bear, with black pupils that moved when you shook them. The eyes, sold by the hundreds, came in all sizes. When he asked his mother if she would buy him a box of extra-large eyes and she told him no, he wished something terrible would happen to her. His rage was often disproportionate to the moment, as was his love, but those days were all so long ago, the sudden memory of the white-hot anger he felt toward his mother both frightened and saddened him. His mother had been dead a dozen years now.

Jason knew that a blow to the head sometimes caused vivid but fleeting memories to come swirling back to a person, but he had suffered no such injury, only a vague lightheadedness that came with falling in love. Her name was Marie, and she lay in bed next to him, on her back, with her eyes shut. Jason resisted the urge to touch her, fearful of revealing his chief flaw as a boyfriend: the penchant to cling. If he could have his way, he would glue one of his palms to her flesh; he would trail her everywhere, be always on her heels—but he knew that this was an ugly way to behave, and it had driven away more than one girlfriend. What he saw as devotion often came across as pathetic desperation.

Marie had fallen asleep during *River of No Return*, a movie starring Robert Mitchum and Marilyn Monroe. During the filming, Monroe had nearly drowned. She'd worn waders to protect her costume, but when she slipped and fell into the river, the waders filled with water, pulling her under. Jason had paused the DVD to tell this trivia to Marie, only to realize, after he'd concluded the story, that she was already asleep. Now, through the barely open bedroom window, he heard feral cats rambling across the back yard, the whispers of high grass against their fur floating up to him. They were probably returning to the storage hut, one of them carrying today's fresh kill on its dry, sandpapery tongue—a mole, most likely, though possibly a field mouse. The small rodents sometimes showed up on Jason's stoop without their heads. The cats, barely hidden in the unmowed lawn, would watch him retrieve it. He suspected this pleased them: Jason discovering their grisly gift, even though the fresh corpse always went straight into a Ziplock baggie and then into a much larger Hefty trash bag full of litter and leaves. Four months ago, he had begun feeding one stray cat. Now he had six—two adults and four kittens. Half the cats were black, the other half tigers.

"What are you thinking?" Marie asked. The TV still glowed, though nothing was playing.

"You're awake," Jason said.

Marie nodded. She was spooky that way. You'd think she was sound asleep, but then she'd open her eyes and ask you a question. Jason was about to tell her what he was thinking, but Marie shut her eyes again, as if the conversation had already come to an end.

Jason knew why he loved her. It was a simple thing, really. He felt he'd known her his entire life, or at least since they were children, even though they'd met only six weeks ago in the cafeteria near campus. In the short time they'd been together, Jason had told her things about himself he had admitted to no one, like the time he had been so angry with his mother for not buying him a toy he had wanted, he took his father's .38 caliber handgun from the banker's box inside the broom closet and pointed it at her. He was only six and was probably imitating behavior he had seen on TV, but even now, all these years later, the thought of what he'd done caused his stomach to cramp up. What if the gun had been loaded? What if he had pulled the trigger? His father had come up behind him and quickly snatched the gun away, and Jason had been sent to his room for the night without dinner. After the incident, the gun had been moved to a more secure hiding place, and no one ever mentioned what had happened, but it was one of a handful of episodes that still weighed on Jason.

For reasons Jason was unable to pinpoint, he couldn't stop talking when he was around Marie. He'd never felt this way around anyone before, and it was a relief to unload some of the things he'd been carrying around since childhood.

Marie, on the other hand, remained silent, but it wasn't a judgmental silence. She was a vessel, taking in all that Jason had to offer. The things she told him in return were sparse and unambiguous: She preferred spring to fall; her favorite food was Italian; she needed a new car but couldn't afford one just now; she'd never been married and didn't want children.

"They're not for me," she had said, as though they had been talking about a style of shoe.

Marie opened her eyes again now, as eerily as before.

"I know you're thinking something," she said. "I can feel it." Staring at the ceiling, her gaze seemingly trained on a crack in the plaster that Jason had failed to notice until this very second, she said, "Tell me your secrets."

"I'm thinking about that missing dog. Have you seen the signs?"

She nodded.

Jason said, "I'd really like to look for her."

"Now?" Marie asked.

"If you don't mind," Jason said.

It was three in the morning by the time they left the house, each holding a flashlight. The dog's name was Molly, but they didn't call out for her. Instead, they listened for the jingle of a collar, looked for the suspect shadow behind hedges.

After an hour of creeping through strangers' yards, crouching to peer dog level, Marie said, "We'll look again tomorrow."

Jason wanted to take hold of Marie and not let go. He'd never been this attracted to anyone he'd ever dated or longed for. The pull was gravitational. Unable to hold out any longer, Jason reached over and touched Marie's arm, revealing in one swift and impetuous gesture more than he'd meant to.

(

Jason was an assistant professor of history at the state university in southern Illinois near where he'd grown up, a part of the country he had tried but failed to escape from. His area of research was the Japanese internment camps during World War II—or, more specifically, the phenomenon of America's collective amnesia in the aftermath of a crime against humanity. For the six years of work toward his Ph.D., Jason had burrowed into his subject, interviewing over a dozen survivors—mostly men and women who had been children when their families were forced to move to a camp but also a few who had been young adults at the time.

Now in his sixth year at the university—his tenure year—Jason had failed to publish a book. In fact, he hadn't so much as unboxed his dissertation during his time at State, publishing only one essay in a scholarly journal and two book reviews. A pittance.

Though he went through the motions for his tenure review, allowing senior faculty to observe his classes and interview his students, Jason braced himself for the inevitable outcome—that he would be let go. Secretly, he hoped the department would deny him tenure. After all that he'd put himself through—two advanced degrees and a good tenure-track position at a research university—Jason wasn't sure that this was how he wanted to spend his life. To be denied tenure might just be the best possible outcome he could hope for.

At home, in his back yard, he sat in a lawn chair and watched the feral cats. He held a cup full of Purina Cat Chow and shook it, hoping to lure one of them over, but they remained at the entrance of the outbuilding, the adults and the kittens, unmoved by the bribe. When he spoke to them, they shut their eyes, as if the sound of his voice soothed them. Jason invested all of his hope in their response, certain that one day the cats would come close enough for him to pet them.

"Look at you," Marie said. "Keeping a watchful eye on your brood."

Jason hadn't heard Marie's car, hadn't heard her footsteps. She was as quiet as the cats—quieter. In the short time they'd been together, they'd already fallen into a routine: Marie would show up after he came home from campus; they'd go for a walk together, searching for the lost dog; Jason would fix them something to eat while Marie napped; they'd make love as the food simmered; they'd eat; they'd watch TV;

they'd fall asleep together on Jason's bed. At some point in the night, however, Marie would slip away, returning to her own apartment. He wasn't sure where she lived or what she did. When they had first met at a gallery during the city's annual art walk, she had said, "If we're going to make this relationship work, save any boring questions you have for another girl." He took her words to heart.

"You can stay all night, you know," Jason had told her more than once.

Each time, Marie nodded but didn't say anything. When he was younger, Jason might have described Marie to his friends as spooky, the sort of girl you were more likely to keep your distance from than date. And yet now, as he and Marie took their daily walk together, Jason strategized on how to keep this odd, mysterious woman in his life.

"Look," she said. "A possum."

A dead possum lay in the road, its stiff fur moving to the ebb and flow of the breeze.

"You're running out of time," she whispered.

"Who?"

"You," she said.

"For what?"

"To domesticate the kittens," she said. "It's a small window before they turn feral for good."

"How long do you think?" he asked.

Marie shrugged. "A couple of weeks? A month?" She crouched and placed her palm on the body of the possum. "Still warm," she said.

Jason spent Friday morning on campus reading up on how to domesticate feral kittens. Marie was right: Time *was* of the essence. Once a cat had crossed over, it would not only become difficult to domesticate, it might prove to be deadly to the cat, which was likely to run continuously in a panic or ram its head into doors or walls, trying to escape.

From his research, Jason also discovered that many cities, in an attempt to decrease the feral cat populations, had catch-and-release programs. A person could sign up for a humane trap designed to do no harm to the animal. Once trapped, the cat would be taken to the catch-and-release center where, along with dozens of other cats, it would be spayed and neutered by veterinarians who had donated their spare time to the cause. The cat would be given appropriate shots and, while still anesthetized, receive a light grooming. Later that day, the cat could be retrieved, kept in a safe place overnight, like a garage or basement, and then released the next morning or afternoon so that it could return to its colony. During his office hours, Jason made a few phone calls, only to discover that no such program existed in his town, or, for that matter, in any nearby town.

After wrapping up his Survey of Twentieth-Century American History course, Jason decided to ask a student who volunteered at the local animal shelter if he could borrow one of their traps. Her name was Lucy, and she was disconcertingly covered from her neck on down with tattoos of vines and other foliage.

"I don't think I'm supposed to loan them out," she said, but then she smiled. In her bottom lip alone were three silver hoop earrings. "Give me an 'A'?" she asked. She was a senior, knocking out a general studies class that she should have taken two years ago, her last gen ed requirement.

Jason smiled and said, "We'll see."

They arranged to meet in the Barnes & Noble parking lot on Saturday morning, and Lucy, in a moment of uncharacteristic formality, offered an ivy-twined hand for Jason to shake. Although the sensation of her soft palm didn't match the gnarled and vine-laced flesh, there was something about the incongruity of what he saw as opposed to how it felt that was strangely familiar to him. He couldn't place the memory, but a feeling of melancholy came over him that was so intense, it disturbed him.

"Good enough," Jason said, nodding, turning away.

Jason had met Marie at art walk when the two of them were standing together and studying a modern day take on the famous dogs-playing-poker paintings. In this version, the dogs were sitting side by side at a bar and playing video poker.

"Jesus, that's depressing," Jason had said, and when he turned to Marie, he saw that she was crying. He was about to speak when Marie turned to him and said, "If we're going to make this relationship work, please save any boring questions you have for another girl."

The cafeteria where they ended up after visiting five more galleries together was the last of its kind in town, offering meat loaf for dinner, vegetables ladled up from silver tubs by old women wearing hairnets, and lime Jell-O desserts with dollops of whipped cream on top—an entire meal for less than five dollars. The building that housed the cafeteria was slated to be demolished in two months, at the end of the fall semester, to make way for a new twenty-four-hour fitness center. Marie tried to pay for her food with a credit card when the cashier, who may well have been ninety, pointed to the "cash only" sign.

Jason found it charming that the place had refused to budge out of the 1950s, let alone into the twenty-first century, but he also knew that this was likely the reason for its demise. Modernize or die, he thought.

Marie said, "Well, then. I guess I need to return it."

Jason stepped up and offered to pay for her meal, but the only way Marie would accept his generosity was if he gave her his address.

"I don't like to owe anyone anything," she said. "And I'd like to keep it that way."

"Fair enough," Jason said, and in a rare moment of confidence, he added his phone number below his address.

Jason marveled at the randomness of their meeting. He imagined a time in their future—five, ten years from now—when he could tell this story to their friends in a way that might sound apocryphal, like the 1959 meeting of Marilyn Monroe and Nikita Khrushchev, about which Marilyn had said, "He looked at me the way a man looks at a woman."

On their dusk-lit search for the lost dog, Jason and Marie passed the dead possum again, but this time they didn't stop.

"Civilized cities pick up dead animals," Marie said. "They don't just leave them rotting on the road."

"Key word," Jason said. "*Civilized.*" He turned to Marie, hoping to catch her smiling at him, but her eyes were wet and her nose was starting to run. "I'll call the city," Jason said. "On Monday."

After it had gotten dark, they sat in lawn chairs inside the circle of light from the street lamp and watched the ferals.

"They're coming closer," Jason said. "Look."

The kittens shortened their distance between the outbuildings and where Jason sat by half, while the bigger cats hung back, fastidiously licking their front paws. The kittens sat and stretched in the grass but refused to come any closer. Jason shook the cup of food again, trying to entice them, but Marie took hold of his wrist and made him stop.

"That's as close as they want to come," she said. "Be happy." She turned to him and forced a smile, and there was something about the way the streetlamp lit up her face, along with her expression, that convinced Jason that he had in fact once known her, but he still couldn't place when or where, and he was too afraid to ask.

Jason leaned forward and shook the cup again.

It had come to Jason in the middle of the night. Lori Jenkins. That's who Marie was, who she really was: the once-missing girl, now a woman, from his childhood. The girl from the telephone-pole flyers. The girl everyone thought had died but had come back. The miracle girl.

That was twenty-five years ago, but it was her. It was Lori. She had changed her name to Marie. She lay beside him now, asleep, remaining in his bed longer than she had ever stayed since they'd begun seeing each other. He wondered what other secrets were inside her head. He wondered what a person who carried with her such a profoundly disturbing past was capable of.

Jason tried falling back to sleep, but it wasn't until an hour before his cell phone's alarm clock was to begin chirping that he finally drifted off. When he woke up an hour later, Marie was gone. It was as though a symbiotic relationship existed between Jason's state of unconsciousness and Marie's ability to flee, and in order for one to wax, the other needed to wane.

There wasn't much information about Lori Jenkins' abduction on the Internet—nothing, at least, that he didn't already know. It had happened before Amber Alerts went into effect, before the national media became obsessed with missing children to boost their ratings. Furthermore, it had happened in southern Illinois, a part of the country few people cared about.

Jason searched for information about abductions, and what he learned was that girls Marie's age—the age she had been when she had been kidnapped—were three times more likely than boys to be victims, and that the captor was almost always a man with a history of sexual misconduct, violence, and substance abuse. Not surprisingly, the main reason for abduction was sex.

Lucy was already in the parking lot now, sitting in an old hatchback and sipping from a thermos. Her car was plastered with a few dozen bumper stickers, all with a left-wing bent, a few radically so, and when Lucy stepped out of the car wearing a tank top that revealed even more tattooed leaves and prickly vines, Jason wondered what it was about Lucy—what dark compulsion—that kept her from letting something simply be.

"Well, hell-*looooo*, professor!" Marie said to Jason before they stepped out of Jason's car. Marie had texted earlier to say that she would go with him to Barnes & Noble to pick up the trap from Lucy. For reasons Jason couldn't put his finger on, he really wanted to come alone but couldn't think of a reason for asking Marie not to join him, but now he knew why he had felt as he did as he sensed a wordless and unnecessary rivalry brewing between two women who had only just met.

"Lucy?" Jason said. "This is Marie. Marie; Lucy."

Lucy smiled at Marie, then glanced toward Jason, as if to say, *So this is who you're having sex with.* He could tell that something curious pulsed behind her eyes by the extra-deep breath she took and the way her eyebrows were raised. She walked around to the rear of the car and popped the hatch.

"Here it is," she said. "I'll need it back by Monday, though. I didn't tell anyone I took it."

"Will do," Jason said. "I appreciate it."

Lucy gave Marie one last once-over before getting into her car and driving away.

On their way home, Marie said, "She was disappointed you weren't alone."

Jason laughed.

"What I mean," Marie said, "is that she probably thought she was special because you'd asked her for a favor."

"OK," Jason said, smiling.

Marie said, "Don't patronize me."

"Don't *what?*" Jason asked. He couldn't help it—he laughed again. "I'm not. I swear."

"Let me out," Marie said.

"Are you kidding me?"

"No," Marie said. "Let me out or I'll scream."

Jason pulled over to the side of the road. Marie opened the door and got out. She walked ahead of the car without looking back. Jason sat there, unable to think of what to say or do. He finally leaned over and shut the door, then drove away, passing her without slowing down.

In moments like these, when he knew that pleading would result in a deeper retreat, he felt himself trying to stay afloat but being pulled under no matter what he did, whether he fought or relaxed.

"God damn it," Jason said and hit the steering wheel with his palm. "Christ," he said. "Christ almighty."

Last week, Jason had stocked up on a variety of Chef Boyardee and Franco-American canned foods for lunches, if only because the sight of their labels brought to mind summer nights in childhood when trucks crept up and down side streets, misting the air with insecticide, or Sunday afternoons when there was nothing to do but watch black-and-white movies or World Wide Wrestling.

Back home with the humane trap, alone, Jason heated up a can of ravioli, stirring the pot like a witch in *Macbeth*. The old familiar smell—a smell from childhood—rose up to him. Beginning in the fifth grade, Jason started seeing Lori Jenkins' flyers around town, everywhere. The photo on the flier was a headshot of a nine-year-old girl with wind-swept hair—a photo chosen, he suspected, so that everyone could get a good look at her face. Above her photo was one word: MISSING. She lived two towns over from Jason, and she had been abducted, according to the flier, on the same day as his tenth birthday. The flier hung in the window of every store in town, on the bulletin board of Safeway's breezeway between the two sets of automatic doors, and on at least one telephone pole for every block.

Jason fell in love with Lori Jenkins that year, as he'd fallen in love with so many other girls when he was ten, but his love for her was more profound as he imagined being the one who found her walking with a stranger; he imagined how she would give him a look that said "Help me" or "I'm not supposed to be with this person," and he imagined wrestling her away from danger. He would free her. And because he had saved her, she would fall in love with him in return.

Over the two years that she had been missing, the flyers remained up, although the ones in the storefront windows turned yellow from the sun, and the ink on the ones on the telephone poles blurred from the rain and snow. The flier on the Safeway bulletin board stayed intact but would get covered over with fliers for used boats or guitar lessons, until someone—Jason never knew who—repositioned Lori's flier, returning it front and center. At the end of two years, the flier was a constellation of holes.

Jason eventually came to believe, like so many others, that Lori would never be found, or if she was found, she wouldn't be alive, but one afternoon in the fall, when all the town's children were in school, a girl was discovered standing in the middle of a busy intersection. She was wearing a sheer pink nightgown, no shoes or socks, and her fingernails and toenails were all painted the same shade of red as her lipstick. It was Lori Jenkins. She was eleven years old, and she was alive.

"A miracle," Jason's homeroom teacher, Mrs. Hammond, said the next day. "Like Jesus resurrected."

Marie returned two days later as Jason was busy fixing the trap. He had spooned out canned tuna onto a paper plate and set it behind the raised piece of sheet metal that was to trigger the cage to shut as soon as a cat stepped on it.

"I don't want to talk about it," Marie said.

"OK," Jason said, pulling the lever that set the trap. "We won't."

Marie sat down next to him and said, "Are they coming closer?"

Jason shook his head. "I sense a setback," he said.

"Be patient," Marie said.

Jason nodded, but he wasn't sure he had ever been that patient. His neediness was like an addiction that needed feeding. For Marie's sake, he nodded. He resisted the urge to pick up the cup of food and shake it, but the entire time he remained there, it was the only thing he could think about, and it took all his willpower not to do it.

On Sunday, the cats were nowhere to be seen. The trap was empty. Jason's heart sped up at what he feared—that the cats had crossed over to the other side, and that no matter what Jason did or what he offered them now, they would never cross back. The window for domesticating them had slammed shut.

Marie drove over to console him.

"Let's go for a walk," she said.

The first few minutes of the walk were spent in silence. Neither mentioned the cats or even the missing dog. Jason knew that Marie was comfortable without words, but Jason wasn't. Even in class, whenever Jason asked his students a question, he couldn't bear the silence for longer than a few seconds before he offered an answer, even though he knew that he was supposed to let the silence linger until someone finally, mercifully spoke up. The one time he forced himself to remain silent, Lucy had stared at him with great sympathy, the way a person looks at someone who has lost a beloved pet.

"I did everything by the book," Jason told Marie.

Marie said, "You should never think that intellect is superior to instinct. Instinct will always win."

Marie was only making an observation, but the way she put it made Jason feel defensive. Would she have said that to him if he wasn't a professor? Was it a slight against his academic background, about which he had his own misgivings?

Marie paused at the site of the dead possum. The possum had been run over so many times, it was nothing but fur and concrete now. Someone who had not been tracking the dead animal's decay would have had no idea what they were looking at. It looked as though the road itself had begun to sprout a patch of fur.

The sight of the indiscernible possum brought to mind all those times Jason rode his bike in grade school past dead animals, so many dead animals that he became immune to the sight of them, unless it was a dog or a cat, in which case he would stop his bike, get off, and check for a collar. If there was a collar and a tag identifying the owner, he would find the owner's house and, like a miniature soldier during wartime, deliver the unfortunate news of the death to the person who answered the door. Often, the response was anger or disbelief. Sometimes, it would be laughter, as though his presence were part of a larger gag orchestrated by friends. Occasionally, the response was hysteria, and Jason would watch as his existence to the bereaved disappeared entirely in the face of grief. More than one grade-school teacher had told his mother that he tried too hard.

"He needs to temper his desires," Mrs. Hammond had told his mother during a parent/teacher conference, and his mother had reported this news afterward without any elaboration, the way another parent might have said, "Do your homework on time."

"I'm calling the city tomorrow," Marie said now.

Jason said, "I'm not really sure what they can do at this point."

"It's not what they could do," Marie said. "It's what they should have done."

Two blocks in the distance, Jason thought he saw one of the black ferals crossing the street, but he decided not to mention it to Marie, who was busy taking photos of the possum, using her foot to provide scale for someone who might desire perspective.

☾

When Jason was eleven, his mother sat across from him while he ate a grilled-cheese sandwich that she had made for him. The cheese was pimento, a word he normally liked to repeat over and over until it sounded like the strangest word that had ever existed. The more he said it, the more devoid of meaning the word became. "Pimento!" he would say. "Pimento! Pimento!" But on that day, he was unnerved by his mother silently watching him, so he ate his sandwich slowly, trying not to finish it in two or three large bites, as was his way.

"I found this hidden inside a magazine in your room," his mother finally said, revealing a folded sheet of paper. He knew before she opened it what she was holding: a flier for Lori Jenkins. But it wasn't just a flier of her. He had pasted a photo of himself next to her photo, and he had drawn hearts around the two heads. He had also drawn bodies onto the two heads, but the bodies were not wearing any clothes.

Jason stared down at the sandwich in his hands, which could have been someone else's hands holding someone else's sandwich. Then he stared beyond them to the tablecloth with the geometric designs, and he tried to lose himself in the various triangles and circles and squares, but the designs only reminded him of other vague memories of impatience and boredom. He tasted cheese and acid at the back of his throat.

"This isn't healthy," his mother said. "This poor girl. This poor, poor girl. Her parents are worried to death, and you're ... I don't even *know* what you're doing. It's not right, though."

Jason nodded. He knew, even as he defamed the flier, that what he was doing wasn't right, but it made him happy to think about the two of them together, and absent the actual Lori Jenkins herself, the flier was the closest thing he had to being with this girl he loved.

His mother tore up the flier and stuffed it in the garbage. When she was done, she said, "I won't tell your father." She paused. She stared at him, as though he were a stranger. "This time," she warned.

The next day, Jason found another flier of Lori on a telephone pole, one of the newer flyers that hadn't yet begun to suffer from the elements. He removed it, folded it, and tucked it away. At home, he lifted from his parents' room a framed photo of himself from the third grade. He detached the backing, pressed the folded flier against the back of the glossy eight-by-ten, and then refastened the backing. He returned the frame exactly as he had found it.

It wasn't until his mother had died and his father had moved a thousand miles away that Jason, going through the things his father had left behind, remembered what was hidden inside the frame, and when he removed it and unfolded it, the sight of Lori Jenkins resurrected a host of complicated feelings that he had thought had long vanished from his life—namely, what it was like to fall in love with the specter of a person instead of the person herself.

That night, in bed in the dark, when Marie opened her eyes and said, "I know you're thinking something," Jason replied, "I am."

"Tell me," Marie said.

"I wonder where all the missing dogs go," Jason said. "The ones that survive. I'm sure some are taken in by strangers, but others probably roam in packs. When I first moved into the house, there was a note under a rock at the end of my driveway. It said, 'Beware. A pack of dogs is loose.' That's all it said. I looked up and saw that everyone on the street also had a note pinned to the ground with a rock. Imagine. Someone had taken the time to do that."

"Did you ever see the pack of dogs?" Marie asked.

"I didn't," Jason said. "No." He paused before pushing on. "When I was a child," he said, "I fell in love with a girl I had never met."

"A lot of boys do," Marie said. "They fall in love with women they see on TV shows."

"It wasn't like that," Jason said. He wasn't sure if he should continue, but he was afraid if he stopped now, she would become angry with him. He said, "She was a missing girl. Her flier was everywhere." He took a deep breath and held it. He listened for a response from Marie, but there was none. He said, "Her name was Lori Jenkins, and she'd been abducted. For two years, I stared at her flier and wondered what she was like. I wondered if she was still alive." Jason wanted to impress upon her the depth of his love for this girl whom he had never met, so he said, "I wanted to be the one who found her. I wanted to be her hero."

"I see," Marie said.

"Do you?" he asked. "Because it doesn't put me in a good light. I think the other children thought I was—what's the best word?—peculiar. Do you think I'm peculiar?" he asked.

"Not at all," Marie said.

"Really?" He was relieved to hear her say this.

Marie said, "I think you're like everyone else."

"Oh," he said. "OK then."

"I don't mean that in a bad way," Marie said. "Most people aren't unique."

Jason turned onto his side so that his back faced her. He brought his knees closer to his chest and tucked his arm under his head.

"Don't be that way," Marie said, but Jason couldn't help himself. He knew that he was sulking, and his behavior embarrassed him, but he couldn't help it. He offered up his emotions the way a child might.

"I'm tired," he said, finally. "That's all."

For the first time, Marie spooned behind him, holding him tight, but when Jason awoke only a few hours later, she was already gone.

In the morning, Jason sent Marie a text to apologize, but he received an auto-reply that his message couldn't be delivered. He called her, but all his calls went straight to voicemail. He never knew where she lived, so going to her place wasn't an option, and he didn't know where she worked. He sat at his kitchen table, stirring his coffee, thinking how, after all these years, he had found the missing girl, but now that she had disappeared, he knew he would never find her again. It was a statistical improbability.

Fall bled into winter and then into spring. To Jason's surprise, he was granted tenure. A colleague came by his office to shake his hand and said, "I guess this is it then. I guess this is where you'll die." He said it jokingly, but Jason felt ill at the thought. The next year, Jason was on committees to recommend or deny tenure to his junior colleagues, and he envied their freedom, ever-diminishing though it was. "Leave before it's too late," he wanted to warn them.

A year had come and gone without a word from Marie. As he had predicted, she was gone forever. That fall, he and Lucy were living together. She was no longer a student, having graduated the previous May. He knew what his colleagues would think if they ever found out, but it wasn't like that. She was renting a spare room from him while she figured out her next move. It was a good arrangement for both of them. They were roommates, even though she was younger than him by a dozen years, had more energy, more interests, and often referenced celebrities and cultural phenomena he didn't know. But she had never seen a Marilyn Monroe movie, and she did not know who Nikita Khrushchev was. He had told her the story of their unlikely meeting, but he left out what Marilyn, who had found the Soviet premier repugnant, had said to her maid afterward, "He squeezed my hand for so long and hard that I thought he would break it. I guess it was better than having to kiss him."

On the night of the first snowfall of the season, they stood together in the back yard. She had removed the earrings from her lip. Her winter coat and gloves covered the inked skin. In this light and under these circumstances, she looked unlike anyone he had ever met. He imagined she was someone from his future, someone he would meet and fall in love with one day. A feral cat—perhaps one of the ferals he had hoped to lure to him last year—had given birth to five kittens, and the kittens were in the old storage hut next to their mother. They occasionally made mewing sounds—squeaks, mostly—but their eyes were still sealed shut.

Lucy took a flier from her pocket and said, "I found this in the house." As she unfolded it, Jason expected it to be a flier for Lori Jenkins. He still had one tucked away behind his third-grade photo, but how could Lucy have found it? When she handed it over, Jason realized that it was the flier for the missing dog.

"Did they ever find it?" Lucy asked.

Jason shook his head.

"Poor fella," Lucy said. She took his hand in her gloved hand and said, "You must be cold."

"A little," Jason said.

Lucy said, "We'll have better luck catching these ones. I have cat-catching skills heretofore unseen in this back yard." She smiled up at him. She often spoke using formal diction in an ironic way. It was one of the things Jason liked about her.

Beyond the hut, three back yards down from his, stood a woman he thought might have been Marie—something about her posture suggested so—but when the woman turned to face Jason, he saw that it was the new neighbor. He remembered now seeing a moving truck the night before while on his walk, its front tire parked over where the possum had once been. They had a dog, too, a big old St. Bernard, and Jason hoped that if he ever appeared on his new neighbor's doorstep, he would be bringing good news in the form of a happy dog that had only gotten loose. Jason waved, and the neighbor returned the gesture. Lucy, whose view of the neighbor was obstructed by the hut, said, "They'll wave back when their eyes open. Until then—patience, my dear man. Patience."

Contributors' Notes

Gale Acuff has had poetry published in *Ascent, Chiron Review, McNeese Review, Florida Review, South Carolina Review, Carolina Quarterly, South Dakota Review*, and other journals. He has authored three books of poetry: *Buffalo Nickel* (BrickHouse Press, 2004), *The Weight of the World* (BrickHouse, 2006), and *The Story of My Lives* (BrickHouse, 2008).

Notwithstanding his spare output, with only two volumes of poetry, *Diary of House Arrest* (2003) and *Blue Bicycle* (2015), **Hasan Alizadeh** (b. 1947, Mashhad, Iran) has left a poetic signature on modern Persian poetry distinguished by lyricism and colloquialism. Alizadeh embarked on a literary career initially as a short-story writer and cultivated his writing talents alongside the notable Iranian novelists Reza Daneshvar and Ghazaleh Alizadeh in the literary circle that developed in their hometown of Mashhad. Since the early 1990s, Alizadeh has focused mostly on poetry. In Alizadeh's poems, a labyrinthine memory, structured by the intricate architecture of old Iranian bazaars and mosques, continually revises itself in spontaneous narrations of love and death.

Garrett Ashley's work has appeared in *Sonora Review, Yemassee, Red Rock Review*, and *SmokeLong Quarterly*, among other places. He is a doctoral candidate in fiction at the University of Southern Mississippi.

Kathryn M. Barber grew up in the mountains that follow the Tennessee/Virginia state line, near the Carter Fold. She holds an MA in English literature from Mississippi State University and an MFA in fiction from the University of North Carolina Wilmington. Recently, she said farewell to the beaches of North Carolina and returned to

Starkville, Mississippi, where she teaches composition and creative writing at Mississippi State. She appears on the mastheads of *Ecotone*, *Southern Humanities Review*, and *Press Pause Press*.

Walter Bargen has published twenty-three books of poetry. Recent books include *Until Next Time* (Singing Bone Press, 2019), *My Other Mother's Red Mercedes* (Lamar University Press, 2018), and *Too Quick for the Living* (Moon City Press, 2017). His awards include a National Endowment for the Arts Fellowship, a Chester H. Jones Foundation Award, and the William Rockhill Nelson Award. He was appointed the first poet laureate of Missouri (2008-2009). www.walterbargen.com.

Melissa Benton Barker grew up in San Francisco and in Sasebo, Japan. She currently lives in Ohio with her family. Her work appears in *Wigleaf, Vestal Review, SmokeLong Quarterly*, and elsewhere. She has been nominated for Best of the Net and for the Pushcart Prize. Her chapbook, *Elemental*, was a semifinalist in the annual Tar Open Chapbook competition at *The Atlas Review*.

Charli Barnes is a freelance illustrator and graphic designer and is creative director for Christian County Library in southwest Missouri. She has a BFA in graphic design and illustration from Missouri State University and currently resides in Springfield. Work can be found online at www.charcoal.studio.

Hanna Bartels is an MFA candidate at Queens University of Charlotte, where she is fiction co-editor of *Qu Literary Magazine*, and received her BA in creative writing from Northwestern University. Her fiction is forthcoming in *The Sun*.

J.A. Bernstein is the author of a novel, *Rachel's Tomb* (New Issues, 2019), which won the AWP Award Series and Hackney Prizes, and a chapbook, *Desert Castles* (Southern Indiana Review, 2019), which won the Wilhelmus Prize. His stories, poems, and essays have appeared in about seventy-five journals and anthologies, including *Shenandoah, Boston Review, Chicago Quarterly, Lumina*, and *Kenyon Review Online*, and won the Gunyon Prize at *Crab Orchard Review*.

B.J. Best is the author of three books and four chapbooks, most recently *Yes* (Parallel Press, 2014). A fifth chapbook, *Everything About Breathing*, is forthcoming from Bent Paddle Press. He lives in Wisconsin.

Melissa Boston's poetry has appeared in *Midwestern Gothic, I-70 Review*, and others. She lives in Fayetteville, Arkansas.

Savannah Bradley is a Kansas City-based poet and graduate student in the M.F.A program at University of Missouri- Kansas City. Bradley is the recipient of the Durwood fellowship at UMKC and has also had work in *Bear Review* and *Barrow Street*.

A.M. Brant's poems have appeared in *Salt Hill Journal, Blue Earth Review, Ninth Letter*, and elsewhere. She teaches writing at the University of Pittsburgh and women's and gender studies at Carlow University. She lives in Pittsburgh.

Jason Lee Brown is the author of the forthcoming story collection *Midwest Everyman*, the novel *Prowler: The Mad Gasser of Mattoon* (Zetabella Publishing, 2014), and the novella *Championship Run* (The Fly Came Near It, 2016). He is the editor-in-chief of *River Styx* literary magazine, co-director of the River Styx Reading Series, and series editor of *New Stories from the Midwest*.

Sarah Browning is the author of *Killing Summer* (Sibling Rivalry Press, 2017) and *Whiskey in the Garden of Eden* (The Word Works, 2007). She is co-founder and for ten years was executive director of Split This Rock. An associate fellow of the Institute for Policy Studies, she is the recipient of the 2019 Lillian E. Smith Writer-in-Service Award, as well as fellowships from the DC Commission on the Arts & Humanities, the Mesa Refuge, the Virginia Center for the Creative Arts, and the Adirondack Center for Writing. For thirteen years, Browning curated and co-hosted the Sunday Kind of Love poetry series at Busboys and Poets in Washington, DC.

Danielle Burnette's short fiction has appeared in *The Examined Life Journal, The Saturday Evening Post, PRISM International, Soundings*

Review, Lunch Ticket, and a love story anthology published by Flash: The International Short-Short Story Press.

Justin Carter is a writer and instructor in Denton, Texas. His poems appear in *The Adroit Journal, Bat City Review, The Journal, Redivider,* and *Sycamore Review.*

Clayton Adam Clark works as a public health research scientist, studies clinical mental health counseling at University of Missouri-St. Louis, and volunteers for *River Styx* magazine. *A Finitude of Skin,* published by Moon City Press last year, was his debut collection, and now he is working on his second book. In addition to *Moon City Review,* his individual poems have appeared in *Poetry Daily, The Massachusetts Review, Mid-American Review,* and elsewhere.

Mary Christine Delea's poems have appeared in *Mid-American Review, Room, New Ohio Review, Prose Poem Project, The New Guard,* and many more. Her full-length book, *The Skeleton Holding Up the Sky,* was published by Main Street Rag in 2006.

Regina DiPerna's work has been published in *Boston Review, Missouri Review, Passages North, Gulf Coast, The Cincinnati Review, Salt Hill,* and others. Her chapbook *A Map of Veins* was published in 2018 by Upper Rubber Boot Press. She lives and works in New York City.

Maggie Dove is a cross-genre Southern writer by way of south Florida. Her work has appeared or is forthcoming in *Hobart, JMWW,* and elsewhere.

Dawn Dupler's poetry can be found posted on the buses of St. Louis, on the trains of the city's MetroLink, or in journals such as *Natural Bridge, Paper Nautilus, Chiron Review, Whiskey Island Magazine,* and others. She left the field of engineering to teach English.

Taylor Fedorchak is the current poetry editor for *Puerto del Sol.* She is a second-year MFA candidate at New Mexico State University. Her work has appeared in publications including *Glass: A Journal of Poetry, Bluestem Magazine, Arkana, Gravel,* and *decomP.*

Amelia Fisher is a graduate assistant in the master's of English program at Missouri State University.

Rebecca Fishow is a writer, artist, and educator. Her work has been featured in *Quarterly West, Tin House, Joyland, The Believer, SmokeLong Quarterly, Jellyfish Review,* and other publications. Her chapbook, *The Opposite of Entropy,* was published by Proper Tales Press. She holds an MFA from Syracuse University and teaches creative writing at the Barbara Ingram School for the Arts in western Maryland. Find her at rebeccafishow.weebly.com.

Jeannine Hall Gailey served as the second poet laureate of Redmond, Washington. She's the author of five books of poetry: *Becoming the Villainess* (Steel Toe Books, 2006), *She Returns to the Floating World* (Kitsune Books, 2011), *Unexplained Fevers* (New Binary Press, 2013), *The Robot Scientist's Daughter* (Mayapple Press, 2015), and *Field Guide to the End of the World* (2016), winner of the Moon City Press Book Prize and the SFPA's Elgin Award. Her web site is www.webbish6.com. Twitter and Instagram: @webbish6.

John Gallaher's poem "Elegy for the Oil Industry" is from his forthcoming book, *Brand New Spacesuit* (BOA, 2020). Other recent poems appear in *New England Review, Poetry, Pleiades,* and others. He lives in rural Missouri and co-edits *The Laurel Review.*

Caroljean Gavin's work has appeared in places such as *Barrelhouse Online, Bending Genres, The Conium Review,* and is forthcoming from *Pithead Chapel* and *X-R-A-Y Literary Magazine.* She can be found on Twitter: @caroljeangavin.

Rebecca Ruth Gould's poems and translations have appeared in *Nimrod, Kenyon Review, Tin House, The Hudson Review, Waxwing, Wasafiri,* and *Poetry Wales.* She translates from Persian, Russian, and Georgian and has translated books such as *After Tomorrow the Days Disappear: Ghazals and Other Poems of Hasan Sijzi of Delhi* (Northwestern University Press, 2016) and *The Death of Bagrat Zakharych and Other Stories by Vazha-Pshavela* (Paper & Ink, 2019).

Madison Green is an undergraduate at Missouri State University and writes both poetry and fiction. This is her first publication.

Jennifer A. Howard teaches and edits *Passages North* in Michigan's snowy Upper Peninsula. Her collection of flash sci-fi, *You on Mars*, was published by the Cupboard Pamphlet in 2017.

Justin Jannise's work has been published in *Copper Nickel, Yale Review, Columbia Journal, New Ohio Review, The Awl*, and other places. He is the editor of *Gulf Coast*.

Christen Noel Kauffman lives in Richmond, Indiana, with her husband and two daughters and holds an MFA from Northern Michigan University. Her work can be found or is forthcoming in *Willow Springs, Booth, The Cincinnati Review, DIAGRAM*, and *The Normal School*, among others.

Danielle Kotrla is an MFA candidate at Virginia Commonwealth University. Her work can be found in *The Pinch, Pidgeonholes*, and others.

Marcia LeBeau's poems have been published in *Painted Bride Quarterly, Hiram Poetry Review, Rattle, SLANT*, and elsewhere. Her work has also appeared in *O: The Oprah Magazine*. She holds an MFA in poetry from VCFA. She recently launched the Write Space, a literary hub for co-writing, workshops, and events in the Valley Arts District of Orange, New Jersey.

Gary Leising is the author of the book *The Alp at the End of My Street* from Brick Road Poetry Press (2014). He has also published three poetry chapbooks: *The Girl with the JAKE Tattoo* (Two of Cups Press, 2015), *Temple of Bones* (Finishing Line Press, 2013), and *Fastened to a Dying Animal* (Pudding House, 2010). He lives in Clinton, New York, with his wife and two sons, and teaches creative writing and poetry as a professor of English.

Elizabeth Leo was a poet, teacher, and gardener. She received her MFA in poetry from West Virginia University. A Philadelphia native, she lived in West Virginia until her death in 2019. Her poems are forthcoming in *Radar Poetry*.

Tessa Livingstone is a southern Californian poet who holds an MFA from Portland State University. Her poems have previously appeared in *Capulet Mag*, *Five:2:One*, *Geometry Literary Journal*, *Whiskey Island Magazine*, and *Portland Review*. Her poem "Grant, 1970" also won first place in *Blue Earth Review*'s summer writing contest and is forthcoming in their next issue.

Angie Macri is the author of *Underwater Panther* (Southeast Missouri State University Press, 2015), winner of the Cowles Poetry Book Prize, and *Fear Nothing of the Future or the Past* (Finishing Line Press, 2014). Her recent work appears in *Cimarron Review*, *NELLE*, and *Superstition Review*. An Arkansas Arts Council fellow, she lives in Hot Springs and teaches at Hendrix College.

Kim Magowan lives in San Francisco and teaches in the Department of Literatures and Languages at Mills College. Her short story collection *Undoing* (2018) won the 2017 Moon City Press Fiction Award and her novel *The Light Source* (2019) was published by 7.13 Books. Her fiction has been published in *Atticus Review*, *Cleaver*, *The Gettysburg Review*, *Hobart*, *Wigleaf*, *Smokelong Quarterly*, and many other journals. She is the fiction editor of *Pithead Chapel*. www.kimmagowan.com.

Liz Marlow's poems have recently appeared or are forthcoming in *The Carolina Quarterly*, *The Greensboro Review*, *The Rumpus*, *Silk Road Review*, and elsewhere.

Autumn McClintock lives in Philadelphia and works at the public library. Poems of hers have recently appeared or are forthcoming in *Cimarron Review*, *Denver Quarterly*, *The Georgia Review*, *Permafrost*, *Sonora Review*, and others. Her chapbook, *After the Creek*, was published in 2016 by Finishing Line Press. She is a staff reader for *Ploughshares* and associate poetry editor of *Doubleback Review*.

John McNally's story "Catch and Release" will appear in his next collection, *The Fear of Everything*, scheduled to be published fall 2020. McNally has published seventeen books as writer or editor, including *The Book of Ralph: A Novel* (Simon and Schuster, 2004), *Troublemakers: Stories* (Iowa, 2000), and, most recently, *The Promise of Failure: One Writer's Perspective on Not Succeeding* (Iowa, 2018).

Jessica Mehta is a citizen of the Cherokee Nation, a multi-award-winning poet, and author of over a dozen books. She's also the editor-in-chief of *Crab Creek Review* and owner of an award-winning small business, MehtaFor, a writing services company that offers pro bono services to Native Americans and indigenous-serving non-profits. Learn more at jessicamehta.com.

Amelia Morand returned to her hometown of Santa Fe, New Mexico, after finishing her MFA at the University of Montana. She serves as the senior fiction editor of *CutBank*. She has work in *apt, Brevity, Hobart, Lunch Ticket,* and *Pithead Chapel*.

Owen Neace is poet, teacher, translator, and MFA student at the University of Alabama. His work has appeared in *Prick of the Spindle* and *Milanga o muerte*, among other publications.

Elizabeth Nonemaker is a writer, journalist, musician, and an MFA candidate in Creative Writing at the University of Maryland College Park. She serves as the managing editor of the multimedia music journal 21CM.org. As a composer, Nonemaker has written for chamber ensembles all over the country and has earned residencies at the MacDowell Colony and the Helene Wurlitzer Foundation.

William Palomo is the son of two immigrants from El Salvador. *Wake the Others*, his first collection of poetry, will be published by Black Lawrence Press in March 2020. He is a translator and founding editor of *La Piscucha Magazine* and a book reviewer at *Muzzle*. He has performed his poetry at the National Poetry Slam, CUPSI, and V Festival Internacional de Poesía Amada Libertad in El Salvador. Follow him @palomopoemas and palomopoemas.com.

Kimberly Ann Priest is the author of *Still Life* (PANK, 2020), *Parrot Flower* (Glass, 2020), and *White Goat Black Sheep* (FLP, 2018). She is the winner of the 2019 Heartland Poetry Prize, and is an assistant professor at Michigan State University and poetry editor for the *Nimrod International Journal of Prose*.

A.R. Robins works as a teacher in Missouri. Her fiction is published or forthcoming in *Gone Lawn*, *Potomac Review*, *Opossum*, *The Big Muddy*, *The Swamp*, and others. Her poetry is published in *Crack the Spine*, *Trailer Park Quarterly*, *The Cape Rock*, *Atlas and Alice*, and others.

Michelle Ross is the author of *There's So Much They Haven't Told You* (2017), which won the 2016 Moon City Press Short Fiction Award. Her fiction has recently appeared in *Alaska Quarterly Review*, *Colorado Review*, *The Pinch*, and other venues. Her work was selected for Best Microfictions 2020 and the Wigleaf Top 50 of 2019. She is fiction editor of *Atticus Review*. www.michellenross.com.

Leigh Camacho Rourks is a Cuban-American author who lives and works in Central Florida, where she is an assistant professor of English and humanities at Beacon College. She is the recipient of the St. Lawrence Book Award, the Glenna Luschei Prairie Schooner Award, and the Robert Watson Literary Review Prize, and her work has been shortlisted for several other awards. Her fiction, poems, and essays have appeared in a number of journals, including *Kenyon Review*, *Prairie Schooner*, *RHINO*, *TriQuarterly*, *December Magazine*, and *The Greensboro Review*. Her short story collection, *Moon Trees and Other Orphans*, was released in 2019 by Black Lawrence Press.

Rebecca Schumejda is the author of several full-length collections, including *Falling Forward* (sunnyoutside press, 2009), *Cadillac Men* (NYQ Books, 2012), *Waiting at the Dead End Diner* (Bottom Dog Press, 2014), and most recently *Our One-Way Street* (NYQ Books, 2017). She is currently working on a book forthcoming from Stubborn Mule Press. She is the co-editor at *Trailer Park Quarterly*. She lives in New York's Hudson Valley with her family. www.rebecca-schumejda.com.

Jordan E.C. Seyer is a senior at Missouri State University. She is double-majoring in painting and art history. Currently, Jordan works at the Brick City Gallery. Recently, her piece "Comfort" was featured in the First Friday Art Walk's Annual First Friday Art Walk Anniversary Contest in October of 2019. Her work has also been featured on the cover of Jacob Seyer's 2018 album *Migration*. After her graduation in the fall of 2020, she plans on moving to Kansas City, Missouri, to pursue a career at the Nelson-Atkins Museum of Art.

Andy Smart is a fourth-generation south St. Louisan. His work has appeared in *Two-Thirds North, Red Fez, River Heron Review*, the anthologies *Show Me All Your Scars* (In Fact Books) and *Come Shining* (Kelson Books), and is forthcoming in *Lilly Poetry Review*. He is a candidate for an MFA at the Solstice Low-Residency Program in Creative Writing at Pine Manor College.

Karaline Stamper is a poet, linguist, and copywriter from San Diego. More of her work can be found in *Sweet Tree Review, Manastash*, and *Acorn Review*.

Daryl Sznyter is the author of *Synonyms for (OTHER) Bodies* (NYQ Books, 2018). Her poetry has appeared in *Diode, Harpur Palate, Poet Lore, The American Journal of Poetry, Best American Poetry Blog*, and elsewhere. She received her MFA from the New School. She currently resides in northeastern Pennsylvania

Kayvan Tahmasebian is a poet, translator, literary critic, and the author of *Isfahan's Mold* (Sadeqia dar Bayat Esfahan, 2016). His poetry has appeared in *Notre Dame Review, Hawai'i Review, Salt Hill*, and *Lunch Ticket*, where it was a finalist for the Gabo Prize for Literature in Translation & Multilingual Texts in 2017. With Rebecca Ruth Gould, he is co-translator of *High Tide of the Eyes: Poems by Bijan Elahi* (The Operating System, 2019).

Nancy Takacs is the recent recipient of a Pushcart Prize. Her book *The Worrier: Poems* (University of Massachusetts Press, 2017) received the

Juniper Prize for Poetry and was the 2018 winner of the 15 Bytes Book Award for Poetry.

Caitlin Rae Taylor holds an MFA from the University of North Carolina Wilmington, where she served as fiction editor for *Ecotone* magazine and publishing assistant for Lookout Books. She is currently the managing editor for *Southern Humanities Review* at Auburn University. Her work has appeared online in *Germ Magazine*.

Catherine Uroff's short fiction has appeared in a variety of literary journals, including *Hobart, Prairie Schooner, Valparaiso Fiction Review, Bellevue Literary Review*, and *The Roanoke Review*. She won the 2018 *Prairie Schooner* Glenna Luschei Award and was a finalist for American Short Fiction's Short Story Contest and the Snake Nation Press Serena McDonald Kennedy Award.

Hannah V Warren is a doctoral student at the University of Georgia, where she studies poetry and speculative narratives. Her forthcoming chapbook, *[re]construction of the necromancer*, won Sundress Publications' 2019 chapbook contest.

Sam Herschel Wein lives in Chicago. His chapbook, *Fruit Mansion* (Split Lip Press, 2017) was the winner of the 2016 Turnbuckle Chapbook Prize. He is the poetry editor for *The Blueshift Journal* and runs a new journal, *Underblong*, with his best friend, Chen Chen. Recent work can be found in *Hobart, Mojo,* and *Connotation Press*, among others.

Terin Weinberg is an MFA candidate at Florida International University in Miami, Florida. Weinberg serves as a poetry reader for *Gulf Stream Magazine*. Weinberg's poems are forthcoming in *The Shore, The Normal School*, and *Flyway: Journal of Writing & Environment* and have been published in journals including *Barely South Review, Red Earth Review, Dark River Review, New Southerner*, and *Waccamaw*.

Jennifer Wortman is the author of the story collection *This. This. This. Is. Love. Love. Love.* (Split Lip Press, 2019), and a recipient of a National Endowment for the Arts fellowship. Her work appears in *TriQuarterly*,

Glimmer Train, Copper Nickel, Normal School, DIAGRAM, Brevity, and elsewhere. She lives with her family in Colorado, where she serves as associate fiction editor for *Colorado Review* and teaches at Lighthouse Writers Workshop.

G.H. Yamauchi has had work published in *Electric Literature's The Commuter, SalonZine,* and the *Tipton Poetry Review.* Some of her drawings and photos can be found at www.subwaycommute.com.

Rosetta Young is a doctoral candidate in the English department at the University of California, Berkeley, where she also received an MA in fiction writing in 2016. While at UC-Berkeley, she won the Roselyn Schneider Eisner Prize in Prose for a full-length short story collection, the Joan Lee Yang Memorial Prize for a group of poems, and the Elizabeth Mills Crothers Prize in Literary Composition for a stand-alone short story. Her work has appeared in *Hanging Loose Magazine, West 10th* and *The Gallatin Review.*

CPSIA information can be obtained
at www.ICGtesting.com
Printed in the USA
FSHW011005090221
78343FS